The New
Complete
GREAT DANE

by Noted Authorities

Illustrated

Twelfth Printing

1975

HOWELL BOOK HOUSE INC.
730 Fifth Avenue
New York, N.Y. 10019

Foreword

IT is with the greatest pleasure that we submit this new edition of *The Complete Great Dane* to admirers of the breed. It is our sincere hope that this book will merit the same warm reception accorded by the fancy to its first edition.

Grateful thanks are expressed for the chapters submitted by Miss Gerda M. Umlauff, Hamburg, Germany; Miss Muriel Osborne, Surrey, England; Anne Fitzgerald Paramoure; Mrs. Peggy Seitz; J. Wen Lundeen; and Mr. John G. McEdward and the Great Dane Clubs of California. Their researches and writings have enabled us to add a definitive modern history of the breed to the earlier material. The Section on leading sires, dams and winners of the past seven years will be of continuing interest and value to the breeders of today and tomorrow.

Sincere appreciation is also due Mr. Donald Gauthier for his permission to use his drawings to illustrate the Standard, and to the many fanciers who kindly granted the privilege of using their pictures of noted dogs.

May *The New Complete Great Dane* provide a never-ending source of useful information to the fancier and novice alike whose canine interests are centered in this beautiful working dog—the Great Dane.

HOWELL BOOK HOUSE, New York

iii

Table of Contents

PART I

PART II

GENERAL CARE AND TRAINING OF YOUR DOG

ASSYRIAN HUNTING DOGS

Ancient Assyrian Dogs

THE excavations of Assyrian palaces and monuments have given us evidence and knowledge of the ancient culture of the once predominant tribes of Western Asia. These excavations are of interest to the dog fancier chiefly because of the evidence of the early existence of Dane-like dogs. All Assyrian kings were great builders, from comparatively simple private homes to decorative temples and magnificent palaces. On the walls of these buildings we find pictures of dogs illustrating special incidents. The chronicle of the empire is depicted thus, telling us of warlike rulers who were fond of triumphal marches with many followers—women, soldiers, horses and coaches, and chained prisoners. The pictures also show the Assyrian kings sacrificing to their gods and hunting wild animals. The very high culture of the Assyrians is indicated in the pictures of men wearing finely embroidered and woven garments some of which were jeweled. Their manufactured goods were made of gold, silver, and ivory, and their carpets and weaving, which were exported to Greece, were often imitated there. It is possible that Assyrian dogs went through the same channels, because we know that at a later date Greeks and Romans also had Dane-like dogs.

We are especially interested in the figures of Assyrian dogs whose origin as offspring of Indian dogs is frequently

7

Dalmatian D.

Danish D

Small Danish D.

Mongrel Turkish D

8

mentioned in ancient writings. Many scientists believe that the highland of Tibet was the original country of all Dane-like dogs, and therefore say that Indian dogs are identical with the dogs of Tibet who lived at the foot of the Himalayas. Tibetan dogs who lived in a warmer climate would, of course, very soon lose their long tufted hair.

On the other hand, dogs with Dane-like figures, independently of others, existed in the middle of Russia, Poland, and middle Germany. This has been proven by excavations of big, heavy dog skulls. Dogs with heavily built bodies lived in those regions where the natural conditions and the necessity of fighting wild animals made life hard to bear.

Two pictures of old Assyrian monuments are preserved. The one relief-plate came from a Babylonian temple built two thousand years B.C. and reconstructed later by Nebuchadnezzar. It shows an Assyrian man leading a powerful Dane-like dog on a twisted leash, while the second picture shows dogs pursuing two horses who have been hit by arrows. This Assyrian fighting dog is very similar to the Tibetan dog of today in his massive body, heavy bones, accented dewlap, and the skull with its broad forehead, excessive jaws, and powerful lower jaw. He was probably used as a fighting dog, a personal watch-dog, and perhaps also as a bear or lion hound.

The second depiction of the hunting scene is a wall relief of an Assyrian castle built about 900 B.C. Quite the contrary of the above-mentioned representation, this dog figure has a much frailer body, more refined in all parts, and with greater elegance in its whole form. The head has no wrinkles and the ears are small. This canine figure evidently personifies the slim type used for hunting swift game, and, though Dane-like, does not conform as to size.

History further proves that after the conquest of Babylon by the Persians the taxes from four towns were required for the upkeep of the king's pack of hounds. The Greeks and Romans followed in the footsteps of the Assyrians and Persians, adopting also their Dane-like dog figures. These have been repeated in a number of breeds and confirms the view that the Tibetan dog, the Mastiff, the Great Dane, the New-

STUDY OF A DOG
By Vittore Pisano, 1425

BRONZE DOG BY BENVENUTO CELLINI, ABOUT 1535.
Reproduced from a drawing by Nicola Samel

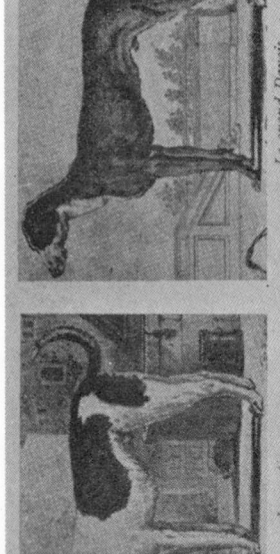

Le matin   Le grand Danois
BUFFON'S ILLUSTRATIONS, 1750.

THE DANISH DOG
By Sydenham Edwards. Published in 1803

foundland, and the Saint Bernard are of the same family.

It is also probable that the cultured Romans with their high standards of living were interested in raising pure-bred dogs for fighting, and also the more slimly built hunting dogs. For these purposes they imported British dogs who were very famous in that day. It is reported that these imported dogs were able to break the neck of an ox. Their ancestry went back to the Molossian dogs which the Phoenicians had taken to Britain in the sixth century A.D., and, as a result of their descendants' being crossed with the native dogs, the breed became very famous. They were taken by the Romans to fight in the circus, and in order to procure the best specimens the Roman emperor had a special official called the "Procurator Cynogie," who lived at Winchester. It was his duty to select both the heavy and more slightly built dogs which were to be exported to Rome. In earlier years the Romans had gotten most of their dogs, Molossians principally, from Epirus in North Greece, but as Britain became more and more the source of supply they undoubtedly also imported Mastiffs and Deerhounds. In any event, the dog of Tibet, the Molosser, and the Mastiff are important in the history of Dane-like dogs, and without doubt the Mastiff was the ancestor of all European Dane-like dogs. On old Greek vases and Roman small bronzes we find bull-dog-like canine figures which prove that the same dogs could be found in the south, probably imported from the east. It is strange that in the north, especially, the breed had grown so much larger.

The broad-jawed dogs who became victors in the Roman circus against the Molossers are mentioned for the first time in A.D. 200 by Gratius Faliscus. The Celts probably took such a breed in the form resembling the Mastiff to Ireland and England where, being cross-bred with the Irish Wolf-hound, they became the most famous dogs of Europe. They were always greatly favored at the courts because they had such beautiful figures. About the year A.D. 100 the Cimbern also had broad-jawed dogs for use in war and hunting, and to kill one of them would bring about severe punishment.

Great Danes in Denmark, 1686

Dogs of the Middle Ages

A HISTORY of the hounds of the middle ages gives us a very impressive picture of hunting at that time. Enormous packs of boars lived in mid-European forests, and not infrequently bears and wolves were included in the princely booty. The hunters rode on noble horses, and running before them packs of personal and chamber hounds led the hunt. People from all the surrounding villages were required to serve as drivers for the hunter. Courage and strength, agility and endurance were demanded of the hounds in those days, and these qualifications made them very valuable. This fact can be observed in the "alemanischen" laws of the seventh century which record the heavy penalty for the theft of a boarhound, or, as they were sometimes called, a boar-hound or a bulldog. The first records concerning the boar-hounds are found in the descriptions of the Spanish and French writers of the twelfth and fourteenth centuries.

The native boar-hounds had evidently been cross-bred with numerous imported English hounds. The English hounds were high-legged, strong animals which had been bred in kingly courts at the beginning of the fifteenth and sixteenth centuries. They originated from the crossing of a Mastiff with an Irish Greyhound. The greatest number of the male boar-hounds worked together in the attack to divide the masses of boars so that eventually a group of

13

THE PARABLE OF DIVES AND LAZARUS
Artist: Domenico Feti
National Gallery of Art, Kress Collection

hounds would drive a single boar toward the hunters who were concealed behind screens. The most powerful and strongest hounds were chosen for the real attack, being suddenly loosed from behind the screen and sent against the boar. The dogs would get a firm hold on the beast, and then it was killed by one of the hunters, either on foot or from horseback, with a so-called boar-spear.

The training of young boar-hounds began when they were still in the company of old dogs, who taught them how to catch wounded young bears by the ears. Later on they were exposed to the strong, wild boars, but first they put on protective jackets. These were sort of bombazine harnesses lined with linen and filled with hair, rags, or fishbones. At Madrid in Spain one can see exhibits of dog armor in the weapon collection of the museum.

Proof of the remarkable abilities of the boar-hounds is found in the results recorded from the hunting grounds of the Landgrafen (Earl) Philipp and William IV of Hessen in the Habichtswald, Reinhardswald, and Kaufunger Forest. It is no wonder that one of these young nobles paid fifteen Florin for a hound in the year 1538. We have a record that in 1556 Landgraf Philipp had caught seven hundred and twenty-six wild boars up until November thirtieth, an achievement only possible with the skill of excellent boar-hounds. In 1559 he wrote to Duke Christopher of Würdenberg: "Our home-bred hounds have afforded us much pleasure during this hunting season, and we have bagged about eleven hundred and twenty boars." In the year 1563 the greatest number of wild boars was hunted, Philipp and his hounds taking twenty-five hundred and seventy-two. The greatest number of boar-hounds belonged to Duke Henry of Braunschweig, who in 1592 appeared at the hunt at the Oberweser with six hundred male dogs. At all royal courts there were special kennels for the packs of boar-hounds.

At the big boar-hunts there were very often more dogs needed than the hunters had available. This accounts for the fact that all shepherds, in addition to maintaining their own dogs, had to keep a strong male for boar-hunting to be available to the ruling prince upon demand. Otherwise

THE MISFORTUNES OF CEPHALUS
Artist: Bernardino Luini
National Gallery of Art, Kress Collection, Washington, D. C.

their flocks of sheep were taken from them. During the season for boar-hunting Landgraf Moritz, the scientist, sent a hunter throughout the land. This hunter had power of attorney to collect male dogs from shepherds, butchers, and others who kept dogs. If, contrary to the specifications, little, disqualified curs were offered, their owner had to pay a penalty of five sheep. This obligation of the shepherds and other keepers of dogs dated far back into another century. It was customary in the seventeenth century to send the royal dogs, or at least a portion of them, to the millers to be fed. The millers, like the butchers, also had to raise a certain number of dogs to be delivered to the ruler. It was also the duty of royal officials to keep several dogs.

In the seventeenth and eighteenth centuries importations of English dogs stopped because in Germany home-bred hounds were being used more and more. At this time it was considered necessary to use two light-weight hounds against a young boar. Against a two-year-old, three or four dogs were needed, and against a three-year-old boar, four to six hounds were required. Earlier paintings show even more. They were nearly always depicted with rough hair, but resembled the Great Danes in figure and sometimes in the lines of the head. The painter, Snyders, has included two types of dogs in his work—the light, and the heavier variety for attacking animals. As the European noblemen tried to outdo one another in having especially good and heavy dogs, the breed spread over all the continent, as is witnessed by their representation in stories and pictures. For example, we have the pictures which Van Dyck and his pupil, Castiglione Giovanni Benedetto, painted for the Duke of Mantua. Or we might mention the pictures of Gaston Phebus, which show that these dogs were known in France as the "Allant Gentil."

Under William VIII of Hessen-Kassel, boars were found in large numbers, but as time went on their number became fewer and fewer. Part of the reason may have been the very severe winters of 1784 and 1785, in which many boars died. Also Landgraf William IX made strict laws about the

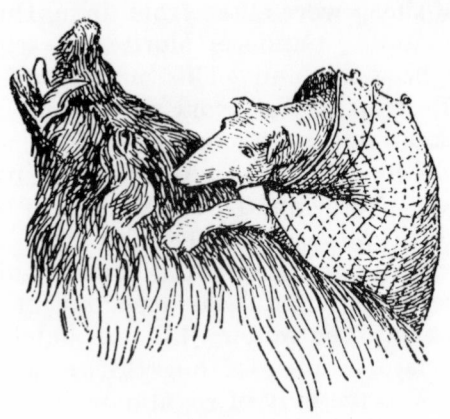

Boarhound in quilted Coat
(From a Tapestry in the Louvre by Bernard van Orley, 1527-33)

The PANTHEON AND OTHER MONUMENTS of Ancient Rome
Artist: Giovanni Paolo Panini
National Gallery of Art, Kress Collection, Washington, D. C.

damage caused by game and the habitual use of firearms. With the decrease of the boars, naturally the boar-hounds began disappearing. They were still kept at the courts in small numbers, but gradually became private property. Finally there were packs of hounds kept at the Solitude near Stuttgart and at Ballenstedt in Harz. They had ringed tails, coarse features, rough hair, and their bodies were not very well formed. A so-called "game-master," who, during the years 1860-1870, belonged to the Kurhessischen Jägerhof, has given us the details of the last boar-hounds. They were energetic dogs of yellow, red-yellow, and brindle colors, with black muzzles, and some of them were high-legged. In 1876 the last of these dogs was sold, and the breed probably completely disappeared.

The heirs of these dogs, however, are the Great Danes. So we should be grateful to these dogs of the middle ages who are responsible for the Great Dane, a superior breed which combines perfect measurements, elegant features, and a proud bearing into a completely beautiful and noble appearance.

PORTRAIT OF A GENTLEMAN
Artist: Antonia Mor
National Gallery of Art, Mellon Collection

20

History of the Great Dane
During the Nineteenth Century

HERE is scarcely another breed of dogs whose name has changed so frequently as that of the Great Dane. In Germany the Great Dane is now called "Deutsche Dogge," and we know that the word *Dogge* had its origin in the early English word *Dogca* which later became *dog* in English and Dutch, and in French *Dogue*. The English word *dog* was known as early as 1050, but was not used in low German until the second part of the sixteenth century. At first it was written *dock* and had the masculine form, but later on was given the feminine gender. Today it is still in the masculine form in the Danish language.

In the sixteenth century the Great Danes were most frequently called "English Dogges." About the year 1680 when these dogs were bred in great numbers at the German princely courts, the largest and best Danes were called "Chamber Dogs" (*Kammerhunde*), and they wore gilded collars. The second best dogs were called "Life Dogs" (*Leibhunde*), and wore collars with a silver finish. All collars were richly trimmed with fringe and padded with velvet. At a later date all other dogs were known as "English Dogs," and still later the name *Hatzrüde* replaced the old German word *Fanghund*. *Fanghund,* of course, referred to the work of the Dane, just as did the names *Boarhund* and *Saupacker*.

In spite of these different names we can follow the path which the Great Dane has taken from the earliest days of

21

AT BAY
(*From the painting by Benno Adam*)

A WILD BOAR HUNT

sporting dogs in Germany until the present. The first German dog show occurred in 1863 at Hamburg, and we are informed that "some very grave-looking Doggen took part in the event." Of these "grave-looking Doggen" eight were called "Danish Doggen" and seven announced as "Ulmer Doggen." The czar of Russia purchased two of these Danes.

In the next exhibition at Hamburg-Altona in 1869 fifteen "Danish Doggen" and twelve "Ulmer Doggen" were shown. In the year 1876 at the great dog show in Hamburg there were twenty-four "Danish Doggen," and forty-five "Ulmer Doggen." The truth is that of all these dogs not one had ever seen Denmark, nor had any of them even been born there, as their papers indicated. They all belonged to citizens of Hamburg and had been bred partly in Berlin and partly in Württemberg (South Germany). At the time of the 1876 show the judges declared that it was impossible to separate dogs of the same breed into different classes as if belonging to a different breed. They therefore proposed to call the Great Dane the "Deutsche Dogge," as it had really been for centuries.

This name, however, did not prevail, and different names were continually being used until the dog show at Hanover in 1879. Many breeders met there and decided to call the heavier Danes "Danish Dogs" and the lighter weight Danes "Ulmer Doggen." In spite of this decision brindle Danes were often referred to as "Hatzrüden" or "Wolf Dogs," while the fawn-colored and sometimes the blue Great Danes were called "Danish Dogs" regardless of weight. At that time the black and white spotted Danes were bred principally in South Germany, while breeders in North Germany preferred the blue dogs. Thirty years later, however, there were more harlequin kennels in North Germany.

The year 1880 finally brought the new official name for the Great Dane, and since that date until today in Germany he has been officially known as the "Deutsche Dogge." Fanciers also like to call the Great Dane the "Apollo of the Dog World," which is a charming but unofficial title. In France the Great Dane is known as "Grand Danois," while in 1892 the English called him the "German Mastiff," and in

23

VAN DYCK'S "MASTIFF"
From the picture of the children of Charles I.
The dog is undoubtedly of boar hound or Great Dane type.

Denmark he was known at the "Great Danish Dog." There was therefore very often confusion pertaining to the Danish Dog who is related to the Deutsche Dogge. In France the naturalist Buffon used for the first time the name "Grand Danois," or Great Dane, in conjunction with the remark that under the influence of the Danish climate the greyhound had become a Grand Danois!

When, in 1874, the famous German breeder, Mr. Max Hartenstein, bought a Great Dane at Stuttgart, a new age began for this breed. His first dog was called a "Württembergischer Hatzrüde" with the name Bosco; and his second dog, a female purchased in 1876, was named Bella. Until 1895 Hartenstein bred many Great Danes and showed many excellent specimens. He did not hesitate at any time to buy the best breeding material regardless of cost, and began an illustrious course for the Great Dane, especially at Württemberg.

His most famous dogs were Faust I and his three daughters Goldperle, Otter, and Schwalbe. His best black Great Danes were Peter, Cora II, Sandor II, and Nigra. The best of his blue Danes were Faust I, Faust II, Faust III, Thibo, Falkner-Palvia, Prima, Perle v. Plauen, Schwalbe, Otter, Maximus, and Flora Plavia. His best brindles were Rex, Mustapha, Stella, Ilka II, who was sold in England for fifteen hundred marks, Armida, Girofla, Goldperle, Ruth, Bella Vista, Venus v. Plauen, and Primas. The best of his harlequins were Bravo (porcelain tiger), Dorina, Milo (dark blue harlequin), and Dora. The best yellow Great Danes were Bosco, Electra, Mora, Bachus, and Sandor.

In 1878 a Mr. E. Mebter, a breeder in North Germany, started a kennel of Great Danes. He followed certain principles consistently in his breeding, with the result that many of the pedigrees in the stud book show the name of his kennel. His most affluent time was in the years between 1880 and 1890. For example, he exhibited in 1880 in Berlin, entering thirty-two Great Danes; and in the years 1881, 1883, and 1885, he exhibited in London, on each occasion showing twenty dogs. In 1887 at St. Petersburg in Russia he exhibited twenty-two Great Danes at the various shows.

25

Danish Mastiff

Mr. Mebter's best dogs were Nero I and Nero II, Sultan I and Sultan II, Mentor I, Pluto, Apollo, Cedric, Tiger, Cyrus I and Cyrus II, Brutus, Bella I and Bella II, Minka I and Minka II, Euphrat, Viola, Vineta, Juno, Zampa II, Ceres, Judith, and Tyra.

Another breeder from South Germany was Mr. B. Ulrich who produced many Great Danes, and for a long period of time always had the best specimens. His most noteworthy period was between 1882 and 1887. His male Danes proved to have a great influence on the German breed. They were Harras II and his son Corvin, Harras I, Helios, Hannibal, Halfdan, and Hermes. His best females were Nora-Doos, Bella II, Ilka, Senta, Noritta, and Noriega.

The fourth big kennel was founded in 1886 by the well-known Mr. Aichele in Berlin. Mr. Aichele preferred blue Danes, and his kennel was called Schwalbennest. His best dogs were Falkner I and his son Talisman v. Schwalbennest, and the blue females Blaue Donau, Iris, and that especially fine female, Vesta. Blaue Donau he bought in 1902 at Vienna, and Iris and Vesta were sisters born of Otter I (Faust Hartenstein and Flora) and Falkner I. The blue Grille whom he bought in Vienna in 1895 was sold to an English buyer one and a half years later.

Other breeders of the latter part of the nineteenth century were Prinz zu Solms, Dr. Bodinus, Dr. Caster, and Messrs. Burger, Essig, and Cohn.

In the year 1882 the Second International Dog Show took place at Hanover, and fortunately we have a complete description of this event. It is interesting to note in the judges' report how many Great Danes were there, and that a single breeder had twenty-two entries. The principal faults noted in the show dogs were too much dewlap, too strong lips, and pointed muzzles. About half of the sixty-five Great Danes were rated very good, as was frequently the case in those years at the end of the century, and some tiger dogs were mentioned as being of especial interest.

It is recorded that it is very difficult for breeders of Danes to get a proper position assigned to them between the "Bullenbeiser" and the "Greyhound." The *Dog Magazine* of 1882

27

300 years ago the famous VAN DYCK (Netherlands) painted
the Duke Wolfgang William v. Neuberg with a Great Dane,
which resembles very much the type we know today.

states: "Sometimes Great Danes are entered as 'Ulmer Doggen,' 'Danish Dogs,' or 'Hatzrüden,' but everyone who is at all informed is aware that only the name 'Deutsche Dogge' is correct. In recent shows the St. Bernards and Newfoundlands did not make a good impression, but the Great Danes were uniformly good in coat, color, and conformation of their bodies. It is a pity that we so seldom have 'English Doggen' (Mastiffs) shown here. When we think of the great shows in England when eighty to a hundred Mastiffs, all of great weight, may be seen at one show, we realize what an excellent appearance our elegant 'Deutsche Dogge' would present by way of contrast." A concluding remark states that a fancier paid five hundred *Taler* for one of the Great Danes which had been exhibited.

In 1887 a dog show took place at Stuttgart, and there were three hundred Great Danes entered. As far as we know this is the largest number of Great Danes ever entered at one show. In 1888 the still extant "Deutscher Doggenclub" was founded at Berlin, and this was the first club to be devoted exclusively to one breed. Many dog shows, with numerous entries of Great Danes, now occurred, and we mention the following at Berlin in 1888—one hundred and eight Great Danes; at Frankfurt/M in 1888—one hundred and ten Great Danes (best brindles, Harras II and the female Nora-Doos, owner Ulrich); at Cologne in 1889—one hundred and sixteen Great Danes (best breeders' groups belonged to Messrs. A. Latz, Euskirchen, and S. Cohn, Hamburg). Mr. Hartenstein's dogs, Neckar, Otter, and Ruth, took the first prizes in the show of 1889 at Kassel. In the fall of 1889 a dog show was held at Cannstadt, Württemberg. On this occasion the Great Dane male Hannibal received a prize which was given by His Royal Majesty King Karl.

Other events attracting Great Dane breeders and fanciers were the following shows: at Charlottenburg in 1890—one hundred and thirty-three entries; at Frankfurt/M in 1891—one hundred and five entries (first prizes awarded to the brindle Ella-Hansa, owner S. Cohn, Hamburg; the yellow Halfdan-Doos, owner B. Ulrich, Doos; and Bella-Göppingen, owner H. Gaiser; the grey Falkner-Plavia, owner A. Latz,

29

VELASQUEZ'S MASTIFF
Philip IV of Spain

Euskirchen; the harlequin Diana-Dortrecht, owner F. A. Onderwater); at Berlin in 1894—one hundred and forty-five entries; at Berlin in 1897—one hundred and two entries; at Pankow in 1899—one hundred and nineteen entries; and at Berlin in 1902—one hundred and twenty-three entries. Just prior to most of these shows—about 1892—the breed standard was published, probably for the first time.

We wish now to summarize the information we have at hand about the most important Great Danes of the years 1885 to 1893. Dr. Caster's brindle Harras I, the grandsire of Hannibal, was born in 1883. He had neither unusual height nor excellent color, but he had such a wonderful body that he always took first prize after the judges had observed him carefully. The male Dane Harras II, whose owner was Mr. B. Ulrich of Doos, was the winner in 1886 of prizes at Vienna, Munich, and Leipzig.

We are fortunate to have the measurements of some of these ancestors of the Great Danes of today. Harras v. Nero, whose breeder was Mr. Eisele of Stuttgart, had a shoulder height of 79 cm (2½ cm—1 in.), head length of 27 cm, muzzle length of 12 cm, the elbow was 42 cm from the ground, the flank was 56 cm from the ground, the total length of the body from the shoulders to the end of the legs was 87½ cm, the circumference of the chest behind the shoulders was 93 cm, and the length of the tail 57 cm.

Juno, whose owner was Ch. Essig of Leonberg, was a lightweight female whose body was slim and very beautiful. She was shown at the dog show in Munich in 1886, and caused quite a sensation because of the coquettish way she held her head and because of her color which was white with yellow and brown spots. Her measurements are as follows: shoulder height, 74 cm; length of head, 26 cm; length of muzzle, 13 cm; flanks, 53 cm from the ground; elbow, 43 cm from the ground; entire length of the body horizon from the shoulders to the end of the legs, 81 cm; circumference of the chest, 90 cm; forehand around the legs, 24 cm; and length of the tail, 52 cm.

Hannibal I was a very good male brindle owned by B. Ulrich of Doos. His sire was Moreau (Dr. Caster's Harras

31

Photograph of about 1890

I from Hertnecks Liza) and his dam was Flora, born in 1887. Hannibal I was probably one of the best Great Danes of his time in Germany. He was sold in 1892 for a high price in England, and from there to Moscow. At the end of the last century many great Danes, mostly from Württemberg, were sold to England, and a little later many were purchased by the United States, France, and the Netherlands.

We can easily see that Germany was the country in which the breeding of Great Danes was done most intensively. It is to the credit of the German breeders that they have created a dog with both great strength and elegance in appearance, not to mention his lovable character. The Great Dane is admired all over the world, and in the future will continually make friends for himself.

Considering the perfection to which the Great Dane had been brought in his native country, it is not surprising that the first World War inflicted grievous wounds on this breed. Those dreadful years of hunger which caused the death of so many of these great dogs brought breeding to a standstill, but did not completely stifle interest in the Great Dane. Nineteen-eighteen and the years following were very difficult for the breeders of the Great Dane because, though they were anxious to build up the breed again, there were so few animals left worth using for breeding purposes.

The best brindle males at that time were Bosko and Dolf v.d. Saalburg, and the best harlequins Japha and Jagla Moguntia. The serious breeders had to lay out a great deal of money if they wanted to get good breeding material. The owner of the well-known kennel v. Kaiserhof purchased a blue stud male at Wiesbaden in 1923, paying the enormous sum of nine hundred dollars for him. This kennel has been in existence for the past thirty-six years and continues to prefer the blue Danes. Other kennels of this era were v.d. Alster with its outstanding harlequin male König Midas v.d. Alster, Kohlenstein, and v.d. Meibenburg.

With two exceptions there have never again been so many Great Danes exhibited at the dog shows as there were at the end of the nineteenth century. In 1929 at Stuttgart there were 130 Great Danes, and in 1935 at the World Dog Show held at Frankfurt/M there were 150 Great Danes. In 1945 at Vienna there were only forty-five Great Danes entered, and this number is representative of most other years since the turn of the century. The report states that the dogs entered at Vienna were of good quality.

In 1936 at the Champion show at Cologne fifty-four Great Danes were exhibited, the yellows and brindles being for the most part the best quality. In 1937 at Hamburg thirty-six Danes were entered, and of these the yellows were the best. The *Reichssieger* (Champion) show at Munich in the same year had seventy-one Great Dane entries, and Switzerland showed Great Danes of very good quality in the rings on that same occasion. Another report, however, makes mention of light eyes, deficient legs and hindquarters, and poor carriage. At the World Dog Show at Paris in 1937 the harlequins did not prove to be so good as other colors.

In July, 1938, very good Great Danes, mostly harlequins, were exhibited at Groningen in the Netherlands. After the *Reichssieger* (Champion) show in 1938 at Cologne, a show at which seventy-two Danes had been entered, the following report came out: "The breed makes little progress for there is a lack of really outstanding stud males. Too many light eyes were observed at the show. With few exceptions the spotted great Danes which were exhibited had the blood of brindle dogs in their pedigrees, and they therefore had brown spots and stains which were especially noticeable in the sunshine. Through breeding with the brindles, the heads of the harlequin Great Danes were improved, but on the other hand the harlequins often had steep fronts which proved detrimental."

In 1938 a dog show took place at Hanover at which there were twenty-two Great Dane entries of which twelve received the rating of "excellent." It was stated that all of them on the average were of good quality. Among the best dogs of the year 1938 were the Great Danes: Candax v. Hoch-Eberstein 28008, yellow; World Champion Hellas Kadow 26832, yellow; Zeus Hexengold 28632, brindle; Kato LOF 519, black; Champion Saturn v. Petzenschlob 27571, blue; Fürst v. Urbachriesen 27234, harlequin; Dango v. St-

Anna 26608, harlequin; Champion Silver Borussia 26230, harlequin; Hilde v. Urbachriesen 21378, harlequin; Draga v. Birkenhof 28199, harlequin; Ingo Hassia 27709, yellow; Cerberus v. Birkenhof 28030, brindle; Elfe v. Eppelein-sprung—Noris 27469, yellow; Champion Dolly v. Oden-wald 18924, yellow; Burzel v.d. Saarhuttenstadt 27346, brindle; Inge v. Dalberg 26120, harlequin.

In the course of time many Great Danes naturally found their way to the United States of America, and did very well at the American dog shows. At the end of the year 1936 a list was published with the names of those Great Danes who received championship titles in the U.S.A. From the first time Great Danes were exhibited in the U.S.A. until 1936, three hundred and eighteen of them received this title. Among this number one hundred and eighteen of them had been bred in Germany.

REH, RIESE and RUNGNIR v. LOHELAND
with owner, Frau M. von Rohden, Fulda, Germany

The Status of Great Danes
In Germany

GERDA M. UMLAUFF

ITH the coming of the second World War, which meant food shortages, air raids, tremendous loss of life and material possessions, not to mention a myriad other troubles, there was a time of great difficulty and sorrow for the German breeders of Great Danes. How could they maintain their beloved dogs, how could they feed them sufficiently while men were in need? The owners of Great Danes had not the remotest idea how it could be done, but were resolved to keep their dogs as long as possible. Incredible as it may seem, a number of dog shows took place in all parts of Germany during the years 1939-1944. We mention some of them:

> 1940 Stuttgart with 40 Great Dane entries
> 1940 Hamburg with 22 Great Dane entries
> 1941 Hamburg with 30 Great Dane entries
> 1941 Stuttgart with 51 Great Dane entries
> 1941 Mannheim with 13 Great Dane entries
> 1941 Berlin with 30 Great Dane entries
> 1942 Hamburg with 37 Great Dane entries

At some of the shows the quality of the dogs was very good on the average. Interestingly enough, the years of war did not do as much harm to the breeding of Great Danes in Germany as one would have expected. In fact the condition of the breed was much better after World War II

37

THORA v. BIRKENHOF

OZELOT v. BIRKENHOF
and puppies

than in 1918. When one asks how this was possible, a famous judge of the Great Dane and well-known leader of the Hamburg group of the Deutscher Doggen-Club e. V. von 1888 replies: "The principal reason that the Dane came through the war years so well is the fact that among the breeders and members of our club we have so many women. To them belongs the credit that the Great Danes today are in so much better condition that after the first World War. In a certain sense they fought for their pets, sharing their last bread and potatoes with them. In many instances they made long journeys into the country to find farmers and butchers who would be willing to exchange meat for cigarettes in order that they might feed their dogs."

In many cases their dogs were the only possessions they were able to save during the war, though in some instances the Danes were taken away for war purposes. In peace time they had tried using Great Danes to pull little carts or for work in the country, and during the war they were used to pull machines.

The lack of medicines did not do as much harm to the Great Danes as to other breeds, so we have heard. But it is a pity that a number of valuable Great Danes (and humans) were killed during the bombing of Hamburg. Due to the events of 1945 there were further heavy losses of the best specimens in Berlin, Stettin, Konigsburg, and the Erzegebirge.

With the capitulation in 1945, the old name of the "Deutscher Doggen-Club e. V. von 1888" was restored, while the word "Fachschaft" was eliminated. This club has now approximately eight hundred members in the western zones, and for some time a little magazine called *Mitteilungsblatt* has been published monthly.

Nearly one thousand Great Danes on an average are registered in the stud book each year. They are mostly yellows and brindles of the best quality, upon which we shall comment later. With one exception, dogs without pedigrees have not been registered in the stud book. This one case was a female who without question was the type of the Danes before the first World War, and it was decided to register

WURTEMBURG GREAT DANES OF THE 1880'S

her because of the possibility and probability that she would be used to advantage for breeding at the present time. Caution was exercised, nevertheless, and she was registered as foundling (*findling*), with the stipulation that all her litters must be inspected by two judges. The expression "foundling" must be included in the pedigree of all her puppies.

The allied soldiers have been very much interested in the Great Danes of Germany, and for some time the Deutscher Doggen-Club has been receiving letters from various parts of the world asking for German-bred Danes. The United States and Switzerland are interested in yellow and brindle Great Danes, while India and Spain prefer harlequins or, in some few instances, quite white dogs.

The new currency has worked much hardship on the money of the Doggen-Club, but on the other hand this may facilitate the elimination of those breeders who have been interested in breeding Great Danes in recent years only for the sake of the money involved. As soon as it is apparent that it is becoming increasingly difficult to sell Danes for large sums of money, only those breeders with high ideals and a real love for the Great Dane will remain in the club.

It has been said that many people do not dare to buy a Great Dane because, as has often been observed, this breed catches cold very easily. The German breeders feel that it is possible there are certain bloodlines among the Danes which tend to be subject to colds, but, with a cautious hardening of the animals representing these bloodlines, much improvement can be hoped for in this regard. It is difficult, however, to promote this "hardening" among show dogs, for if they are kept constantly in the fresh air they may develop too long hair (*Unterwolle*) which is considered undesirable in show dogs.

There is no doubt that at present the best Great Danes are in North Germany, especially in the blue, yellow, and brindle colors. This may be due to the high standards set by the club, which in the year 1948 made the following regulations: The stud male must be at least twenty months old, and the

Blue Great Dane of German breeding,
FABEL vom KAISERHOF
A daughter of Ch. Edfa v. Kaiserhof

Fawn female, 3 years old, of
Swiss breeding from Kennel
"vom Gschweich"

ZISKOW KADOW
Owned by Frau von Rhoden

female eighteen months old before they may be used for breeding. Each female may be used only once a year for breeding, and if she is not twenty months old she may raise only four puppies from her litter. Older females may raise six puppies. If the breeder does not observe this regulation he will not receive any pedigrees certified by the club for his puppies.

One must have a great deal of knowledge in order properly to breed harlequins and blue Danes, especially since the latter require improvement in their eyes. The crossing of yellow and brindle Danes with harlequins, or the crossing of yellows and brindles with blue Danes is forbidden in Germany. Only in a very exceptional case will a serious breeder be permitted to perform such a crossing even once, hoping for some remarkable improvement. All Great Danes who do not have the right coloration (see details in the chapter on the Blueprint) will no longer be registered in the German stud book. Formerly several dogs of the same kennel could have the same name, distinguished only by a I, II, or III in connection with the name, but the regulations now forbid this practice.

The aim of the German Great Dane breeders is now and always has been to produce strong and beautiful dogs, and it is therefore necessary to reject weak stud dogs. The breeder and owner of the Great Dane must especially try to avoid tail injuries among his dogs. A tail whose end is more or less hairless, without a point and full of wart-like scars is indeed an unpleasant sight. In some unfortunate cases one or more tail vertebra are missing, which gives the tail a stumpy, unfinished look, and this in turn spoils the whole appearance of the animal. The tail should be slender but never too long. A long tail will be inherited, and if the dog is excitable its tail will be easily injured. Stud males, therefore, whose tails are unsuitable must be rejected for breeding purposes.

The stud male must overcome the faults and supplement the deficiencies of the female in whom a good figure, dark eyes, and good bloodlines are essentials. Both the stud dog and the brood bitch must be perfectly healthy, not nervous

Great Danes working in the Hagenbeck Circus in Germany

WOTAN v.d. KREUZSCHANZE,
34838
One-year-old fawn Great Dane male
Germany

VIGIL de BELVOIS
Male Great Dane of French breeding

or shy, must not have steep forehands, loose shoulders, coarse necks, overshot or undershot teeth, or cuneate heads.

Today the quality of the harlequin Great Dane in Germany is not so very good, for being cross-bred with yellow and brindle dogs some twenty years ago did much harm. There is especially a lack of good stud males whose heredity is excellent and who could be very helpful to the breed. Most of the harlequins are to be found today in South Germany. The breeding of this color is particularly difficult, because in the litters there are usually several puppies not as spotted as is desirable. An old breeder once said, "Only twenty-five percent of the litters are good, the other seventy-five are either too white or too black." Others have said, "If among all the litters there is only one good puppy one must be satisfied, but once there were two champions among brothers and sisters."

The chief faults found today among the Great Danes in Germany are in connection with the teeth, for they are often overshot. Dogs with teeth faults receive only a rating of "deficient" at German shows. Another fault which we have observed recently is that of too short heads.

Grayish tiger-colored and porcelain-colored Great Danes are not registered in the stud book, for they, like white Danes, are in many cases deaf. Black Great Danes are always judged in a class by themselves at the shows. They are not bred especially, but appear among the harlequins now and then.

The best German kennels of today are: for yellow and brindle, v.d. Hummelburg and v. Hause Birkehagen; for harlequin, v.d. Stadt Hamburg and Munchhausen; for blue, v. Kaiserhof and v.d. Föhrde.

The best stud males of today are: brindle, Dolf v. Hamburger Michel 33545 (sire Cäsar v. Nessal 31608—dam Champ. Gitana v. Frauenberg 31135). He carries the blood of Kant Doggensport and is the sire of Champ. Dina v.d. Hummelburg 34051. Black (for black and blue) Despot Funcken v.d. Heide 33350 (sire Simba Funcken v.d. Heide—dam Treantsima v.d. Heide) carries the blood of Jagla Moguntia and Dolf v.d. Saalburg and from his dam's side Blaumeise Funcken v.d. Heide.

45

PRINZ v.d. RHOEN

CHAMPUS aus dem **SCHAUMBURGERWALD**
Winning German harlequin

How German Champions are Made

CHAMPIONSHIP titles in Germany have varied somewhat at different periods. Judging by the early stud books, around the year 1900, the term "champion" was used for a time, but was apparently superseded by the more native term "Sieger," which means literally a conqueror or victor. The Pinscher-Klub, founded in 1895, at Cologne, published the first volume of its studbook at the end of 1902. This contains minutes of its earliest meetings. At Erfurt on September 15, 1900, a decision was made regarding the awarding of Sieger titles. They were to be conferred on dogs winning three first prizes in the Open class, under three different approved judges at recognized shows and two first prizes in the Sieger class, and non-members of the Klub were eligible. This is the same requirement as in Volume I of the studbook of the Bayerischer Schnauzer-Klub, founded in 1907, which appeared in 1910. The Cologne and Munich clubs amalgamated in 1922 as the Pinscher-Schnauzer-Klub and their first studbook, published in 1923, states that the title of Sieger (or its feminine equivalent, Siegerin) shall be awarded to dogs winning three first prizes with the rating "excellent" under three different approved judges at recognized shows. The title of "Jahressieger" or Year Champion was to be awarded at the annual specialty show by an approved Klub judge to the best dog in all classes, with a rating of excellent." The same requirements applied to the "Jahressiegerin" title for bitches. By 1925 the term "Klubsieger" was applied to dogs receiving the first type award. There could be as many of these in a given year as fulfilled the requirements, and the Jahressieger was usually, though not always, a Klubsieger also. By 1925, likewise, Miniature Schnauzers were divided by color, so that a double set of Jahressieger titles was awarded, one for blacks and one for pepper and salts.

In 1902 Oberleutnant Emil Ilgner (retired) published "Gebrauchs-und Luxushunde." In this he lists 17 breed specialty clubs which published their own studbooks, in addition to the D.H.St.B., the all-breed stud book, comparable to the AKC studbook in this country, and the D.G.St.B., the all-breed studbook for working dogs. He does not state when the specialty clubs were founded but the Dachshund Club had already (in 1902) published ten volumes of its studbook, the German Wirehaired Pointers five, the Foxterriers nine, the St. Bernards and Collies three each, while the German Shepherd Dog Club was founded in 1899 and the Pinscher-Klub, as above stated, in 1895. The Deutschen Kartell für Hundewesen was founded by a group of clubs, among which the S.V. was a charter member. It corresponded to the AKC and even though the specialty clubs kept their own studbooks the AKC required the Kartel stamp on all German registrations before German dogs were accepted for registration over here. Probably the various clubs made their own rules for sieger titles, at least in the early days, but Ilgner makes no mention of what they were. The first volume of the Pinscher-Klub records the award of the title of "Champion" in 1899 at Cologne and also at Amsterdam in Holland in 1901. The S.V. for many years awarded only two titles annuallly, "Sieger" for dogs and "Siegerin" for bitches.

In 1933 the Nazi government muscled in on the dog fancy, as on so many other things. The Kartell became the Reichsverband für das Deutsche Hundewesen, in the Reichsfachgruppe Deutsches Hundewesen (RDH), and the specialty clubs belonging to it each became a Fachschaft or "Section." The Jahressieger title or its equivalent became Reichssieger, and was awarded at the annual Reichssieger show. The

Klubsieger title became Fachschaftsieger. In 1937 the RDH became a member of the Reichsverband Deutscher Klein-tierzüchter (German Reich Organization of Small Animal Breeders). Orders were given that in breeding both parents should have received the rating of "very good" or "excellent" from a judge approved by the Section. In the case of working breeds at least one parent must also have an "Ausbildungskennzeichen" or training certificate. This rule went into effect July 1, 1937, according to Felix Ebner in his "Schnauzer und Pinscher," published in that year. He also stated beginning January 1, 1938, a working certificate would be required for both parents.

The terms Siegeranwärter and Siegeranwärterin are used for a dog or bitch which has wins toward a title. Such a dog would correspond to a championship certificate winner in England. The title of Weltsieger (world champion) appears to be awarded at one important European show annually, with competition open to qualified dogs from various countries. The August, 1937, issue of the Mitteilungen of the Fachschaft für Schnauzer und Pinscher gives a report of the World Congress of the Fédération Cynologique Interna-tionale (FCI) at Paris in July and in another item lists German Schnauzer winners at Paris, which included five Weltsieger and Weltsiegerin titles. In July, 1938, it was announced that the Antwartschaft for the Internationale Schönheits-Championat (International Bench Champion-ship) as well as the Reichssieger titles would be competed for at Cologne in October. The report of the Paris show in 1937 mentions an Internationale Championats-Anwärterin. This would seem to indicate that these International Cham-pionships were awarded on a basis similar to the Fachschaft or Klubsieger titles and were not the same as the Weltsieger titles.

RAAN v. LOHELAND

A Short Explanation of German Grammar

By Anne FitzGerald Paramoure

HE translation of foreign pedigrees and show reports is not easy, even for one who is well acquainted with the language in its everyday form. Just as the novice finds many English words used in an unfamiliar sense, so there is a special vocabulary employed by German-speaking breeders and exhibitors. To translate them it may be necessary to plow through ten or twenty variations of meaning in the unabridged dictionary, with no certainty that one will select the correct equivalent, even if it is included, while the ordinary abridged dictionary is likely to be no help whatever. Abbreviations are very frequently used, and may be fully as puzzling as an unfamiliar use of a familiar word.

All German nouns are capitalized, not merely proper names. Adjectives are not capitalized, even though they may form part of a kennel name, unless actually used in place of a noun. The formal second person "Sie" (meaning YOU) is also regularly capitalized. When an adjective is attached to the front of a noun so as to make a single word, however, it is capitalized instead of the noun to which it is attached, as in *Kleintierzuchter*, meaning small animal breeder.

German plurals are not formed by adding *S*, but in most cases by adding *er, e* or *en* to the root of the noun. Sometimes

51

the root vowel is changed by the addition of an umlaut (··) over a, o or u, making it ä, ö, or ü. This may be the only change or it may be in addition to the plural endings already mentioned. The umlaut stands for an *e* which is not written. In proper names or in a word beginning with a capital the *e* is often written in place of the umlaut, and where printing is done with type which does not include the umlauts the *e* itself may likewise be used. The umlaut can be important for three reasons: it changes ·the pronunciation, it may be the only sign that a word is plural and not singular; in a German dictionary or index all names or words which contain an umlaut will be alphabetized as though the letter *e* were printed after the vowel over which it is used. This may mean that a name or word will be found several lines or even pages away from the same name or word without the umlaut. Moreover, the presence or absence of the umlaut may completely change the meaning of a word. For instance, *Mucke* means a whim, while *Mücke* is a gnat. Finally, the feminine of many nouns is formed by adding an umlaut to the vowel and the suffix *in* to the end of the word, so Hund, dog (general or masculine) becomes Hündin, bitch.

Other pecularities which may confuse those not familiar with the language are: nouns have four cases, nominative, genitive (usually ending in *s* or *es* but sometimes in *e, en* or *ens*), dative and accusative. There are three genders, masculine, femine and neuter. Adjectives and pronouns also change their endings.

Another peculiarity is that the perfect participle of verbs is formed by adding *ge* to the *front* of the verb in most cases. Thus the participle of *decken* (meaning to breed) is *gedeckt* (bred) and the word will be found in a dictionary under *d* and not *g*. Compound verbs with *inseparable* prefixes do not add the augment *ge* for the participle, however. On the other hand, compound verbs with *separable* prefixes insert the *ge* between the prefix and the verb root, the participle of *anfangen* (to begin) being *angefangen*. In certain other tenses the separable prefix of the verb in the main clause comes at the end of the phrase or sentence, as for instance.

52

ich fang an (I begin) is a form of *anfangen*. As a compound verb may have quite a different meaning from the simple one from which it is formed, non-Germans unaccustomed to this usage find it extremely confusing to discover at the end of a sentence a prefix which may unexpectedly change the whole meaning. The Teutonic word order which frequently puts the verb at the end of the sentence instead of where other people would expect it is also confusing.

The names of German dogs, which are likely to appear dauntingly long and formidable to those who do not understand the language are much easier to remember if they are broken down into their separate parts. Most of them consist of an individual name, a preposition with or without an article, and a kennel name. Most if not all German breeds require litter registration, all puppies carrying the breeder's registered kennel name, while it is usual for all of a single litter to have individual names beginning with the same letter. Kennels' names often refer to the town, village or local area in which the breeder lives. Sometimes they are related to the name of the breed or the breeder, and puns are not uncommon. Thus Herr Berger, breeder of German Shepherds, used the kennel name *Bergerslust*, meaning "Shepherd's Delight" or "Berger's Delight" as one prefers. The impressive-sounding "Fiffi v. Rhein-Herne-Kanal" is only Fiffii of the Rhine Canal at Herne, where her breeder lived. Wilhelm Schwaneberg took the kennel name "v.d. Schwanburg," meaning "of or from the Swan Castle." The owners of "Neckar-lust," "Neckarstadt" and "Neckartal" all live along the Neckar River. "Zwergschnauzerheim" is nothing but "Home of Miniature Schnauzers."

Up to 1934 many of the large German specialty clubs published their own studbooks. Included among these were the Verein für Deutsche Schaferhunde, devoted to German Shepherd Dogs, and the Pinscher-Schnauzer-Klub, which registered six breeds: Giant, Standard and Miniature Schnauzers, Smooth-haired Pinschers (not Dobermans), Miniature Pinschers, and Affenpinschers. The Deutsches Kartell für Hundewesen (DKH) was the all breed club recognized by the AKC, and the papers of imported dogs

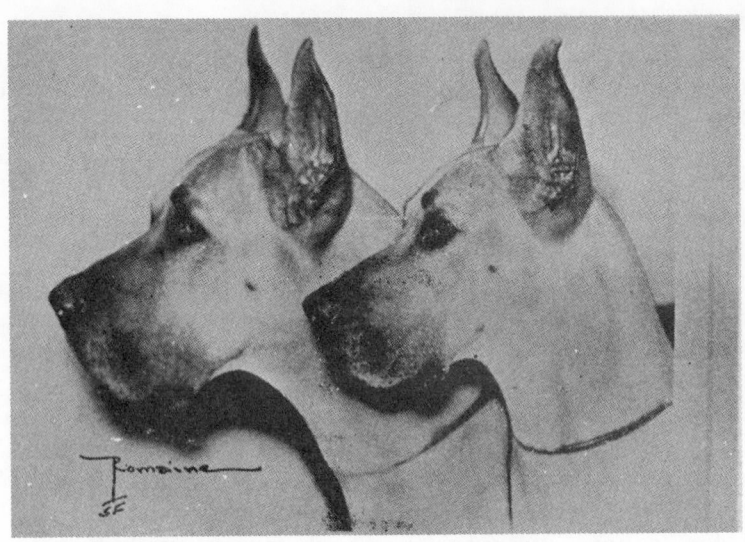

CH. PRINZ ERIC OF WILLOW RUN and
CH. OZELOT v. BIRKENHOF

had to be endosed by them before they were accepted for
AKC registration. In 1934 the Nazi government reorganized
the dog fancy, like so many other things. The national organization became the Reichsverband für das Deutsche
Hundewesen (RDH) and the specialty clubs were absorbed
as Fachschafte or sections of the RDH, though they continued to publish their stud books and breed papers as before, at least up to 1938. What has happened during the war
remains to be seen. On July 1, 1937, the RDH was reorganized as the Reichsverband Deutscher Kleintierzüchter
(RDK). The old styles of *Sieger,* or *Jahressieger* were
changed to Reichssieger, while the Klubsieger title became
Fachschaftsieger. Bitch titles were similarly changed to
Reichsiegerin and Fachschaftsiegerin.

Great Danes in England

BY MURIEL OSBORNE

T is said that Great Danes have been known in Great Britain for at least two hundred years, during which time they have been called "Danish dogs" and "German Boarhounds" as well as Great Danes. It is possible they were also called "German Mastiffs." Regardless of the name, English experts are agreed that "the foundation of present-day bloodlines was laid in the nineties of the last century when some very notable Great Danes were imported."

The breed became very popular, but during World War I it all but died out. After the war, Great Danes were again imported, and in 1938 it was stated that the Great Dane was "the most popular large breed in England because of its short coat, protective strength, obedient disposition, and its fondness for children." In 1938 a Swiss judge, functioning in England, wrote about the ninety-two Great Danes which he had seen. He said: "The Great Danes in England are conspicuous because of their enormous size and splendid walk. I saw giants there which cannot be duplicated on the Continent, but one-tenth of them had some faults in their jaws. In their walk ninety percent were good, and the same was true of the shape of the forehand and hindquarters. Some cowhocks were evident, and some heads were rather flat to the little stop. Tops of noses were too narrow, and head lines sloped backward too much. The Harlequins were first class as to color, but the brindles were much too dark."

55

CH. BONHOMIE OF BLENDON
(at fourteen months)

CH. BONIFACE OF BLENDON
(at fifteen months)

Between World War I and World War II, Great Dane breeding in England was dominated by two powerful kennels, Ouborough and Send, owned respectively by Mr. J. V. Rank and Mr. Gordon Stewart.

The Ouborough Kennel originally had Harlequins, but, by 1930, had turned entirely to fawns and brindles. The Send Kennel went in for all colors. Both owners imported dogs and bitches of superlative Continental breeding to unite with the English bloodlines, and of course these importations were of the utmost benefit to the breed.

At the height of its fame, the Send Kennels of Great Danes numbered over three hundred inmates! This kennel was almost self-contained, having its own bakery where the best wholemeal biscuit was made, facilities for meat storage, a quarantine kennel, a hospital with excellent equipment, and, in fact, everything imaginable for producing and rearing Great Danes. At Send much experimenting with color breeding was carried on, and Mr. Stewart gained a great deal of valuable knowledge through this.

From the world-famous Ouborough Kennels at this time came a succession of champions, one following on the other without pause. While it is difficult to pick out individual dogs of superb conformation, Ch. Vivien of Ouborough, as the dam of Ch. Ruffler, Ch. Bellovien, and Ch. Revive, deserves special mention. She was also the grand-dam of Ch. Ruffian and the famous Ch. Rebeller; who, in her turn, produced Rebellion, the sire of many of the early postwar champions.

At the same time that these great Ouborough champions were making their appearance, the Send Kennel was also producing a wonderful winning line from two imported dogs—one, the fawn Dutch Grand Champion Urlus Volbloed of Send and the other, also fawn, Egon Falkenhorst of Send. Ch. Urlus, in his two years at stud in England, produced Ch. Mavis, Ch. Midas, Ch. Egmund, Ch. Falstaff, Ch. Ulana, Ch. Lancelot of Send, and from the only bitch he served outside the home kennel, Ch. Bedina of Blendon, the first home-bred champion and the foundation of the Blendon strain.

Not surprising was it that the small kennels in those

CH. PENELOPE OF
ALDERWASLEY

CH. JEZEBEL OF WINOME

CH. IMOGEN OF OLDMANOR

CH. BAFFLEUR OF BLENDON

far-off days had to be content with the crumbs that fell from the great ones' tables!

Mrs. Hatfield's Sudbury Harlequins, while owing something to the Send importations, maintained an imposing line of home-bred winners, including the well-known Champions Zarane, Zarina, and Zinona of Sudbury.

Mrs. Lee Booker's Trayshills and my own Blendons contrived to produce an occasional champion. Mrs. Lee Booker bred Ch. Haakon of Trayshill and imported the Swiss Ch. Nicette von Eisenhof of Trayshill. I had Ch. Benvolio of Blendon (a son of Ch. Bedina), who was three years in succession the Best Great Dane at the shows of the Great Dane Club, and his son, Ch. Baffler of Blendon, who was the last Great Dane dog to be made a champion before the outbreak of World War II.

These dogs, and Ch. Baffler's son, Bafflino, mated to the Trayshill bitches purchased by Mrs. Jewell during 1938 and 1939 formed the foundation of her immensely successful Ladymeade strain.

This was the general picture of the Dane world in England at the outbreak of the last war. Throughout hostilities, of course, breeders greatly reduced the number of their dogs, and many of the small prewar exhibitors faded out completely. The leading kennels, however, contrived to breed one or two litters during the war years so as to preserve their strains, and, with the return of peace, breeding recommenced in earnest, with fawns and brindles, as usual, in far the strongest position. Harlequins were at a low ebb, as Mrs. Hatfield had more or less given up her famous Sudbury Kennel after the death of her only son, Roy, who had always handled her dogs for her, and only two kennels, Miss Lomas' "Wideskies" and Mr. John Silver's "Silvernia" were still specializing in this difficult color. In an even worse state were the blues and blacks, which became almost extinct about this time.

To Mrs. Ennals, of the Bringtonhill Kennels, goes all the credit for resurrecting these beautiful colors after World War II. So successfully has she done this that she has produced a champion in each color in recent years.

CH. RYOT OF OUBOROUGH

CH. BLACJACK OF
BRINGTONHILL

A Merrowlea litter of 6-week-old puppies, owned by Capt. and Mrs. E. J. Hutton.

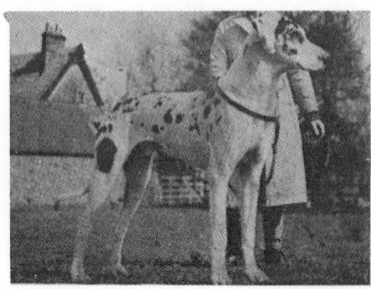

CH. CLOUD OF THE WIDESKIES

CH. FROST OF THE WIDESKIES

60

In case American Dane fanciers do not know the qualifications for an English champion, perhaps I had better state them here. At championship shows the Kennel Club allots two challenge certificates, one for each sex, in each breed which has been given championship status for that particular show. These challenge certificates are awarded to the Best Dog and the Best Bitch. To gain the title of champion, a dog or bitch must win three challenge certificates under three different judges.

All colors, of course, compete against one another on equal terms, so it can be readily seen that the numerically stronger fawns and brindles start with a great advantage over the Harlequins, blues, and blacks.

Before the war, when a mismarked bitch puppy was of superb type, it could be sold cheaply as a pet or given away to a good home, with the reservation that its breeder could have a litter from it, and so its good points were often perpetuated in well-marked offspring. But for financial and other reasons this ceased to be practicable after the war, and only Harlequins of show color, though perhaps of poor type, could be retained. Thus, brood bitches invaluable *from the point of view of type* have been lost to the Harlequin variety. Hence, the Harlequins have had a very difficult task indeed to compete successfully with the fawns and brindles in the show ring.

Miss Lomas was successful in showing a Harlequin well able to challenge the best of the fawns and brindles in the years just after the war, when her Ch. Frost of the Wideskies became a big winner.

The first postwar All Dane Championship Show, held in London by the Great Dane Club in 1946, astonished most people with the number and quality of the exhibits. The late Mr. Gordon Stewart judged and was most agreeably surprised with the Danes. Here, Mrs. Rowberry's Ch. Juan of Winome, the first postwar champion in the breed, gained his first challenge certificate and was Best of Breed. Mrs. Gutherie's Mondaine of Maspound won the similar title for the bitches.

The first postwar bitch champion was Mrs. Clayton's Ch.

61

CH. BONADVENTURE OF BARVAE

CH. TANDYE OF MOONSFIELD

Bon Adventure of Barvae (a big fawn by Rebellion of Oubor-ough ex Bridesmaid of Barvae), who was bred by her owner. Other champions sired by Rebellion and shown about this time were Mr. J. V. Rank's Ch. Rusa of Ouborough, Mrs. Row-berry's Ch. Jillida of Winome, Mr. W. G. Siggers' Ch. Rivolet of Ouborough, and that famous bitch (of which more will be said later), Mrs. Robb's Ch. Ryot of Ouborough.

Into the picture now comes Mr. Rank's Ch. Royalism of Ouborough, winner of numerous challenge certificates and a very potent stud dog that exerted a tremendous influence on the breed. His offspring include eleven champions, of which two became international champions.

Another dog which was to leave his mark on the breed was a fawn, Fingards King of Kings of Blendon, imported by the Blendon Kennels from Mr. David Fingard, Toronto, during 1945. King of Kings was also a tremendously potent stud force that impressed his good qualities on his offspring. This remarkable dog sired (with very limited opportunities) five champions and one other bitch which, to date, has ac-quired two challenge certificates. These five champions, all of which were whelped in three litters, were Ch. Baffleur of Blendon, Ch. Berynthia of Blendon (litter sisters), Ch. Jeep of Winome and Ch. Jezebel of Winome (litter brother and sister), and Ch. Blendon Antoinette of Rydens. Ch. Bonhomie of Blendon, grandson of King of Kings, won the proud dis-tinction of being the only Dane ever to beat Ch. Elch Edler of Ouborough (the Best in Show winner at Crufts in 1953).

Fingards King of Kings of Blendon brought to England some of the best bloodlines of the United States and Canada and gave an extra dash of showmanship and quality to al-most all his descendants.

In 1952, within a few weeks of one another, both Mr. J. V. Rank and Mr. Gordon Stewart died. Their deaths seemed to underline the great change which had been slowly creeping over the English Dane world. From being under the domina-tion of their two powerful kennels before the war, a differ-ent pattern had been emerging and seemed to be crystallized by the deaths of these two famous kennel owners. Mrs. Hat-field also had passed on, and thus another strong personal-

63

ity had disappeared and the Sudbury Kennels had ceased to exist. Now it became the day of the small breeder and exhibitor.

A number of really good kennels have come into being. Having no kennel staff, or perhaps but one helper, these enthusiasts breed and show their own Danes. There is friendly rivalry between a number of kennels that would be judged small by prewar standards, but which are producing Danes of the best type and highest quality.

Mrs. Jewell, well-known to American breeders, took her Ladymeade Danes to California in 1948. Before leaving this country, her big fawn, Hyperion of Ladymeade (sired by Ch. Benvolio of Blendon ex Pandora of Ladymeade) had produced a promising lot of sons and daughters to help the breed over here.

Mention must now be made again of Mrs. Ennals and her work with blues and blacks. Starting during the war with two blue-bred bitches, Black Beauty and Blue Blaze of Bringtonhill, Mrs. Ennals had created a blue and black strain that can hold its own with the best. By using Hyperion of Ladymeade, she produced Bahram of Bringtonhill, a black of immense size and excellent type; Bahram, in his turn, sired the blue bitch, Ch. Banshee of Bringtonhill—the first blue champion bitch in England since Colonel and Mrs. Cowan's Ch. Ranghild of Rungmook acquired the title in 1912.

Ch. Banshee was bred to Ch. Dawnlight of Ickford (both being grand-progeny of Hyperion of Ladymeade), and this mating produced Ch. Blacjack of Bringtonhill, the first black champion dog since Ch. Wotan of Send (bred by Mr. Gordon Stewart) acquired the title in 1931. Mrs. Jewell has imported a black Dane which is a litter brother of Ch. Blacjack.

Mrs. Ennals has also bred a champion fawn dog in Ch. Basra of Bringtonhill (also by Hyperion of Ladymeade), a dog which did a great deal of winning for her.

Miss Lomas' Wideskies Kennels are in the front rank in Harlequins, and she is the only breeder and exhibitor who has made Harlequin champions since the war. Her Ch. Frost of the Wideskies and Ch. Cloud of the Wideskies have kept the Harlequin flag flying at all the leading shows. Homebred,

CH. TELAMAN OF MOONSFIELD
Outstanding English winner and sire of the mid-60's. Owned by Mrs. E. M. Harrild.

An 8-week-old puppy from the
Leesthorpe Hill Harlequin Great
Danes of Leicestershire, England.

CH. MR. SOFTEE OF MERROWLEA

CH. REVERT OF OUBOROUGH

CH. DAWNLIGHT OF ICKFORD

CH. MERRY MONK OF MERROWLEA

they both have Send and Sudbury bloodlines in their pedigrees.

Since the war and before the death of Mr. Rank, the Ouborough Kennels bred and exhibited several more champions, these being Ch. Rusa; Ch. Royalism; the latter's daughters, Ch. Raet and Ch. Rindel (both destined to make history as brood bitches) ; Ch. Ryot; Ch. Relate; and, perhaps the most famous of all, Ch. Elch Edler of Ouborough. Ch. Elch Edler was shown at his first Crufts show as a puppy under the ownership of Mrs. Rank only a month after Mr. Rank's death and won his first challenge certificate at this show. Thereafter, he won his other two challenge certificates at successive shows at which he was exhibited, acquiring his title of champion on the day he was a year old! But his greatest triumph and one of the greatest triumphs in the history of the breed, was his outstanding win at Crufts in 1953 when, handled by his owner, Mr. Siggers, he was made Supreme Champion and Best of All Breeds in Show.

It is sad to note that to win Best in Show at Crufts had been the greatest ambition of Mr. Rank but was destined never to be fulfilled during his lifetime, although it came to pass the year following his death with what was one of the last Danes he bred.

The dam of Ch. Elch Edler was Ch. Raet, who was also the dam of Ch. Relate and Ch. Festival of Ouborough. The latter is now owned by Mr. Jacobs.

Mrs. Robb's Foxbar Kennels in Scotland also go back to prewar days. Her fawn dog, Rebel of Foxbar, became a champion in 1932. After the war, Mrs. Robb took over from Mr. Rank a brindle bitch that was destined to make history — Ch. Ryot of Ouborough (by Rebellion of Ouborough), who won twelve challenge certificates and was Best of All Breeds in Show at the Edinburgh Championship Show in 1949. As well as running up this record, she proved herself a superlative brood bitch and, mated to Ch. Royalism of Ouborough, produced Ch. Raet of Ouborough (previously mentioned), Ch. Rindel of Ouborough, and Ch. Racketeer of Foxbar.

The grand-progeny of Ch. Ryot of Ouborough include the previously mentioned Ch. Relate, Ch. Festival, and Ch.

Elch Edler of Ouborough. Ch. Rindel of Ouborough (Ch. Ryot's other daughter), bred to Ch. Marfre Modern Ransom (by Ch. Royalism), produced a litter of five bitches, of which, to date, one—Ch. Rhapsody of Foxbar—has her full title; another, Marfre Modern Miss, has two challenge certificates; a third, Mrs. Robb's Random of Foxbar, has one; and a fourth, Mr. Siggers' Rhythm of Foxbar, also has one.

Another prewar kennel that is still breeding Danes today is my own Blendon. With three generations of champions before 1939—Ch. Bendina; her son, Ch. Benvolio; and her grandson, Ch. Baffler—the tradition was carried on through Ch. Baffler's son, Bafflino (unshown because of the war), who became the sire of the first postwar champion in the breed, Ch. Juan of Winome.

Ch. Baffler, as well as being the last champion dog before the war, was also the last champion brindle dog in England until his own great-great-grandson, Ch. Bonhomie of Blendon, became a champion in 1951. Ch. Bonhomie has won ten challenge certificates and was Best in Show at the Great Dane Breeders' Association Club Show in London in March 1954—the only Specialist Show of the breed for which the Kennel Club allotted challenge certificates during the year. At this show, Ch. Elch Edler, hitherto undefeated since he was first shown as a puppy in 1952, had his colors lowered for the first time, and amidst intense excitement, was beaten by the four-year-old brindle, Ch. Bonhomie. Ch. Bonhomie is still the only champion brindle dog in England (1954) but, during this year, Mrs. Robb, in Scotland, has made her brindle dog, Racketeer of Foxbar, a champion.

After the importation of Fingards King of Kings, Blendon took the field again with bitches, and Ch. Baffleur won six challenge certificates and was adjudged Best Bitch in Show by Mr. Earl Ross when he judged the Great Dane Club Show in London in 1951.

Ch. Baffleur's sister, Ch. Berynthia, won four challenge certificates, and Ch. Blendon Antoinette of Rydens was adjudged Best Bitch at Blackpool in 1952 by Mr. Tiffin, who awarded her fifth challenge certificate.

Ch. Boniface, a fawn dog by Ch. Bonhomie ex Ch. Berynthia, gained his Junior Warrant; another fawn champion dog in the kennel, Ch. Bronx, is a very tall, rich red grandson of Bafflino's.

Mrs. Rowberry's "Winomes" were also established in prewar days, and her record of champions bred since 1945 include Ch. Juan, Ch. Jillida, Ch. Jeep, and Ch. Jezebel of Winome (the latter now owned by Mrs. Main).

Another kennel making its mark is Mrs. Harrild's "Moonsfield," housing three champion bitches: Ch. Rhagodia of Ouborough (by Ch. Royalism); Ch. Rhapsody of Foxbar (already noted); and the home-bred Ch. Tandye of Moonsfield (another champion daughter of Ch. Royalism). Mr. and Mrs. Allen, of U.S.A. note, have recently purchased a young fawn "Moonsfield" bitch puppy.

The Rev. and Mrs. Davies, whose big brindle bitch, Ch. Imogen of Oldmanor, is well-known, are continuing with the Oldmanor Kennels founded some years before the war by Mrs. Davies and her mother, Mrs. Russell.

Mrs. Mary Jones' Marfre Kennel houses the outstanding dog of 1951 in Ch. Marfre Modern Ransom. Ch. Marfre was Best Dane at Crufts, at the Great Dane Breeders' Association Club Show, and at the Great Dane Club Show, under Mr. Earl Ross during that year. Ch. Marfre is the sire of the litter of five superb bitches out of Ch. Rindel which was mentioned previously.

A breeder-exhibitor who went right to the top soon after the war was Mrs. Laming, of the "Ickford" Danes. Her foundation bitch, Radiance of Ladymeade (by Hyperion of Ladymeade), proved an exceptional brood bitch. In her first litter (by Ch. Royalism of Ouborough) she produced the great Ch. Dawnlight of Ickford and two international champions, Ch. Anndale Royalight of Ickford and Ch. Anndale Moonlight of Ickford. In a second litter by the same sire, Radiance produced Ch. Goldenlight of Ickford.

Ch. Dawnlight has won fifteen challenge certificates and has been eight times Best of Breed. His progeny include Ch, Blacjack of Bringtonhill and Ch. Prudence of Ambergrove.

Ch. Prudence of Ambergrove is owned by Miss Mavis Hicks, a newcomer to Danes, who picked Ch. Prudence out of

69

the litter and reared and showed her. Ch. Prudence, bred by Mr. Perry, is the daughter of Ch. Penelope of Alderwasley, a very beautiful, stylish brindle and a big winner, going back to Ouborough breeding on her sire's side and Mrs. Clayton's Barvae line on her dam's.

Another "novice" owner of a champion Dane is Mrs. Allen, of Elstead, who reared her dog from puppyhood; her Ch. Revert of Ouborough is a model, well-reared Dane. He was chosen to accompany Mrs. Allen's small grandson, little David Weeks, to be presented to Princess Margaret at the Albert Hall and behaved with the most stately dignity imaginable.

Mrs. Bryn Jones is a "one-Dane" owner whose pet is also a champion. Her Ch. Vegar of Ouborough has distinguished herself by winning five challenge certificates, including one at the Great Dane Club Show in 1952 and another at the Great Dane Breeders' Association Club Show in 1953.

This chapter would not be complete without reference to a famous English Dane known to admirers all over the world --Mrs. Woodhouse's Juno. Juno has followed in the footsteps of the Danes of the Send Kennels, which, before the war, were obedience trained and could hold their own against all breeds in obedience tests. They also gave wonderful demonstrations of obedience at shows throughout the country, and by means of films made by Mr. Stewart, taught children the Safety-First Rules for Road Safety.

Juno has done the same things. She has competed successfully in obedience tests and has been in several films. Her latest, in color, is called *Make Me an Offer;* in it, she has played a big part and has acted magnificently.

The Blendons, Ickfords, Bringtonhills, Winomes, and numerous other kennels have, since the war, "de-bunked" the notion that English Danes' coats and colors deteriorate as a result of the English climate. English Danes bred from richly colored, fine-coated stock retain all their depth of color and short, fine density of coat and, without exaggeration, can compare with the best strains from the United States and the Continent in this respect.

But stock with coarse, long coats and pale ground colors,

indeterminate brindle stripes and pale muzzles, will hand down these characteristics to their descendants. It is no use blaming these faults on the weather—unreliable though the English climate is known to be!

Apart from the exhibitor- and breeder-owners of Danes in England, there are countless numbers of people who love the breed purely as pets and companions, for true the world over is the old saying that if you once had a Dane, you never want any other kind of dog.

Stories of English Danes and their quaint ways, endearing habits, and wonderful bravery could fill this chapter all over again! What other breed is at once so big and so gentle, so loyal and so loving, so clever and so faithful? We, who love them so well, hail one another as Dane lovers wherever we may live and, with this great bond between us, must always be friends together—even if we never actually meet at all.

CH. PRUDENCE OF AMBERGROVE

71

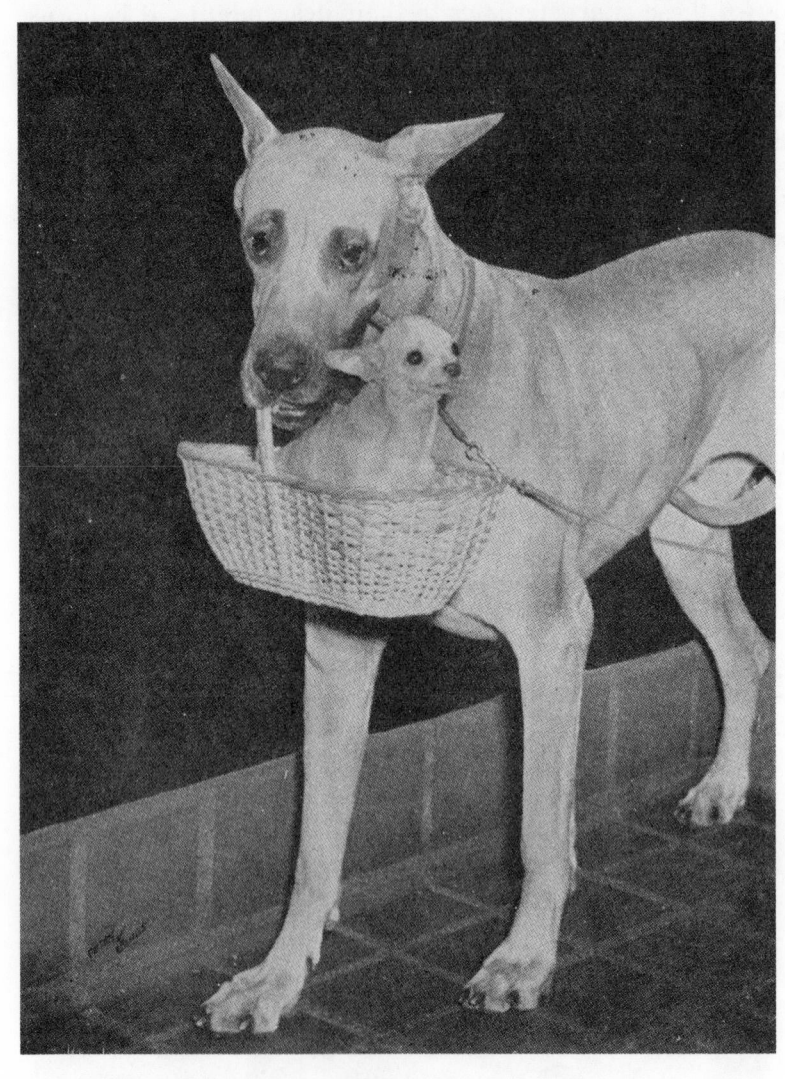

CH. HEIDE OF ROXDANE, Great Dane, and
CH. MERONETTE GRUDIER, Chihuahua
Compliments of Mr. Vincent La Fan, Cleveland, Ohio

72

The Blueprint of the Great Dane

OR the purpose of impressing the populace and inspiring the awe of *hoi polloi*, a Great Dane is not required to be good. He needs only to be big. With a big enough Great Dane on a lead, an owner cannot traverse a block without being surrounded by a gaping group of youths (and elders) and without being barraged with questions, most of them trite if not stupid—a demand for data about the dog.

"How old is he?"

"Don't it cost a lot to feed him?"

"What does he eat?"

"How much does he eat?"

"Is he fierce?"

"Why don't you put a saddle on him and ride him?" This question is always asked as a joke, but the owner has heard it so many times that it has ceased to be funny.

This crowd is not critical of the dog's structure, nor, if the dog is able to ambulate, of his soundness, and seldom of his beauty; but it concerns itself only with size. To be a good Great Dane, a dog must indeed be large, but it is not always the biggest that is the best. There are many other considerations at least as important as size. There is, of course, a certain requisite height at shoulder for a fully adult dog, as we shall see, but we cannot assume that we have a good Great Dane just because we have a big one.

73

Then, how shall the amateur owner of a Great Dane set about to evaluate the excellencies and the shortcomings of his dog? He may exhibit the dog in a dozen dog shows without learning wherein the dog is superior or faulty, as the case may be. Judges of dog shows are too busy to expatiate upon their analyses of the exhibits and to explain their awards to the exhibitors. Moreover, they are loath to incur the animosity of an exhibitor by setting his dog back in the prize list and then enumerating its shortcomings. That is too much like adding insult to an assumed injury. A dog's position in the prize list, especially that of a Great Dane, may or may not be a criterion of his excellence. In most dog shows not enough Great Danes are exhibited, or good enough ones, to enable one to assume that the winning dog is one of great excellence. He may be, and usually is, only the best of the lot.

Consistently to go to the very top of the heap in the larger shows, specialty shows for Great Danes only, or such major events as the Westminster Kennel Club Show in Madison Square Garden in New York or at the great outdoor Morris and Essex Kennel Club Show at Madison, New Jersey, where a numerous entry of fine dogs can be depended upon to be present, is indeed a manifestation of a dog's excellence. At such shows the judges are carefully chosen for their knowl-·edge of the breeds upon which they are called to pass.

However, few persons wish publicly to submit their dog to the criticism of an expert judge without being sure that the dog is one of considerable merit. It makes an exhibitor feel cheap to have his dog turned out of the judging ring not only without a prize but also without more than the casual glance of a judge, who requires no more than that to distinguish a good specimen from a mediocrity or worse. One may not mind losing the top prizes in a class of dogs all of whom are of notable excellence, but one would undergo considerable embarrassment to realize that he had submitted for examination and judgment a dog whose merits were utterly unworthy of the competition in which he was entered. Other onlookers, aware that in any competition somebody must needs be the loser, might pay little attention

74

to the defeat of a wholly unworthy dog, yet the owner might rankle with the knowledge that the Great Dane he had reared and shown as a swan turned out to be only an old gray goose after all.

Then, how is the amateur owner to be sure that his dog is of sufficient merit to warrant his exhibition? How make certain that the pride with which we strut down the avenue with our Great Dane is justified? His size, as we have said, is sufficient to impress the multitude, but how be sure that the dog is not ridiculous in the eyes of the cognoscenti, whose awareness of the requirements of the breed are schooled and trained?

The answer is that the owner should himself examine the dog in the light of those requirements. Such an examination is rather easy to make. While one must have seen and studied hundreds of dogs to become the holder of a license from the American Kennel Club to judge a breed officially, yet one can easily learn to evaluate the merits of one's own or one's friends' dogs and to discuss them intelligently. Indeed, the purpose of this "blueprint" is to provide the reader with the information which, properly applied, will enable him to make such an evaluation.

At the ringside of every dog show in America are to be found dozens of persons fully capable of discussing the merits of the various exhibits. Let a judge come a serious cropper in handing out the right ribbon to the right dog, and these persons will spot the error immediately and be able to give their reasons for it. It behooves every owner of a purebred dog of any breed or variety to make himself conversant with the requirements of an excellent specimen of the breed; to do so enhances the pride he manifests in a good dog, and forestalls him from boasting of merits to which the animal has no claim. Such a person may not choose ever to become an official judge of the breed, but many an enthusiastic owner knows as much about his breed as does the man or woman who assumes to judge it in the show ring.

Incidentally, it may be worth while right here to mention that a pedigree, however long or however excellent it may be, is no criterion of a dog's superiority. The good dog makes the good pedigree, and not the good pedigree the good dog. A pedigree is only the record of an animal's ancestors, tabulated to show the relationships of the animals named in it. A good barrel must stand on its own bottom; and a good dog must be himself a good dog and not fall back upon the name of some eminent grandsire for his claim to merit.

And do not brag about the length of your dog's pedigree. Too many persons, ignorant of canine lore, declare with pride that their dogs have pedigrees, as they say, "as long as my arm." One generation, if the dogs in it are registered in the stud book, is as valid as four or five, since it is easy to trace such a pedigree, by reference to the stud book, as far as one has the time and patience to carry it.

A noteworthy pedigree may provide considerable enlightenment about how best to choose the mates for a dog that is himself one of distinguished excellence. It serves only that purpose and does not make a dog either better or worse than he already is. If we do not know anything about the animals named in the pedigree, it serves no useful purpose at all.

The most nearly perfect bitch in the world mated to the most nearly perfect dog can be expected to produce some mediocre, or even bad, puppies along in the same litter with others that are destined to become famous. All the puppies in the litter, the superior and the inferior, will have exactly the same pedigree; thus we see that, unless it is proposed to derive some glory from a famous brother which may be utterly unlike our own dog, a good (or long) pedigree contributes nothing at all to the superiority of our individual Great Dane. Let us make sure of the merits of the animal himself before we drag out his pedigree or brag too much about it.

The presently accepted standard by which the Great Dane is judged in the United States is "The Official Illustrated Standard of the Great Dane Club of America, Inc." It was formulated by a committee of the club whose name it bears, and was accepted and promulgated by the American Kennel Club in the year 1945. The excellent drawings affixed to that standard, and an integral part of it, were made by Donald E. Gauthier.

The drafting of a new standard for the Great Dane breed and its adoption by the American Kennel Club were not intended in any way to change the specifications for the breed. The same dogs that won under the old standard which the new one supplants could have gone on with their winning careers without interruption. By making a change in the standard of a breed it is possible to throw the breed into chaos and to destroy the ideals toward which breeders may have striven for decades on end. However, in the present case care was taken to preserve the breed just as it was. The purpose of the new standard was better to define the breed's requirements than the discarded standard had done, to tighten up the specifications, and to clarify the wording of the former document.

That new standard is included in this book in a separate chapter, and it should be read and studied (even learned by rote) by anybody who aspires to know what a Great Dane should be like. Standards, however, are brief and technical; they are intended for the perusal and reference of persons who already know approximately the requirements representative of animals of the respective breeds. They cannot spare words for discussions of differences or for reasons why breeds are as they are. The very "official" nature of the standard renders it necessary that its categorical statements about the breed take precedence over any nonofficial statements or opinions. Wherever in this chapter any statement may conflict (or may appear to conflict) with a categorical specification as laid down in the standard, the standard must govern. There is, in fact, no dissent from it.

Before we undertake the survey of any dog, it behooves us to know that the animal is in the best possible condition to which he may be brought. He must be in hard, sound flesh, neither too fat nor, above all, too thin. The amount of flesh, may be in part determined by the quantity and balance of his diet, but his firmness of musculature will be determined by his exercise. An obese animal waddling in his gait or an emaciated skeleton cannot be compared to a bright-eyed, adequately fed and exercised one. The correct nutrition of a large Great Dane is expensive and attention to his exercise is admittedly a problem, but the man or woman who is not prepared to bear the cost of feeding a Dane with ample meat or who has not the space and facilty to give him the exercise to keep him habitually at the top of his form should, for the dog's sake, dispose of him and get a Chihuahua or some small dog that does not require the attention that a Dane demands.

Cleanliness is a matter about which there is some difference of opinion. Some owners of Great Danes consider it harmful to bathe their dogs. Such persons rely upon persistent brushing, with or without dry-cleaning agents, such as corn meal or fuller's earth, to keep their dog immaculate. This is possible but it requires great vigilance and much elbow grease. Bathing actually does a Great Dane no more harm than any other dog. The essential is that he appear for his examination scrupulously clean, however that state may be accomplished.

If exercise has not worn the nails to a state of bluntness, they should be nipped back as far as possible without touching the quick, after which all rough edges should be filed down. Long nails, clattering over the floor, are indicative of inadequate exercise. They spread the toes apart and cause the feet to appear flat.

The teeth should be brushed at least, using a powder made of equal parts of salt and baking soda. If the teeth are clogged with tartar, indicative of too much starchy food in the diet, the dog should be taken to the veterinary dentist to have them scaled.

The anal glands should be kept squeezed out. Their clogging may affect the dog's spirit as well as impair his gait. This process is somewhat painful and it is well to have an assistant to hold the head of so large a dog as a Dane while he undergoes it; but the relief that comes from having these glands emptied more than repays the dog for the momentary unpleasantness.

There is fortunately little trimming to be done on the

Great Dane to improve his outline. His faults are impossible to conceal with hair. Some exhibitors believe that the expression is improved by clipping short with small scissors the long, coarse hairs—the feelers—that protrude from the muzzle. This is a convention and is not considered to be faking; it is a matter of individual choice whether or not it be done.

The conventional and correct collar for a Great Dane is a sound strap of narrow, strong leather, without ornamentation of any kind. A cheap collar of inferior or imitation leather will not suffice for so strong a dog. The Dane is notoriously gentle and easy to control, but it is unwise to risk a fragile collar. A chain collar or a show ring slip lead may be substituted for a leather collar if it is desired, but the old-fashioned, wide, studded collar is no longer used. Nothing must obscure more than is absolutely necessary the graceful lines of the neck of the modern and streamlined Great Dane. The leash for such a dog need not be heavy, if it is made of the best quality of leather. Anybody who can afford to buy and feed a show Great Dane surely will not stint on buying the correct accoutrements for him.

For adequate examination of the dog, at least two persons and a considerable open space are requisite. One of the persons will "handle" the dog, lead him and pose him as the examiner may direct. The usually provided show ring is inadequate for an active dog of the dimensions of a Great Dane to exhibit his gait; but judges are forced to do their best in the space at their disposal. A large, closely clipped lawn or park is the best place for an examination, although a little-used, paved street or a stretch of wide sidewalk will do as well. The area should be as flat and smooth as possible.

If another Great Dane of recognized excellence is available with which to compare the dog under examination, it will simplify the process. However, there are no perfect dogs of any breed, and the examiner is warned not to look for any slavish likeness. Many dogs of only indifferent excellence get by to high awards, even to championships; and the dog employed for comparison must not be accepted as an absolute criterion. The one under survey may well be the better of the two. This is especially true in the matter of gait. Many of the greatest winners in this particular breed do not move with trueness and liberty. Bad action in front or rear is a grievous fault and must be penalized, whether the specimen with which comparison is to be made is sound or not.

You have looked at your dog a thousand times and could recognize him in a throng of similar dogs, but have you ever scrutinized him critically, considered wherein he is right as a member of his breed, and candidly faced the question of his faults? Judging a dog is largely a matter of looking at him intently, recognizing that he is not one hundred percent perfect, and trying to find wherein he is wrong. Most persons possess a sense of symmetry and of the fitness of a thing for its purpose. Little more is required to evaluate the merits of a dog. There may be some purely arbitrary specifications set down in the Standard of the breed, but such specifications are easy to apply. A dog either meets them or fails to meet them. It is other qualifications in which there are various degrees in the approach to perfection that call for exercise of discrimination—such as the determination of just when the desirable elongation of the neck degenerates into weakness; just the point in which great substance causes an animal to appear cloddy; whether a dog is too straight or too bent at the stifle joint. Therein lies the fascination of canine structure and the joy of finding a dog exactly to our liking.

The first thing in making a survey of a dog the size of a Dane is to have him posed naturally at a distance of some twenty-five feet from the examiner. Too many judges, either through the necessity of surveying a class of dogs in a pillbox or through the neglect of looking at them whole, fail to see the over-all ensemble of the exhibits. Later it will be necessary to analyze the parts individually and at close range; but the whole is greater than any of its parts, and, if the dog is wrong as a whole, the perfection of the parts that fail to fit together will not save it. A dog must possess unity and be aesthetically satisfying. He must exhibit style and

80

grace of outline. His head must conform in size to his body; his neck must "flow" into his shoulders; his hinder parts must not be too big for his fore parts and vice versa His back line must be straight from withers to pelvis, without roach or sag.

Often in such a preliminary examination, it is detectable at a mere glance that a dog is unsound. His body may be hung between loose shoulders, he may turn his front feet out in a dancing master stance, he may stand with his hocks pointing inward. In such a case, if it is apparent without moving the animal that his gait is bound to be faulty, one had as well discontinue the survey and discard the dog. It is true that gait is the test of structure, but structure may be so bad that it is not required to move the animal to ascertain that the structure is utterly wrong.

Another fault is an outline foreign to the ideals of the breed. In the Great Dane, this foreign aspect is likely to remind one on the one hand of a Greyhound and on the other hand of a Mastiff. Both are wrong. A Great Dane should be a Great Dane and nothing else. It is alleged, and may be believed, that both Greyhound and Mastiff blood was in earlier times infused into the Great Dane breed, the former to improve its grace and speed, the latter to increase its substance and size. Both are presumed to have been bred out again, and neither should be apparent. However, whippety, weasel-like dogs are often perpetrated as Great Danes, as are coarse and cloddy dogs reminiscent of oversized Bulldogs. The Great Dane should embrace a happy medium of type with lissome grace and activity combined with ample bone and substance. He should have the speed and soundness to overtake the wild boar, and the substantial power to tackle him and hold him at bay until the huntsmen come up.

For this purpose the Great Dane must be a large dog. The minimum height at the withers as stated in the standard is 30 inches for dogs and 28 inches for bitches, with a preference to be given to animals of at least two inches greater stature. Indeed, we want a Dane to be as large as we can have him; and, other things being equal, which they never are, the larger dog must win over the smaller one. But better a well-constructed and sound dog of thirty inches (for a male) at the shoulder, or even slightly less, than a clumsy, coarse, or cow-hocked monster of thirty-four or thirty-six inches.

Great progress has been made in the last twenty years in the breeding of typical dogs of the larger breeds, and even more progress in their adequate feeding for soundness in their growing period. A thoroughly sound Dane only a few years ago was all but unheard of; a tremendously big one was almost certain to be cow-hocked and ungainly. We have now achieved sound Danes of great size, dogs that move as truly as any good terrier, but it requires greater vigilance in breeding and feeding to retain soundness, once we have obtained it, than in varieties of lesser stature.

In the scale of points, five (out of a total of 100) are allotted to size. So long as not more than five percent of our consideration of the Dane is devoted to size, we may be considered safe. The danger is in permitting great size to overweigh more important considerations. Smallness in a Dane is not to be condoned, but mere height at shoulder should not be the criterion of excellence. There are many other things.

Assuming that the dog under our scrutiny has passed muster as a whole, that we find no major part too large or too small for the other parts, that the standing dog shows no obvious evidence of unsoundness, that his stature, symmetry, and substance are at the very least adequate, we may proceed to the examination of the various parts.

The head of the Dane is by no means the most important of its parts, but a dog whose head structure is grossly faulty cannot be considered a characteristic member of its breed. In the standard scale of points the head is appraised at 20 percent of the whole, but no good judge would let a Dane with a bad head off with so small a penalty. The merits of a dog cannot, in any event, be evaluated in numbers, but an otherwise good Dane is ruined by a bad head.

The top skull and muzzle of the Dane should be of approximately equal length; that is, the measurement with calipers (or roughly with the eye) from the stop to occiput should be almost exactly the same as that from the stop to the end of the nose. That measurement cannot be exactly defined, since it will vary in different specimens, both in proportion to the size of the dog and to his structure behind the head. A dog with a tendency to cloddiness will not have so long a head as a whippety-built dog. On the whole, it may be said that considerable length in proportion to the body structure is desirable.

Even more important than the exact length of head is the leanness of the top skull (short of any appearance of weakness) and the fullness and squareness of muzzle. The demarcating stop between the top skull and muzzle must be distinct and abrupt—a step down. Thus the girth of the muzzle is necessarily less than the girth of top skull. The top skull and muzzle may be likened to two loaves of bread of similar length, one somewhat larger in circumference than the other, placed end to end on a flat surface, the disparity in their girth producing the abrupt stop.

The top skull should be essentially flat on top and sides, neither so wide as to appear gross nor so narrow as to be weak. It is better too fine than too common, however. The bitch's head is more refined and delicately chiseled than the dog's. This concession to sex must be made, a bitchy dog being an abomination and a doggy bitch but little more to be forgiven. The muscles on the cheeks should be only visible and never bunchy or prominent. Obtrusive cheeks coarsen the appearance of the whole head and destroy its classical and chaste contours. Such cheeks are usually found to accompany bunchy shoulder muscles. They are not to be excused by the explanation that the dog has been given bones to chew in his puppyhood, since the gnawing of bones does not produce bunchy cheek muscles in a dog that would not otherwise have them.

It is essential that the planes of the top of the skull and the top of the muzzle be parallel. Any deviation from this parallel, whether down-faced or dish-faced, will entirely spoil the dog's expression—as much as will the absence of a distinct stop.

The muzzle should be sharply truncated, perpendicularly to its top plane. The lips should be square, neither sagging and rounded with a string of saliva hanging from them, nor too short and dry. A dog with too profuse a lip is called "lippy," and one with insufficient lip appears "snipey," whether the muzzle formation is adequate or not.

The nostrils are wide and large to afford the dog sufficient breath. Nostrils too small, usually found with small, narrow, pig eyes, give the dog a stingy expression. A "split nose," by which is meant a deeply divided septum, is a disqualification in the show ring, although it by no means disqualifies a dog for breeding purposes.

The teeth should be large, strong, even, and ivory white. They provide an excellent criterion of the width of the muzzle, since there is insufficient space in a snipey muzzle for a full set of even and adequate teeth. Some judges will overlook or forgive pitted and discolored teeth, in the assumption that they are merely the fortuitous results of the animal's having suffered from distemper or other excessive fever. There can be no doubt that the predisposition to them is heritable, and they are as much subject to penalty as is chorea.

The mouth, that is, the occlusion of the teeth, should be even, by which is meant that the upper incisors shall play upon and overlap the lower, but only to the extent that the inner surface of the upper row shall barely touch and cover the outer surface of the lower. It is sometimes known as the "scissors" mouth, as opposed to the "pincer" mouth in which the edges of the incisors of the two jaws merely meet, which results in undue wear and erosion of the teeth.

The standard cites the undershot mouth, in which the lower incisors extend beyond the upper ones, as a "serious fault," as indeed it is if extremely pronounced, but it is a venial fault if it is only the reversal of the scissors mouth, in which the inner surface of the lower teeth meets and plays upon the outer surface of the upper teeth.

In any event, an undershot mouth is no worse than an overshot mouth of similar extent. It is seldom necessary to pull up the lips to see either of these faults in the occlusion of the teeth. The prognathous jaw gives an impression of querulous aggression, which may be wholly out of keeping with the dog's nature; and the pig-jaw of the overshot dog results in an apparent weakness of underjaw which destroys the expression of placid resolution so characteristic of the Great Dane. This shortness of underjaw usually causes the dog to appear lippy, which aspect may be due more to the shortness of underjaw than to an excess of flews.

The eyes of the Great Dane may best be described as "normal," which they seldom are. They are of moderate size, neither bulging from the face nor shrunken and rat-like. They should be set moderately apart, neither in the side of the head nor close together with a stingy expression. They are in the front of the face, looking forward.

The standard specifies "almond shaped" eyelids, which indeed they are, the aperture being of the shape of a fat almond. An elongated-almond-shape implies a slanted or Mongolian eye and is to be found with inadequate stop. The lower lid must not droop below the iris nor must it turn outward to give the dog a Bloodhound expression. The Great Dane is not (or ought not to be) a fierce or vicious dog, and his expression, determined to a large extent by his eyes, should not imply that he is.

The eyes should always be dark in color (save in harlequins, in which one or both may be china-eyes, or walleyes, which may be tolerated but not desired). The exact shade of eye-color is likely to vary with the shade of the coat, but in any event very dark eyes, short of an expressionless blackness, are to be sought. With a light fawn coat, a deep amber eye that would be considered too light in a brindle dog may be tolerated; but, even in a fawn, an almost black eye is to be preferred.

Blue Great Danes are often marred with yellow eyes, and black Danes often enough. Of these colors the standard says "lighter eyes are permitted but are not desirable." "Per-

85

mitted" or not, they give the animal a Hound-of-the-Basker-villes expression, and such an expression, even if not the eye-color itself, should be penalized.

While in the standard scale of points only four are allotted to the eyes, this scale must not be accepted too seriously. A correct eye may contribute immeasurably to the correct expression of a dog, whereas a wrong eye may mar that expression beyond any possible estimate in a scale of points.

No points at all are allotted in the scale to ears, which are notwithstanding described. This omission shows that the scale of points is intended to serve only as a rough guide to the importance of the various parts of the dog, and that scorecard judging is not contemplated by the framers of the standard.

There is no obligation to crop the ears of a Great Dane, even for purposes of exhibition. A neatly cropped dog unquestionably presents a smarter aspect and more alert expression than an uncropped one, but no judge has any moral right to exercise a preference for a cropped dog over an uncropped one merely for that fact alone. Most Danes appearing in American (and German) shows are cropped, and it may be difficult for a judge to visualize what a difference cropping would make in an uncropped one, but he must try.

Cropping of dogs has been forbidden by law in England since 1895, and the smartness of English Danes has suffered as a consequence. English breeders have sought with but little success to produce Danes with small and sufficiently lifted ears to compensate for their inability to crop them. As a consequence English-bred Danes fail in the matter of alertness of expression when compared to no better Danes in countries where cropping is permitted. Some American states have also passed laws that prohibit the cropping of dogs' ears, but these laws are either actually violated or they are evaded by taking dogs into an adjacent state where cropping is permitted for the purpose of having them cropped.

The natural ear of the Great Dane should be moderately

small and fall forward close to the cheek. There should be as much muscular lift in it as is possible, the fold being high on the skull. Such an ear will take a crop and stand better erect than will a coarse, long, hound-like ear that hangs backward at the side of the head.

Ears, when cropped, should stand erect, close together on the top of the corners of the skull, such a stance of the ears causing the skull to appear narrower and flatter than it actually is. The ears should be as long (ribbon-like) as will stand erect.

Cropping of ears is an art. Such surgery should be entrusted only to a veterinary who has had long experience in it, and who is likely to be able to judge what length of ear will stand correctly and what part of the helix it is safe to remove. Short, stubby ears with wide bases are never attractive. Ears cut long and failing to stand up may be shortened somewhat to stand erect. The ear-crop is a man-made feature of a Dane, and, if badly done, it should not be penalized too much. It has naught to do with the dog's natural merits and with his ability to reproduce them.

"Lack of a black mask" is cited in the standard as a fault in the fawn-colored Dane. Such a mask is not truly requisite, but it improves the expression of fawns that wear it, and gives a finish to a classically structured head.

The neck is included in the standard under the heading of "torso," where it does not belong, being a connecting link between the head and the body. It is allotted six points in the scale, which is hardly as much as it merits, since its adequate consideration is often neglected. No part of a Dane proclaims the dog's "quality" or its absence more than does the neck. It must be both long and strong—as long as possible and yet be strong, as strong as possible and yet produce the dignity and high carriage of the head that only a long neck makes possible. The convex crest is present in both sexes, but is particularly marked and stallionlike in the male. Any tendency to ewe-necked concavity is a fault and will reflect itself in the whole forehand assembly. The neck should also be tight skinned and "dry." Looseness of skin under the neck, whether or not it folds into a dewlap, causes the neck to appear short and destroys the beautiful line of its junction with the jaw. Such excess of skin can be surgically removed and, despite that it is faking, it is difficult to understand that it is not more frequently done. Perhaps there is in fact more of it than is detected.

The neck appears literally to flow into shoulders laid back at as nearly 90 degrees to the bones of the upper arm as is possible. The tops of these shoulders are close together and determine a high withers. No other feature can do more to ruin the outline of a Great Dane than a steep, straight, open junction of the shoulder and upper arm. Such a formation has the practical disadvantage of making it impossible for the dog to open the shoulder and take long steps in a free, graceful stride that is so characteristic of the breed.

The Great Dane is a dog of considerable length, measured over all; that is, from the points of the shoulders to the rear of the buttocks. However, he is short from the withers to the pelvis. A dog with steep shoulders and proppy hindquarters may appear short-backed, however long the measurements from withers to pelvis. The major part of the length of the animal should be found before the withers and behind the top of the pelvic bone. The slope of the back line from the withers should be only just perceptibly downward as far as the pelvis with a long sweeping croup gradually dropping to the insertion of the tail. This croup must not be flat, as if it had been hit with a shovel, and the tail should be inserted only a little below the level of the back line.

The dog must not be "over-built," with the pelvis higher than the shoulders. He must not be carp-backed, roached, or camel-backed, which would indicate a constriction of the dorsal muscles; and he will not sag into a sway-back if the line from withers to pelvis is short.

The ribs should extend far toward the rear of the body, leaving a loin short but by no means cramped. The loin must remain long enough to permit the dog to turn and maneuver lissomely and gracefully. The loin is usually found to be too long, rather than too short.

88

The ribs must not appear barrel-like, however frequently "barrel-ribs" may be heard in conversation in praise of a dog. The ribs broaden outward from the spine to provide great capacity for the chest, after which they drop with only a slight convexity to the sternum. The chest must be capacious, but the sides of the ribs are almost flat. Roundness of rib is found with an excessive breadth of chest, and the dog is forced to paddle in his action to avoid interference of elbows and body.

At a point immediately beneath the withers, the body is deep enough to reach at least to the elbow. If it should extend a fraction of an inch lower than the elbow, no harm is done; but too shallow a body is frequently found on an otherwise excellent Dane. Concessions must be made for immaturity, since a dog does not usually attain its full depth of body before two years of age.

From the point of the elbow the underline of the body recedes backward and slightly upward to a slightly tucked-up and well-muscled belly. This tuck-up must not be extreme nor approach the outline of the Greyhound, as so often occurs. A sagging belly, which is most unsightly (except on a bitch in whelp) may usually be remedied by exercise and a change of diet to less bulky food. Few dogs, adequately fed and exercised, develop paunches until their show careers are over.

At the elbow the forearm drops vertically to the pastern, which turns forward almost imperceptibly. A rigid pastern entirely without give causes a dog to appear stilty, but even this is better than a soft pastern with too great a give in it. The very slight turn of pastern saves the dog from excessive fatigue, since it absorbs much of the pounding jolt of prolonged exertion. Occasionally a Dane will be found with so little give in the pastern joint as to knuckle forward awkwardly as is frequently seen in the English Foxhound. This is a minor fault that must be looked for. The feet are comparatively small for a dog of a Dane's great size. Especially must they be deep, tightly knuckled, with toes close together and with thick, horny pads.

Not only must the forearm go straight down from the elbow, but it must be straight forward, the feet and elbows turning neither in nor out. Any tendency to pigeon toes or to slew feet is a serious fault, which will find its compensation in the opposite turn of the elbows.

The correct width of chest in the Dane is that of a normal dog, standing well up on closely knit shoulders and not hung between loose ones. The front should not appear narrow and pinched, nor should it have such width as to cause the dog to waddle in its gait.

The fault most frequently found in the Great Dane is in the structure and use of its hind quarters. Not one in twenty, even among the finest exhibition specimens, is to be found entirely correct in that department. The long femur should drop vertically from its junction with the pelvis and should be joined at an angle of approximately 120 degrees at the stifle joint by the long bones of the lower leg, and the short hock should extend vertically to the foot without angling forward. This provides the dog with considerable angulation in the rear, not quite so much as is found in the best German Shepherd Dogs but considerably more than in the English Foxhound. If forced to choose, an excess of angulation is to be preferred to an insufficiency, especially if the excess is supported by a strong, hard, thick musculature. Quite too many Danes are merely propped up in the rear parts by straight, hamless hindquarters; how they manage to stand, much less to move, is difficult to determine.

In action the hocks should move in parallel planes, and should turn neither inward nor outward. The most prevalent fault in the breed is cow-hocks, due to insufficient musculature to support the angulation. It results in a most ungainly manner of going, painful to the dog and to the acute observer. Yet it must be said that many judges tolerate it in the show ring. Many champions of record possess this failing. If the purpose of the owner is merely to win with his dog, irrespective of its merits, let him not be deterred from exhibiting an otherwise good Great Dane because of cow hocks. With fortune, he will encounter judges who will carry such a dog high in their awards.

The tail should be thick at its insertion, which should be only slightly below the level of the back. It should be moderately short but very strong and should reach not below the joint at the hock. It should be carried in a graceful curve, but never curled, and only in extreme excitement raised above the level of the back, never upright. Dogs with shortened or docked tails are disqualified for exhibition. This is unfortunate, since Danes confined in small quarters frequently suffer from injuries to their tails, the result of their threshing them about, which injures them not at all for breeding purposes.

It is an axiom that gait is the test of structure. A dog adequately made and conditioned cannot move wrong. Any deviation from the normal in the dog's action can be found in the parts and the way they may be put together.

The Great Dane should move directly forward without turning his feet either out or in. He should have a free, easy, and long stride at the trot, lifting his feet sufficiently to clear the ground without the lost motion that comes from hackney-action. This high action is considered stylish and is much admired by the uninformed, but it results in an up-and-down rather than a forward progress.

Seen from the side, the Dane's back should remain straight in action, without bouncing or weaving. The dog's propulsive power is developed in the hindquarters and transmitted through the back to the forehand, which acts only as a point of suspension to prevent the animal from falling on his face. Any undulation of the back in action is a symptom of the leakage of that power between the back and front. That is the reason for our demand of a short line from withers to pelvis.

The natural and correct gait of the Dane is a trot, which a dog should be able to exhibit. Many Danes will, from time to time, fall into an easy, swaying pace in which the two feet on each side are alternately lifted. This is no fault, provided the dog shall demonstrate that he can also trot. Judges are prone to penalize the dog that paces habitually.

Seen from the front, the Dane's legs in action should move in parallel planes, the feet remaining as far apart, and only

91

as far apart, as the elbows. The stride should be long, front and rear, and the hind feet should not overstep or overlap the front feet. This will not occur if the angle of the upper arm with the shoulder blade is adequate.

The correct Dane coat is short, hard, crisp, and dense. It is free from all lint or woolliness. There is little that can be done about trimming it to improve it. A correct diet, freedom from internal and external parasites, cleanliness, grooming, and any means to promote the animal's good health will benefit the coat, which will generally be beyond criticism.

The permissible colors of the Great Dane are purely arbitrary, but the conventions must be observed. Particular attention is called to the official standard for a definition of acceptable "Color and Markings" to which eight points in the scale are allotted. However, a color is either acceptable or it is not acceptable and the points allotted are largely wasted. Attention should also be given to the colors listed under "Disqualifying Faults," found at the end of the standard.

These latter include "white Danes without any black marks (albinos)." This disqualification does not apply to white Danes with dark or spotted nose and pigmented eyes, which are not true albinos. Not one Dane in one hundred thousand is an albino. Indeed, color disqualifications are seldom invoked, although exhibits may be and often are much penalized for their unorthodox colors. The careless and ignorant breedings that produce "crazy" colors and patterns usually also result in dogs with structural faults which are even worse, so that the examiner need not waste too much anxiety lest his Dane is of a bad color if it is structurally correct.

It may not be amiss to mention that brindle and fawn Danes ordinarily are structurally better than those of other colors. Indeed, Danes of those colors constitute a variety (or at least a strain) which should not be crossed, by any but the most experienced and informed breeders, with dogs of any other color or colors. Brindles may be safely crossed with fawns.

Tiger stripings on brindles are particularly beautiful and are desirable if obtainable, but it would be a picayunish and arbitrary judge who could find nothing better than the exact striping or mottling of the pattern upon which to base his choice between two good brindles.

German judges and breeders deem "fading colors" to be evidences of degeneration (rightly or wrongly). In any event, structures being equal, a richly colored fawn is to be preferred to one of a washed-out shade. A silver-blue sheen to a fawn Dane is particularly objectionable, since it indicates a blue ancestor (possibly a blue Greyhound) somewhere in the remote reaches of the pedigree. There is, in fact, little fault to be found with the color itself, but the examiner is warned to look for a racy structure which is usually associated with it.

The absence of the black mask on the fawn Dane is not so much a fault in itself as is the soft and blank facial expression which is usually associated with it. The presence of the mask is genetically dominant. Many good fawns without masks have won high honors.

Few blue or black Danes are exhibited, since Danes of those colors are not as a rule structurally desirable. The color requirements for Danes of those colors is that the colors shall be sound—blues shall be blue; blacks, black. Most blue dogs have unpleasant yellow eyes which mar the expressions.

Blacks are all too frequently the result of a mixture of fawn or brindle blood with harlequin blood. In such cases the black of the harlequin is dominant over the fawn or brindle; and the self pattern is dominant (or incompletely dominant) over the harlequin spotting. Such dogs frequently have white stockings, chests, blazes, or collars, which make them neither fish, flesh, nor herring.

The task of the breeder of harlequins is complicated by the addition of the problem of producing pattern, superimposed upon the problem of structure, which is tough enough in itself. Harlequins, as a lot, are coarser and more beefy than the fawns and brindles, but the rare harlequin of structural excellence, quality, and well-distributed small

93

splotches of sound black upon a white ground is the most spectacular and beautiful of dogs. The requirements of the harlequin are well and fully stated in the standard.

Of the "Disqualifying Faults" not as yet discussed, deafness and spaying are covered by the general rules of the American Kennel Club, although neither is easy positively to detect. Deaf dogs, "listeners" so called in doggy parlance, are particularly alert; and although unable to hear sounds, they respond quickly to jars and to signals. The hearing of a dog is not easy to test, and, in the event of doubt, we must assume that the animal can hear.

Unless the owner of a bitch knows and admits that she is spayed, the judge has no alternative except to pass her as sound. Even surgical scars may not be sufficient evidence that she has been deprived of her ovaries.

"Disqualifying Faults" include "Danes Under Minimum Height"; but, since no minimum height is stated as such in the body of the standard, it is unsafe to disqualify a dog for size. It is better to penalize a small Dane very rigorously than to disqualify it.

"Without visible scrotum" presumably describes a cryptorchid. Such a dog in fact possesses a visible scrotum, but the testicles have not descended into it. Cryptorchids cannot beget progeny, and may rightly be disqualified.

However, the monorchid dog is only unsound and is normally able to produce normal progeny. Under the standard, such dogs must be disqualified, however much the judge may regret such a necessity.

The standard includes three lists of faults as "Very Serious," "Serious," and "Minor." There can be no doubt that the faults named are valid. However, the separations into categories are misleading, since the hint of a fault listed as "Very Serious" may be less harmful and deserving of a smaller penalty than the aggravation of a fault listed as only "Minor." Judgment must be used in assessing faults, and consideration given not only to their presence but to their grossness and intensity. For instance, a slightly "bitchy dog," listed as "Very Serious," may be subject to a smaller penalty than an intensely "doggy bitch," which is listed as only a "Minor" fault.

A standard for a breed of dogs should not be so arbitrary and categorical as to stultify the judge who seeks to apply it. The committee who drafted the new standard for the Great Dane doubtless had that consideration in mind and did not introduce too many cast-iron specifications. The judging of dogs cannot be done by a sorting machine; it must leave much to the personal equation of the judge, to his sense of the fitness of things. It is not so much a science as it is an art.

The Great Dane described herein (and in the standard) is an ideal which in the flesh can be only approximated. The surveyor is again warned not to expect perfection.

The scale of points of the standard, while not to be entirely ignored, is to be accepted only as a guide to the comparative importance of the relative parts of the Great Dane, and, even as such, a guide must not be accepted as absolute. For instance, the tail is allotted but two points in that scale, yet an exceedingly long, twisted tail, set on too high and carried forward over the dog's back can so impair the general picture as to make an award to such a grotesque animal impossible. In fact, the effort to evaluate a dog's excellence by the score-card method, although advocated by at least one otherwise able writer about the Great Dane, is sure to fail. The comparative merits of dogs cannot be expressed in statistical figures.

Better a dog with many minor faults distributed throughout his structure than one with a single gross fault that sticks out like a sore thumb. Better one with a slightly larger or lighter eye than we might wish, a very slightly undershot mouth, a trace of too much lip, shoulders suspiciously loose, feet not quite adequately knuckled, and a trace longer loin than we should like, than another perfect in all points except gross cow hocks, from which the judge is able to take his eyes. The score card might credit the latter dog with the larger number of points, but he must certainly go down in any prize list before the better balanced dog.

The magnitude of the Great Dane causes his faults to appear very obvious. He is likely to be very excellent or impossibly bad. His short, close-fitting coat makes it impossible to hide his faults with hair. If he were smaller, his faults would appear more trivial; if he wore the coat of an Old English Sheep-dog, they might be obscured. The Dane is stark and forthright, for that reason easy to assess. The veriest amateur in canine anatomy, much less the one with an aesthetic sense, can hardly overlook the shortcomings of a Dane, and can hardly fail to thrill at the majesty, dignity, symmetry, soundness and the beauty of a Great Dane of structural excellence. There exists no nobler animal.

CH. PEER GYNT'S ERL KING, sire of CH. STEINBACHER'S KING
Breeder: Jacob Steinbacher.   Owner: Mrs. A. M. Hirsch

Official Standard for the Great Dane

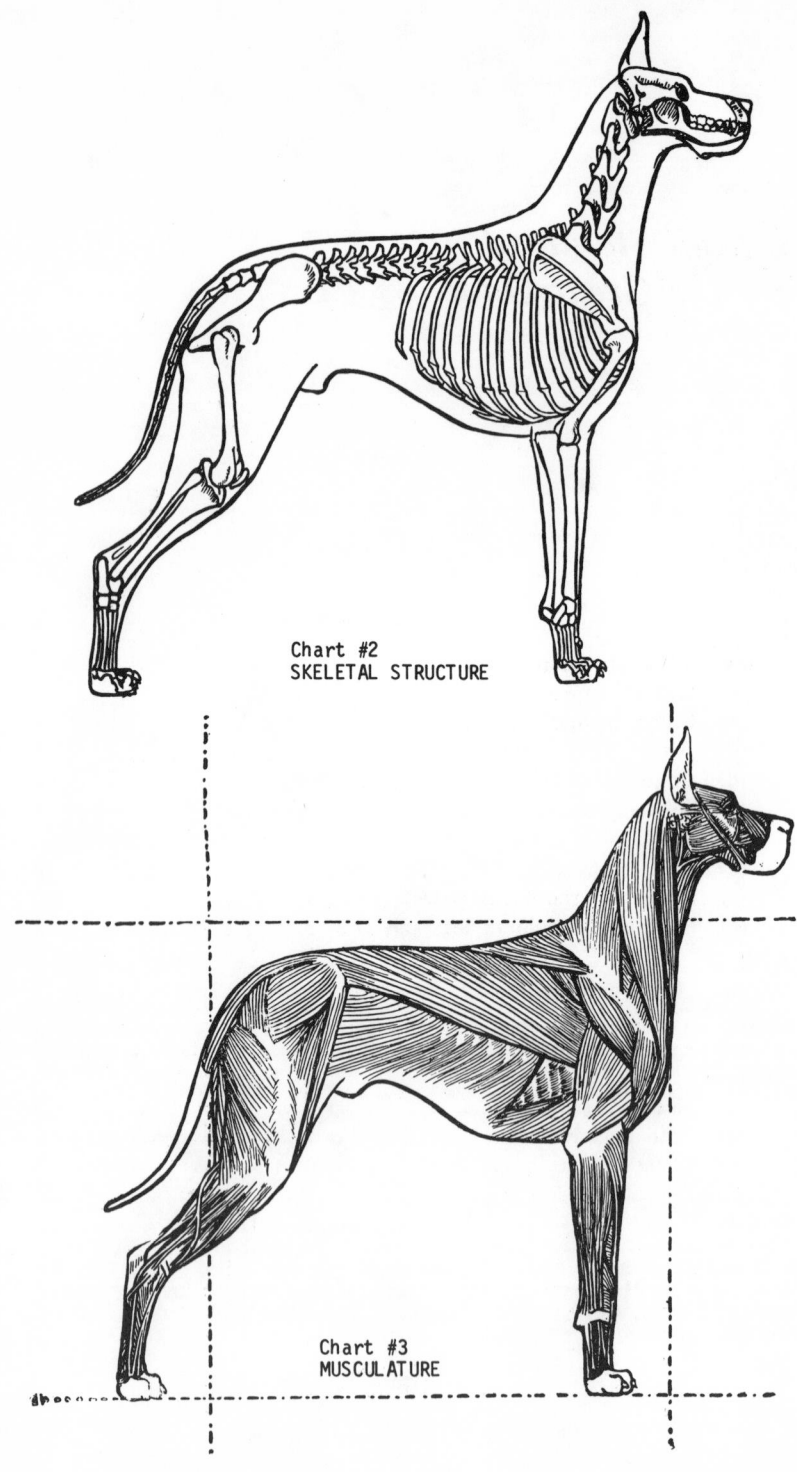

Chart #2
SKELETAL STRUCTURE

Chart #3
MUSCULATURE

Chart #1
APOLLO OF DOGS

1. GENERAL CONFORMATION · · · 30 points

a. General Appearance—10 points

The Great Dane combines in its distinguished appearance, dignity, strength and elegance with great size and powerful, well-formed, smoothly muscled body. He is one of the giant breeds but is unique in that his general conformation must be so well-balanced that he never appears clumsy and is always a unit—the Apollo of dogs. (See Chart #1) He must be spirited and courageous—never timid. He is friendly and dependable. This physical and mental combination is the characteristic which gives the Great Dane the majesty possessed by no other breed. It is particularly true of this breed that there is an impression of great masculinity in dogs as compared to an impression of feminity in bitches. The male should appear more massive throughout than the bitch, with larger frame and heavier bone. In the ratio between length and height, the Great Dane should appear as square as possible. (See Chart #3) In bitches, a somewhat longer body is permissible. Faults: Lack of unity; timidity; bitchy dogs; poor musculature; poor bone development; out of condition; rickets; doggy bitches.

99

b. Color and Markings—8 points

(a) Color: Brindle Danes. Base color ranging from light golden yellow to deep golden yellow always brindled with strong black cross stripes. The more intensive the base color and the more intensive the brindling, the more attractive will be the color. Small white marks at the chest and toes are not desirable. Faults: Brindles with too dark a base color; silver-blue and grayish-blue base color; dull (faded) brindling; white tail tip.

(b) Fawn Danes. Color yellow up to deep golden yellow color with a deep black mask. The deep golden yellow color must always be given the preference. Small white spots at the chest and toes are not desirable. Faults: Yellowish-gray, bluish-yellow, grayish-blue, dirty yellow color (drab color), lack of black mask.

(c) Blue Danes. The color must be a pure steel blue as far as possible without any tinge of yellow, black or mouse gray. Faults: Any deviation from a pure steel-blue coloration.

(d) Black Danes. Glossy black. Faults: Yellow black, brown black or blue black. White markings, such as stripes on the chest, speckled chest and markings on the paws are permitted but not desirable.

(e) Harlequin Danes. Base color: pure white with black torn patches irregularly and well-distributed over the entire body; pure white neck preferred. The black patches should never be large enough to give the appearance of a blanket nor so small as to give a stippled or dappled effect. (Eligible but less desirable are a few small gray spots, also pointings where instead of a pure white base with black spots there is a white base with single black hairs showing through which tend to give a salt and pepper or dirty effect.) Faults: White base color with a few large spots; bluish-gray pointed background.

c. Size—5 points

The male should not be less than 30″ at the shoulders but it is preferable that he be 32″ or more, providing he is well proportioned to his height. The female should not be less than 28″ at the shoulders but it is preferable that she be 30″ or more, providing she is well proportioned to her height.

d. Substance—3 points

Substance is that sufficiency of bone and muscle which rounds out a balance with the frame. Faults: Light-weight whippety Danes; (See Chart #4); coarse, ungainly proportioned Danes (See Chart #5); Always there should be balance.

e. Condition of Coat—4 points

The coat should be very short and thick, smooth and glossy. Faults: Excessively long hair (stand-off coat); dull hair (indicating malnutrition, worms and negligent care).

100

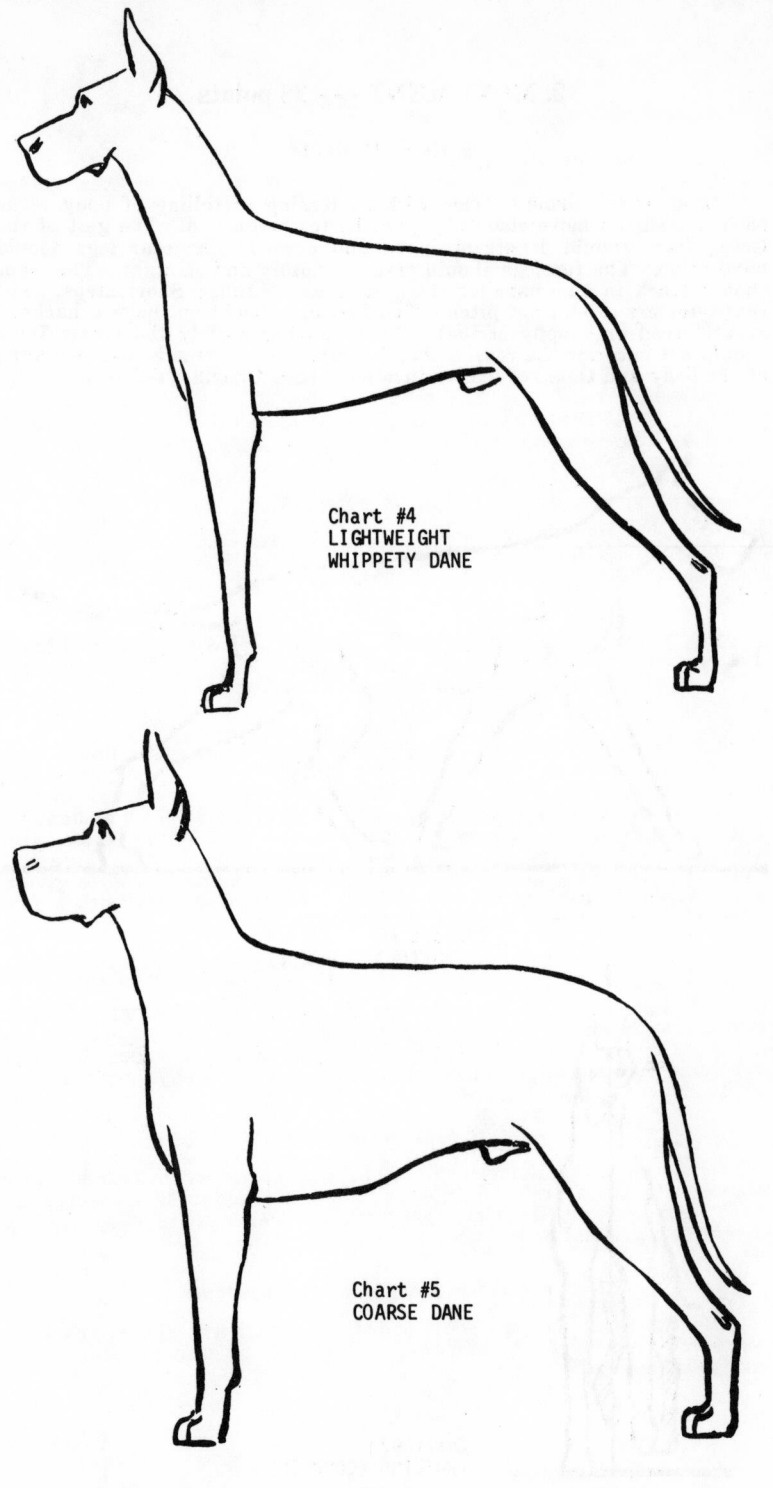

Chart #4
LIGHTWEIGHT
WHIPPETY DANE

Chart #5
COARSE DANE

2. MOVEMENT - - - 28 points

a. Gait—10 points

Long, easy, springy stride with no tossing or rolling of body. The back line should move smoothly, parallel to the ground. The gait of the Great Dane should denote strength and power. The rear legs should have drive. The forelegs should track smoothly and straight. The Dane should track in two parallel straight lines. Faults: Short steps. The rear quarters should not pitch. The forelegs should not have a hackney gait (forced or choppy stripe). When moving swiftly the Great Dane should not pace for the reason that it causes excessive side-to-side rolling of the body and thus reduces endurance. (See Charts #6-7-8-9)

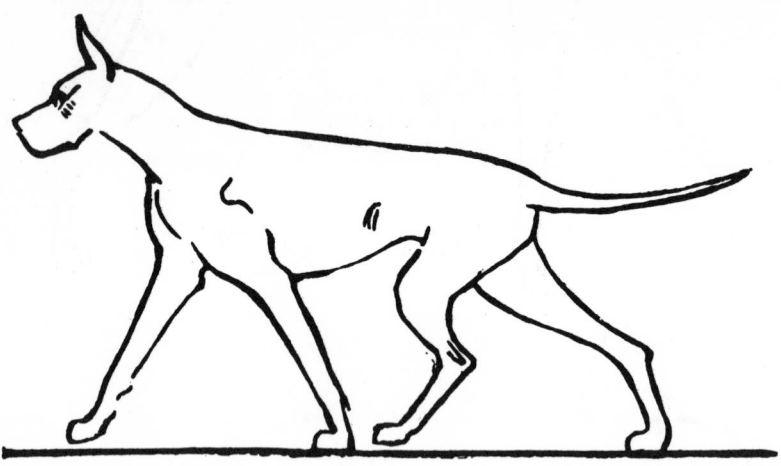

Chart #6
TROTTING (CORRECT)

Chart #7
TROTTING (CORRECT)

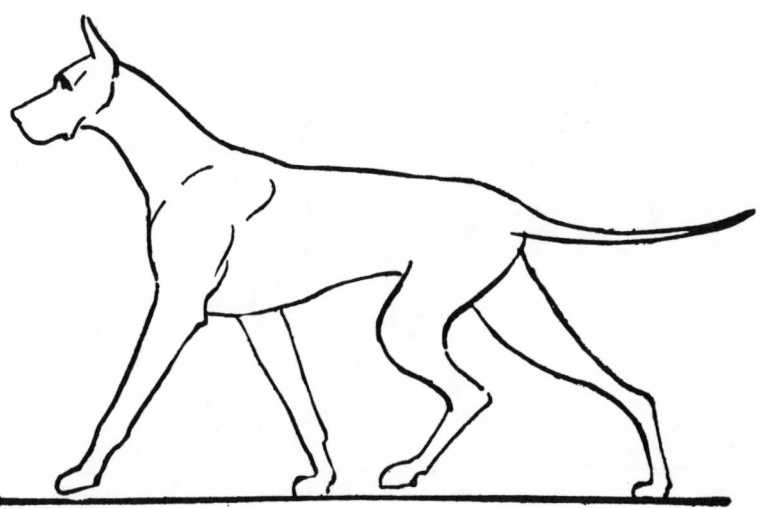

Chart #8
PACING (INCORRECT)

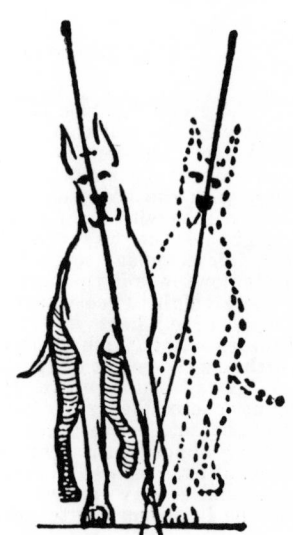

Chart #9
PACING (INCORRECT)

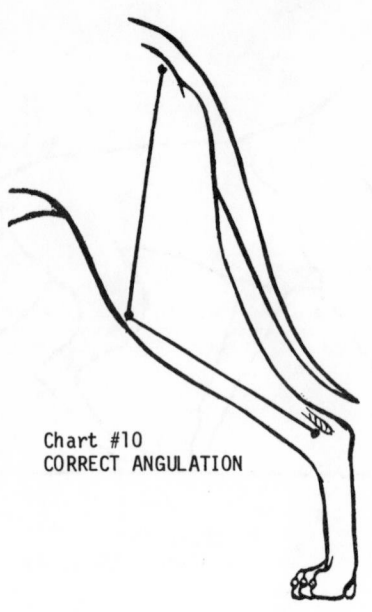

Chart #10
CORRECT ANGULATION

b. Rear End (Croup, Legs, Paws)—10 points

The croup must be full, slightly drooping and must continue imperceptibly to the tail root. Hind legs, the first thighs (from hip joint to knee) are broad and muscular. The second thighs (from knee to hock joint) are strong and long. Seen from the side, the angulation of the first thigh with the body, of the second thigh with the first thigh, and the pastern root with the second thigh should be very moderate, neither too straight nor too exaggerated (See Chart #10). Seen from the rear, the hock joints appear to be perfectly straight, turned neither towards the inside nor towards the outside (See Chart #11). Faults: A croup which is too straight (See Chart #12); a croup which slopes downward too steeply (See Chart #13); and too narrow a croup (See Chart #14). Hind legs: Soft, flabby, poorly muscled thighs; cowhocks (See Chart #15) which are the result of the hock joints turning inward and the hocks and rear paws turning outward: barrel legs (See Chart #16), the result of the hock joints being too far apart; steep rear (See Chart #17); as seen from the side, a steep rear is the result of the angles of the rear legs forming almost a straight line; over-angulation (See Chart #18), is the result of exaggerated angles between the first and second thighs and the hocks and is very conducive to weakness. The rear legs should never be too long in proportion to the front legs (See Chart #19).

104

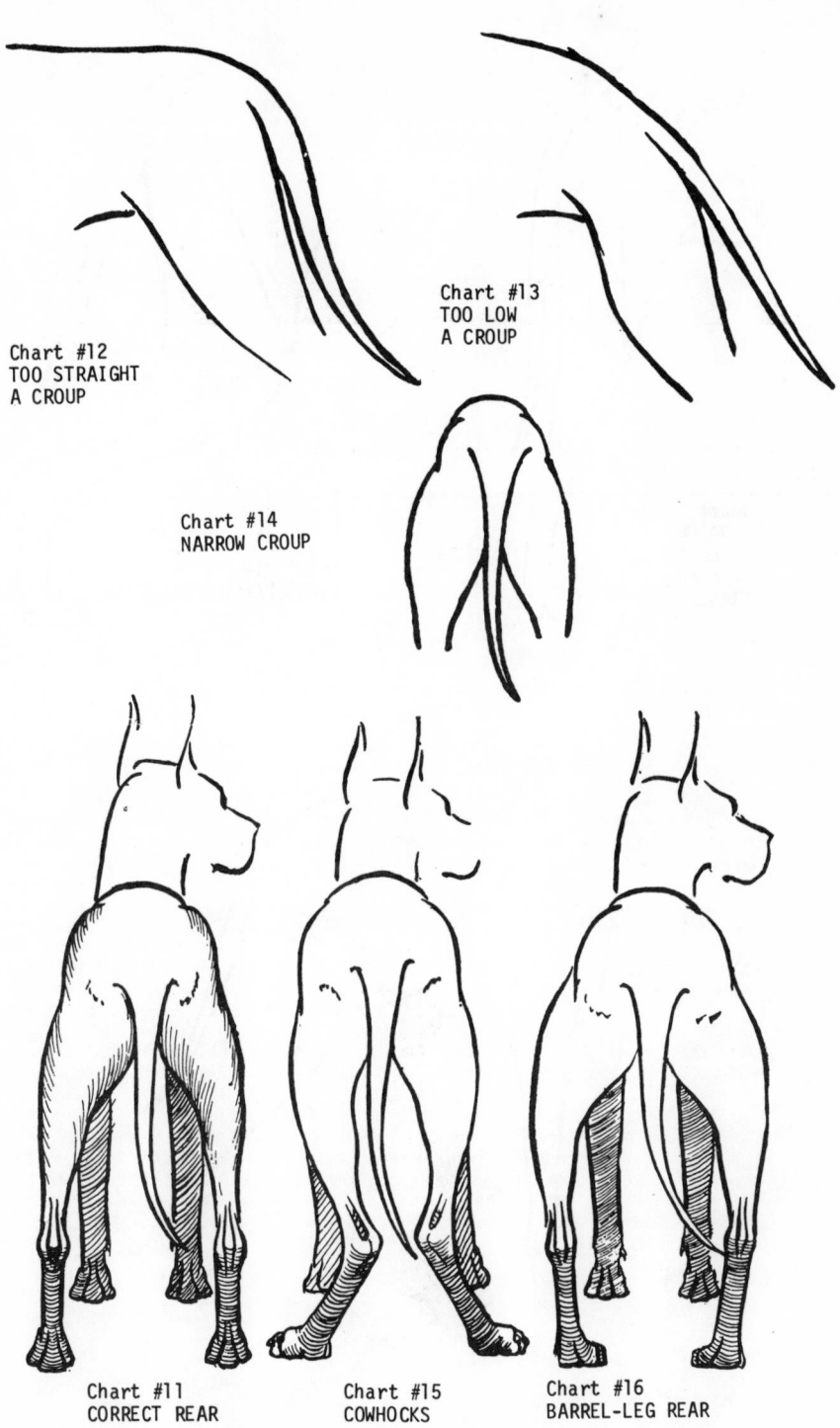

Chart #12
TOO STRAIGHT
A CROUP

Chart #13
TOO LOW
A CROUP

Chart #14
NARROW CROUP

Chart #11
CORRECT REAR

Chart #15
COWHOCKS

Chart #16
BARREL-LEG REAR

Chart #17
STRAIGHT
STEEP REAR,
LACKING
ANGULATION

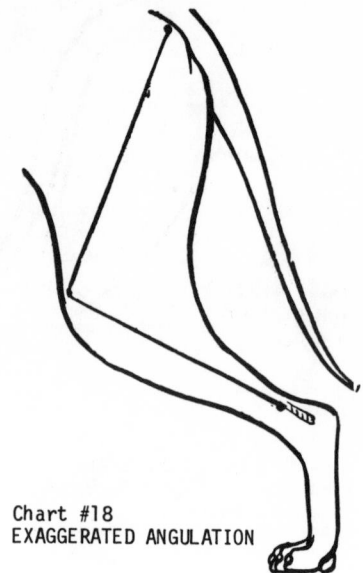

Chart #18
EXAGGERATED ANGULATION

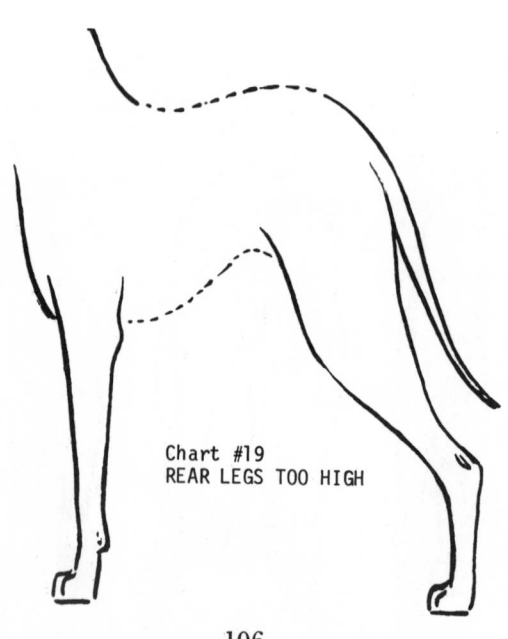

Chart #19
REAR LEGS TOO HIGH

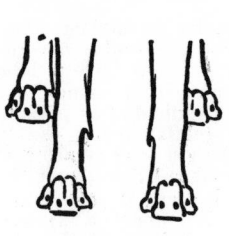

Chart #21
WELL-CLOSED PAW

Chart #20
CORRECT PAWS

Chart #22
WELL-ARCHED PAW

Paws, round and turned neither towards the inside nor towards the outside (See Chart #20). Toes short, highly arched and well closed (See Charts #21-22). Nails short, strong and as dark as possible. Faults: Spreading toes (splay foot) (See Chart #23); bent, long toes (rabbit paws) (See Chart #24); toes turned toward the outside or towards the inside See Charts #25-26). Furthermore, the fifth toe on the hind legs appearing at a higher position and with wolf's claw or spur (See Chart #27); excessively long nails; light colored nails.

Chart #23
SPLAY FOOT

Chart #24
RABBIT FOOT

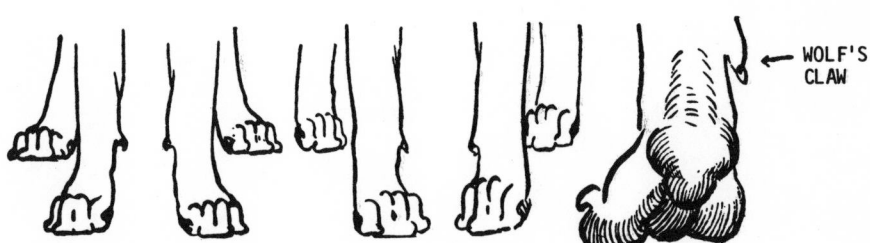

← WOLF'S
   CLAW

Chart #25
PAWS TURNED OUT

Chart #26
PAWS TURNED IN

Chart #27

c. *Front End (Shoulders, Legs, Paws)—8 points*

Shoulders—The shoulder blades must be strong and sloping and, seen from the side, must form as nearly as possibly a right angle in its articulation with the humerus (upper arm) to give a long stride (See Charts #28-29). A line from the upper tip of the shoulder to the back of the elbow joint should be as nearly perpendicular as possible (See Chart #28). Since all dogs lack a clavicle (collar bone) the ligaments and muscles holding the shoulder blade to the rib cage must be well developed, firm and secure to prevent loose shoulders (See Chart #30). Faults: Steep shoulders (See Chart #31), which occur if the shoulder blade does not slope sufficiently; over angulation (See Chart #32); loose shoulders, which occur if the Dane is flabbily muscled, or, if the elbow is turned toward the outside; loaded shoulders.

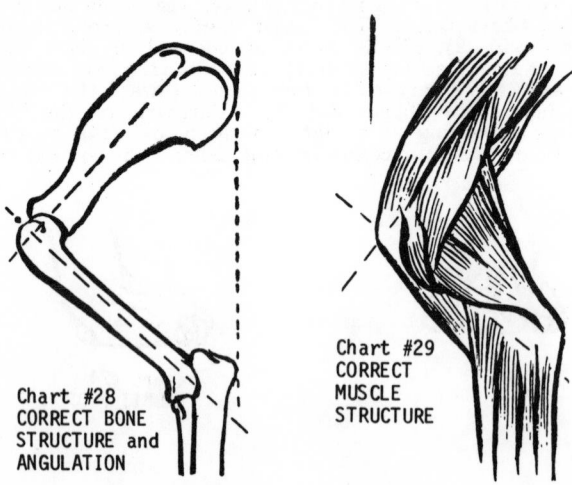

Chart #28
CORRECT BONE
STRUCTURE and
ANGULATION

Chart #29
CORRECT
MUSCLE
STRUCTURE

Chart #30
CORRECT SHOULDER BLADE
STRUCTURE

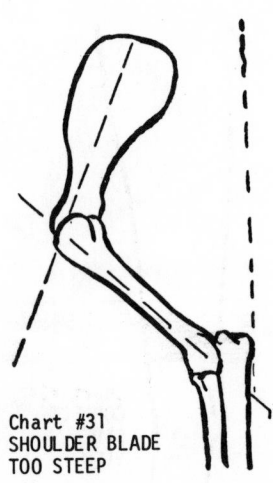

Chart #31
SHOULDER BLADE
TOO STEEP

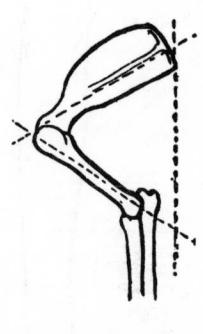

Chart #32
OVERANGULATION

Forelegs—The upper arm should be strong and muscular. Seen from the side or front the strong lower arms run absolutely straight to the pastern joints. Seen from the front, the forelegs and the pastern roots should form perpendicular lines to the ground (See Chart #33). Seen from the side, the pastern root should slope only very slightly forward (See Chart #34). Faults: Elbows turned toward the inside or toward the outside (See Charts #35-36), the former position caused mostly by too narrow or too shallow a chest, bringing the front legs too closely together and at the same time turning the entire lower part of the legs outward; the latter position causes the front legs to spread too far apart, with the pastern roots and paws usually turned inwards. Seen from the side, a considerable bend in the pastern toward the front (See Chart #37) indicates weakness and is in most cases connected with stretched and spread toes (splay foot); seen from the side (See Chart #38) a forward bow in the forearm (chair leg); an excessively knotty bulge in the front of the pastern joint (See Chart #39).

Paws—round and turned neither toward the inside nor toward the outside. Toes short, highly arched and well closed. Nails short, strong and as dark as possible. Faults: Spreading toes (splay foot), bent, long toes (rabbit paws); toes turned toward the outside or toward the inside; light colored nails.

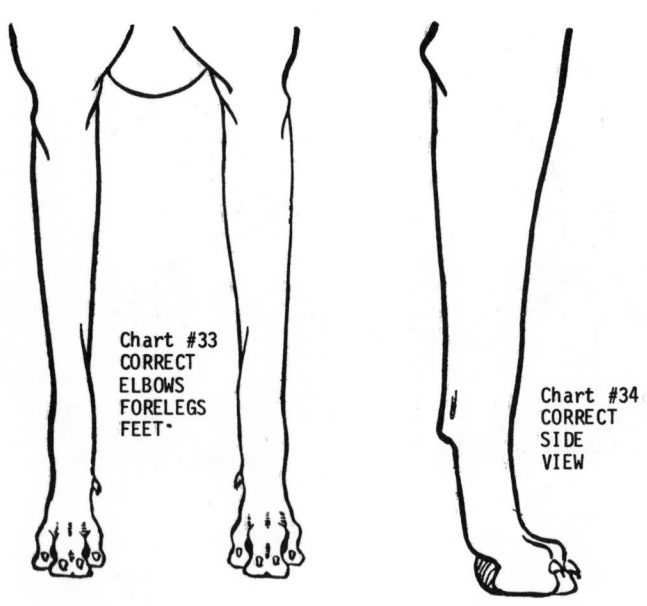

Chart #33
CORRECT
ELBOWS
FORELEGS
FEET·

Chart #34
CORRECT
SIDE
VIEW

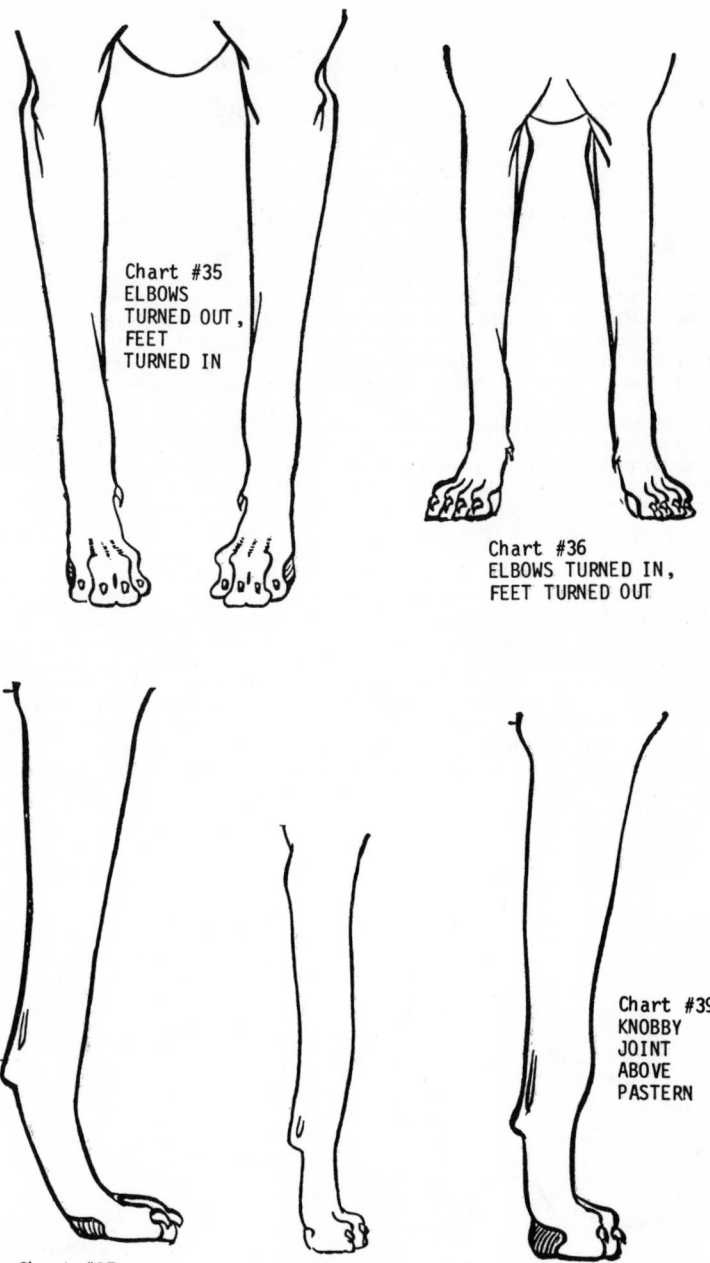

Chart #35
ELBOWS
TURNED OUT,
FEET
TURNED IN

Chart #36
ELBOWS TURNED IN,
FEET TURNED OUT

Chart #39
KNOBBY
JOINT
ABOVE
PASTERN

Chart #37
WEAK PASTERN

Chart #38
CHAIR LEG

111

3. HEAD - - - 20 points

a. Head Conformation—12 points

Long, narrow, distinguished, expressive, finely chiseled, especially the part below the eyes (which means that the skull plane under and to the inner point of the eye must slope without any bony protuberance in a pleasing line to the full square jaw), with strongly pronounced stop. The masculinity of the male is very pronounced in the expression and structure of head (this subtle difference should be evident in the dog's head through massive skull and depth of muzzle, the bitch's head may be more delicately formed (See Charts #40-41). Seen from the side, the forehead must be sharply set off from the bridge of the nose. The forehead and the bridge of the nose must be straight and parallel to one another. Seen from the front, the head should appear narrow, the bridge of the nose should be as broad as possible (See Chart #42). The cheek muscles must show slightly but under no circumstances should they be too pronounced (cheeky). The muzzle part must have full flews and must be as blunt vertically as possible in front; the angles of the lip must be quite pronounced (See Chart #42). The front part of the head, from the tip of the nose up to the center of the stop should be as long as the rear part of the head from the center of the stop to the only slightly developed occiput (See Chart #40). The head should be angular from all sides and should have definite flat planes and its dimensions should be absolutely in proportion to the general appearance of the Dane. Faults: Any deviation from the parallel planes of skull and foreface (See Charts #43-44); too small a stop; a poorly defined stop (See Chart #45) or none at all (See Chart #46); too narrow a nose bridge; the rear of the head spreading laterally in a wedge-like manner (wedge head) (See Chart #47); an excessively round upper head (apple head) (See Chart #48); excessively pronounced cheek musculature (See Chart #49); pointed muzzle (See Chart #50); loose lips hanging over the lower jaw (fluttering lips) which create an illusion of a full deep muzzle (See Charts #51-52). The head should be rather shorter and distinguished than long and expressionless.

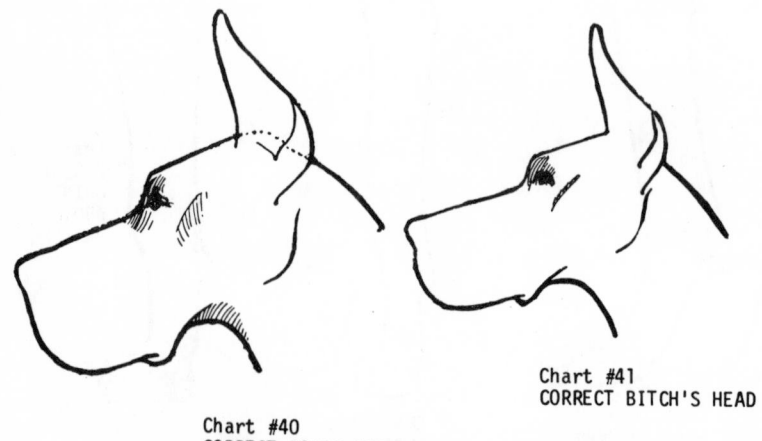

Chart #41
CORRECT BITCH'S HEAD

Chart #40
CORRECT DOG'S HEAD

112

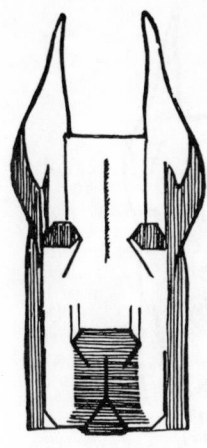

Chart #42
CORRECT SKULL

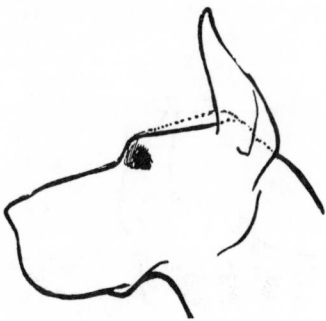

Chart #43
FOREHEAD DROPPING,
BRIDGE OF NOSE DROPPING

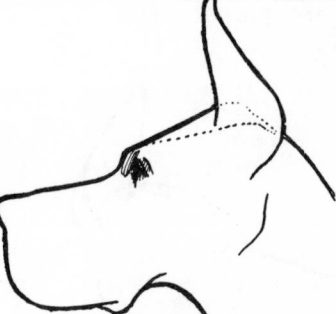

Chart #44
FOREHEAD RISING,
BRIDGE OF NOSE RISING

Chart #45
DISH-FACED

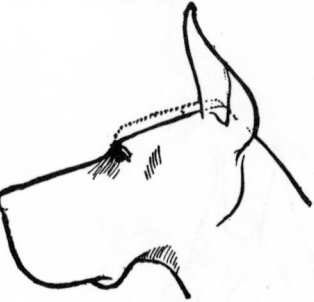

Chart #46
NO STOP

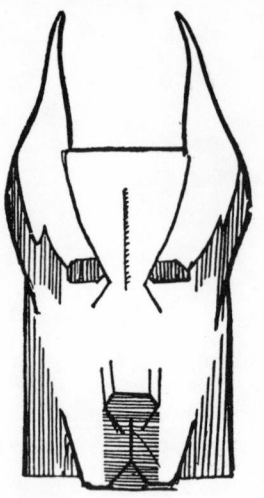

Chart #47
SKULL TOO WIDE (WEDGE-HEAD)
and NOSE TOO NARROW

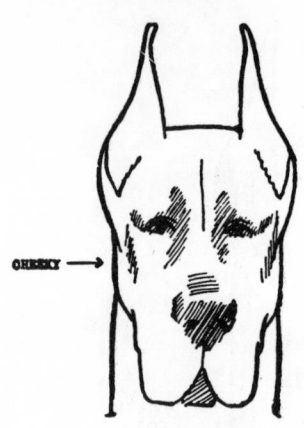

Chart #49
CHEEKY HEAD

Chart #48
APPLE-HEAD

Chart #50
SNIPEY HEAD

Chart #51
CORRECT HEAD

Chart #52
FLUTTERING LIPS

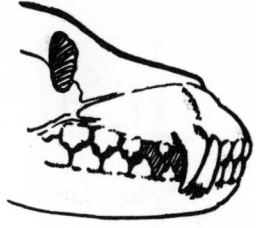 

Chart #53
SCISSOR BITE
(CORRECT)

b. Teeth—4 points

Strong, well developed and clean. The incisors of the lower jaw must touch very lightly the bottoms of the inner surface of the upper incisors (scissors bite) (See Chart #53). If the front teeth of both jaws bite on top of each other, they wear down too rapidly. Faults: Even bite (See Chart #54); undershot and overshot (See Charts #55-56); incisors out of line; black or brown teeth; missing teeth.

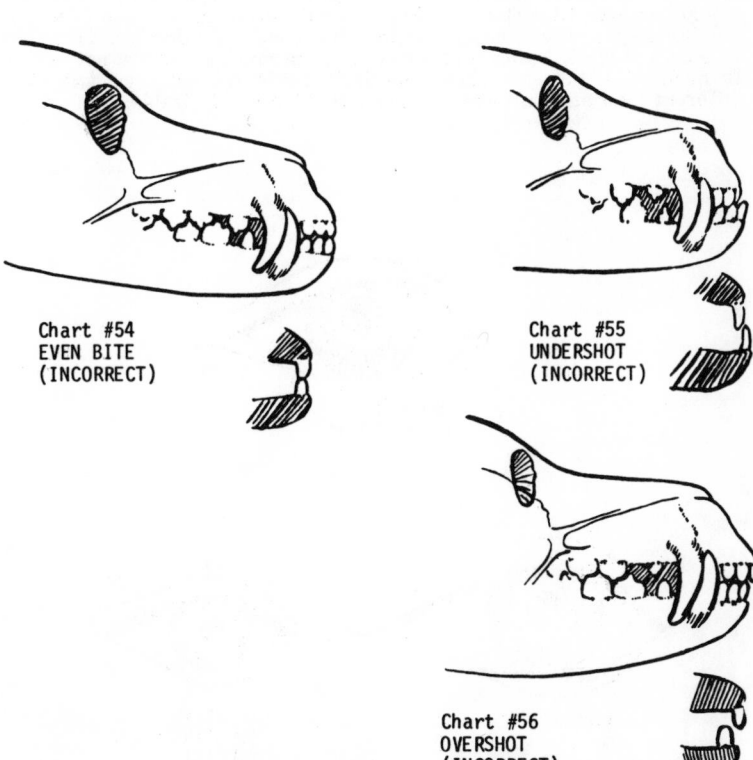

Chart #54
EVEN BITE
(INCORRECT)

Chart #55
UNDERSHOT
(INCORRECT)

Chart #56
OVERSHOT
(INCORRECT)

 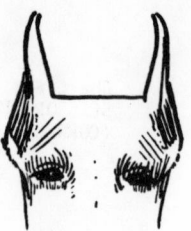 

Chart #57
CORRECT EYES

Chart #58
WIDE-SPREAD EYES

Chart #59
MONGOLIAN EYES

c. Eyes—4 points

Medium size, as dark as possible, with lively intelligent expression; almond-shaped eyelids, well developed eyebrows (See Chart #57). Faults: Light colored, piercing, amber colored, light blue to a watery blue, red or bleary eyes; eyes of different colors; eyes too far apart (See Chart #58); mongolian eyes (See Chart #59); eyes with pronounced haws (See Charts #60-61); eyes with excessively drooping lower eyelids (See Chart #62). In blue and black Danes, lighter eyes are permitted but are not desirable. In harlequins, the eyes should be dark. Light colored eyes, two eyes of different color and wall-eyes are permitted but not desirable.

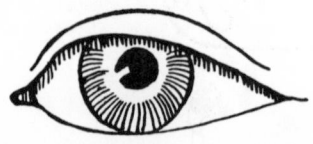

Chart #60
CORRECT EYE

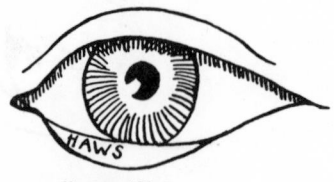

Chart #61
HAW

Chart #62
DROOPING LOWER
EYELIDS

Chart #63
CORRECT NOSE

Chart #64
SPLIT NOSE

c1. Nose (no points)

The nose must be large and in the case of brindled and "single-colored" Danes, it must always be black. In harlequins, the nose should be black; a black spotted nose is permitted; a pink colored nose is not desirable.

(See Charts #63-64)

117

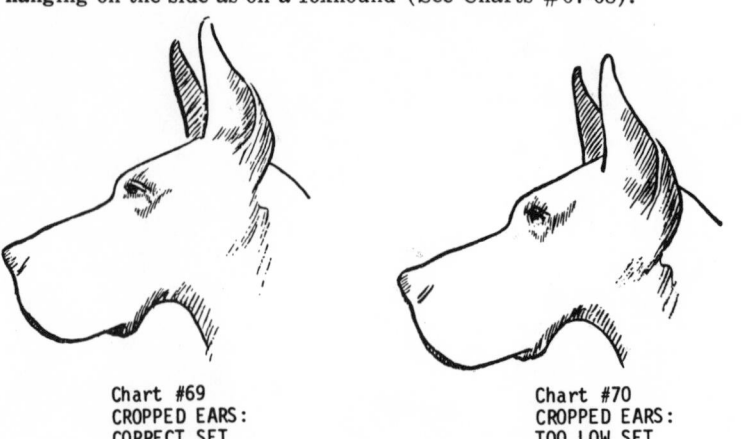

Chart #65

Chart #67
EARS TOO LARGE
SET TOO LOW

Chart #66
CORRECT SIZE, PLACEMENT
NATURAL EARS

Chart #68
EARS TOO LARGE
SET TOO LOW

c2. Ears (no points)

Ears should be high, set not too far apart, medium in size, of moderate thickness, drooping forward close to the cheek. Top line of folded ear should be about level with the skull. (See Charts #65-66). Faults: hanging on the side as on a foxhound (See Charts #67-68).

Chart #69
CROPPED EARS:
CORRECT SET

Chart #70
CROPPED EARS:
TOO LOW SET

Cropped ears: high set, not set too far apart, well pointed but always in proportion to the shape of the head and carried uniformly erect (See Charts #69-70).

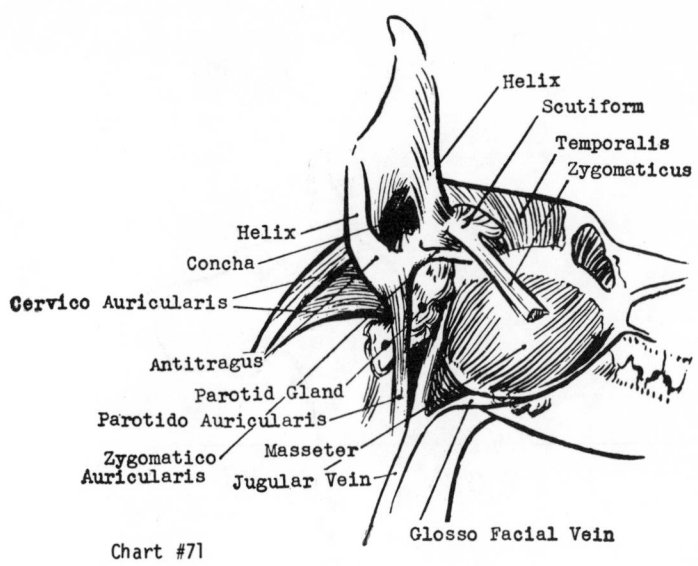

Helix
Scutiform
Temporalis
Zygomaticus

Helix
Concha
Cervico Auricularis

Antitragus
Parotid Gland
Parotido Auricularis
Zygomatico Auricularis
Masseter
Jugular Vein

Glosso Facial Vein

Chart #71

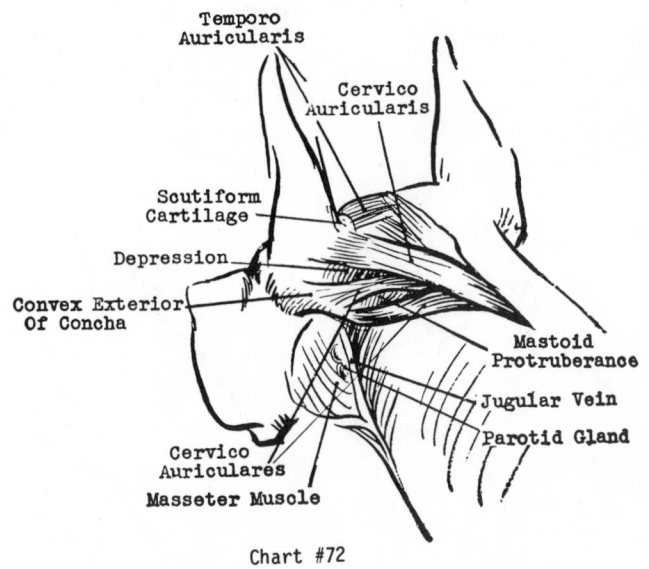

Temporo
Auricularis
Cervico
Auricularis

Scutiform
Cartilage
Depression
Convex Exterior
Of Concha

Mastoid
Protruberance
Jugular Vein
Parotid Gland

Cervico
Auriculares
Masseter Muscle

Chart #72

EAR MUSCULATURE

119

4. TORSO - - - 20 points

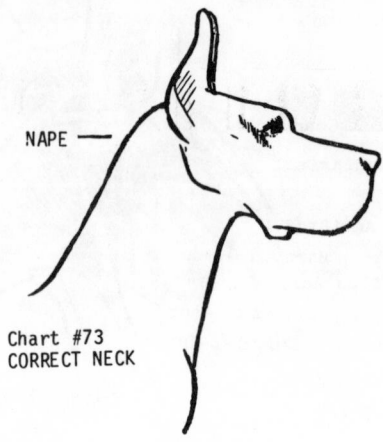

NAPE —

Chart #73
CORRECT NECK

a. Neck—6 points

The neck should be firm and clean, high set, well arched, long, muscular and sinewy. From the chest to the head, it should be slightly tapering, beautifully formed, with well developed nape (See Chart #73). Faults: Short, heavy neck (See Chart #74); pendulous throat folds (dewlaps) (See Chart #75).

Chart #74
SHORT, HEAVY
NECK

Chart #75
DEWLAPS

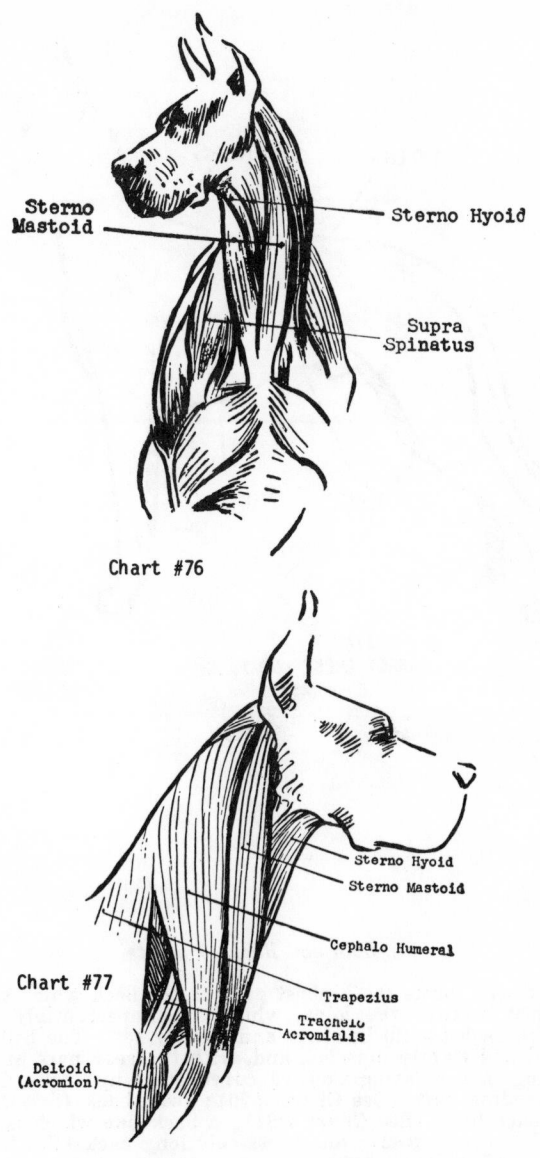

Sterno
Mastoid

Sterno Hyoid

Supra
Spinatus

Chart #76

Sterno Hyoid
Sterno Mastoid

Cephalo Humeral

Chart #77

Trapezius

Trachelo
Acromialis

Deltoid
(Acromion)

NECK MUSCULATURE

121

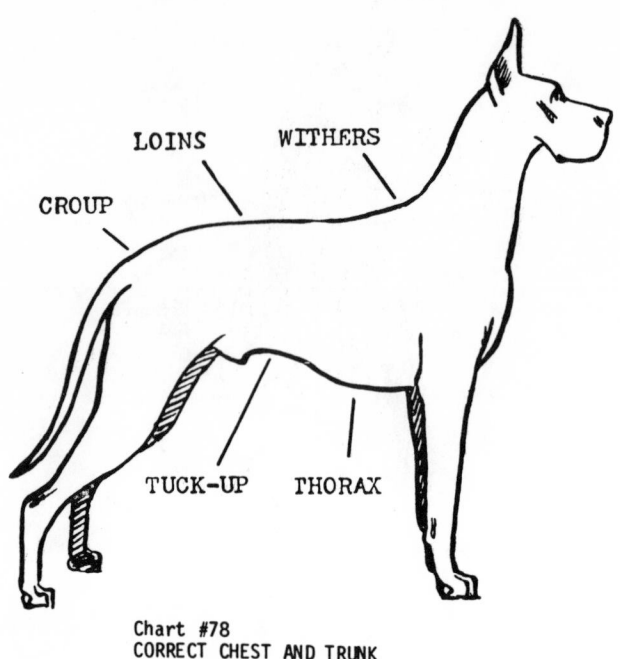

LOINS WITHERS

CROUP

TUCK-UP THORAX

Chart #78
CORRECT CHEST AND TRUNK

b. Loin and Back—6 points

The withers forms the highest part of the back which slopes down-ward slightly toward the loins, which are imperceptibly arched and strong. The back should be short and tensely set. The belly should be well shaped and tightly muscled, and, with the rear part of the thorax, should swing in a pleasing upward curve (tuck-up) (See Chart #78). Faults: Receding back (See Chart #79); sway back (See Chart #80); camel or roach back (See Chart #81); a back line which is too high at the rear (See Chart #82); an excessively long back (See Chart #80); poor tuck-up (See Chart #83).

122

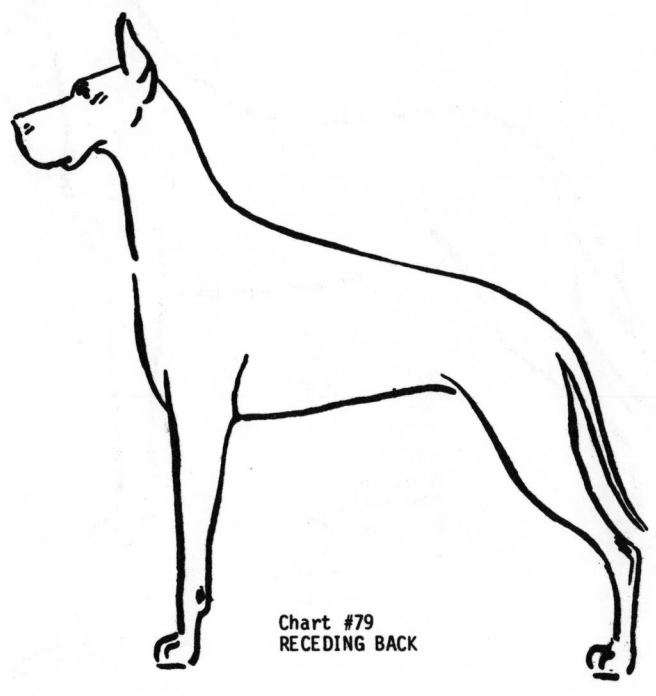

Chart #79
RECEDING BACK

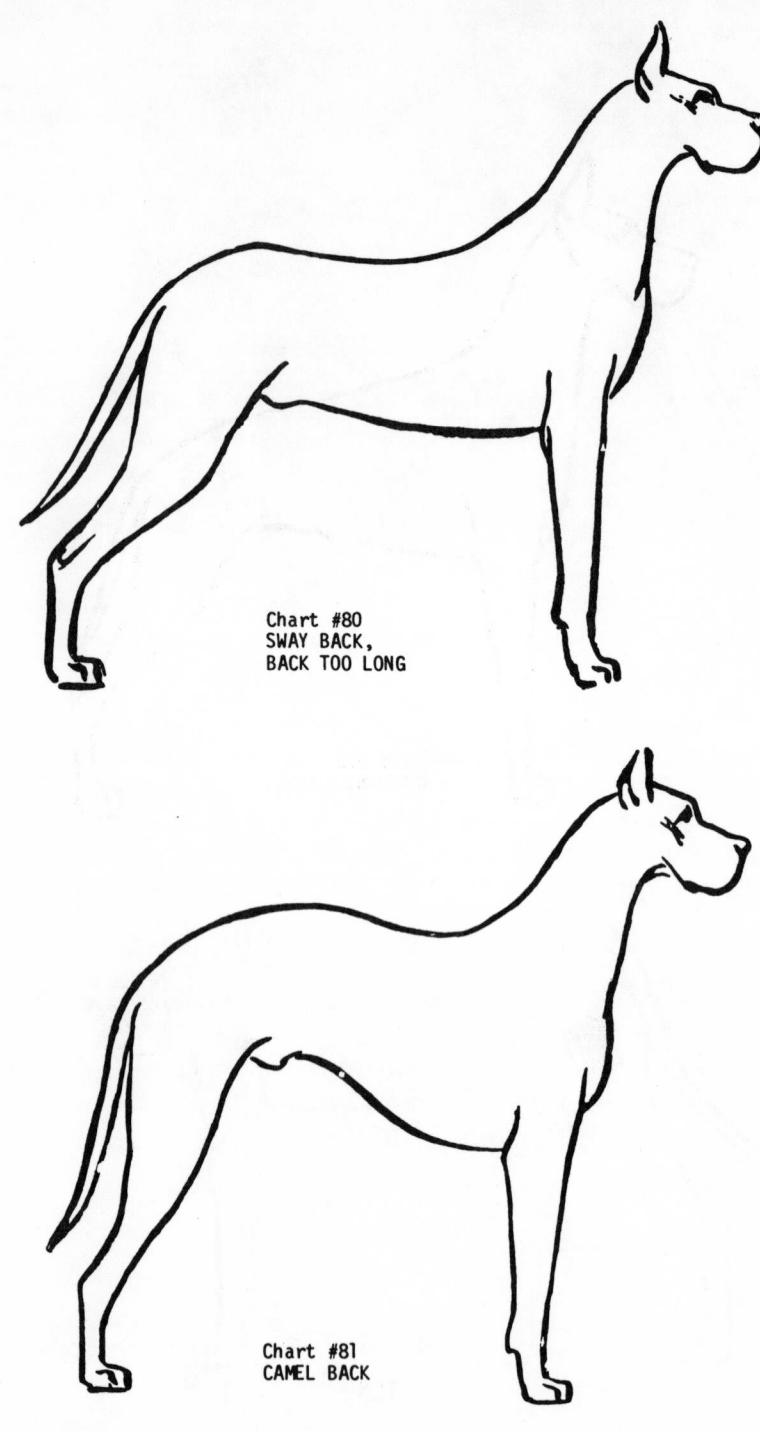

Chart #80
SWAY BACK,
BACK TOO LONG

Chart #81
CAMEL BACK

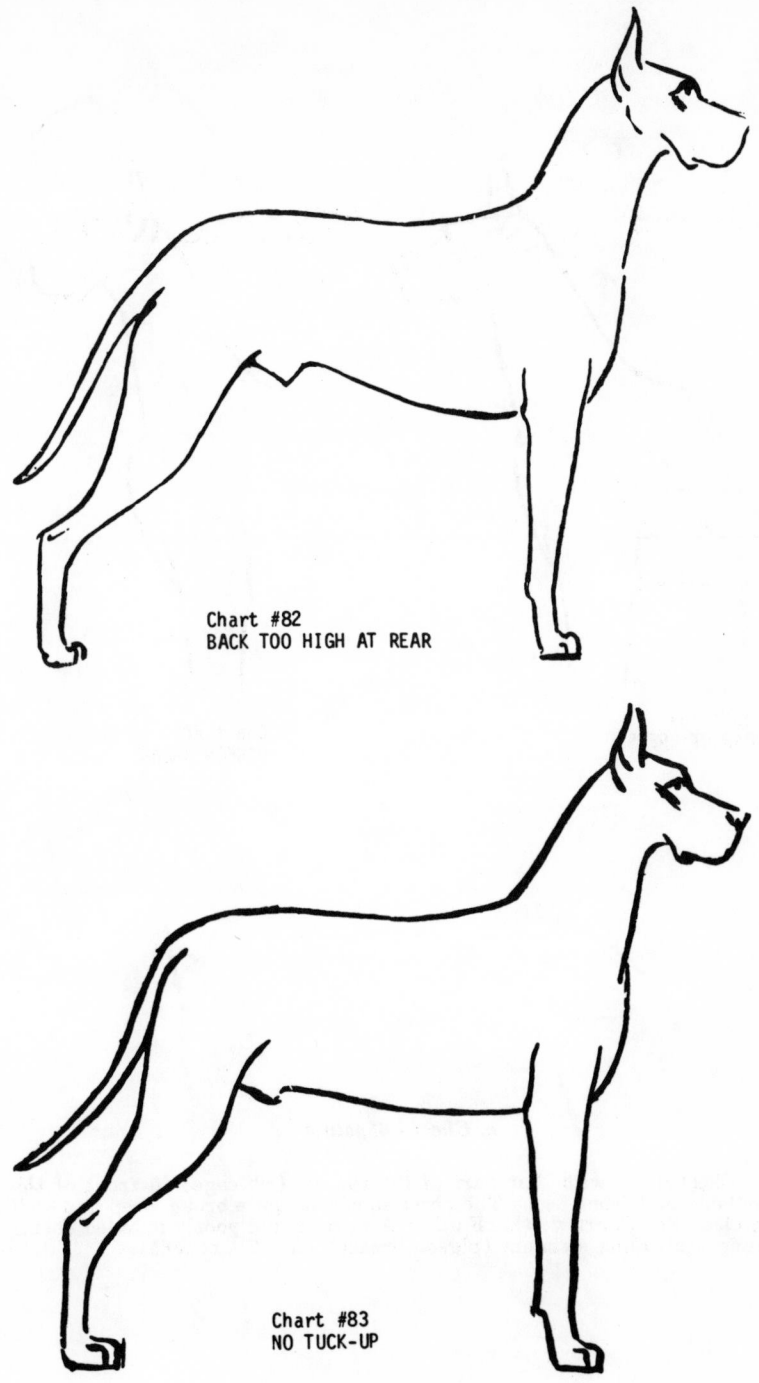

Chart #82
BACK TOO HIGH AT REAR

Chart #83
NO TUCK-UP

Chart #84
CORRECT BREAST

Chart #85
PIGEON BREAST

c. Chest—4 points

Chest deals with that part of the thorax (rib cage) in front of the shoulders and front legs. The chest should be quite broad, deep and well muscled (See Chart #84). Faults: A narrow and poorly muscled chest; strong protruding sternum (pigeon breast) (See Chart #85).

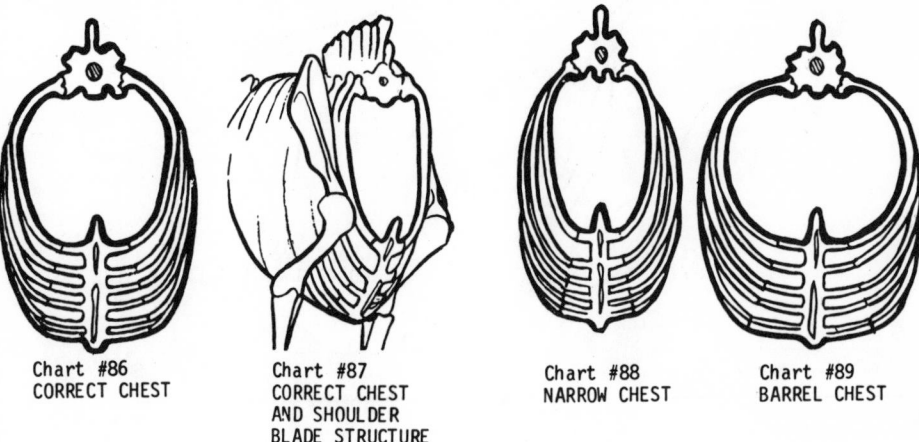

Chart #86
CORRECT CHEST

Chart #87
CORRECT CHEST
AND SHOULDER
BLADE STRUCTURE

Chart #88
NARROW CHEST

Chart #89
BARREL CHEST

d. Ribs and Brisket—4 points

Deals with that part of the thorax back of the shoulders and front legs. Should be broad, with the ribs sprung well out from the spine and flattened at the sides to allow proper movement of the shoulders, extending down to the elbow joint (See Charts #86-87). Faults: narrow (slab-sided) rib case (See Chart #88); round (barrel) rib cage (See Chart #89); shallow rib cage not reaching the elbow joint (See Chart #90).

Chart #90
SHALLOW CHEST

127

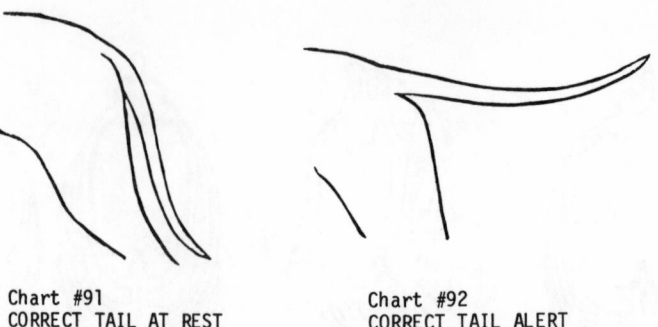

Chart #91
CORRECT TAIL AT REST

Chart #92
CORRECT TAIL ALERT

5. TAIL - - - 2 points

Should start high and fairly broad, terminating slender and thin at the hock joint. At rest, the tail should fall straight (See Chart #91). When excited or running, slightly curved (saber like) (See Chart #92). Faults: A too high, or too low set tail (See Charts #93-94) (the tail set is governed by the slope of the croup); too long or too short a tail (See Charts #95-96); tail bent too far over the back (ring tail) (See Chart #97); a tail which is curled (See Chart #98); a twisted tail (sideways) (See Chart #99); a tail carried too high over the back (gay tail) (See Chart #100); a brush tail (hair too long on lower side). Cropping tails to desired length is forbidden.

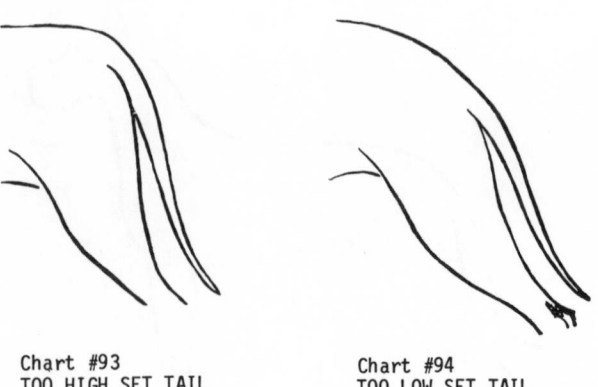

Chart #93
TOO HIGH SET TAIL

Chart #94
TOO LOW SET TAIL

128

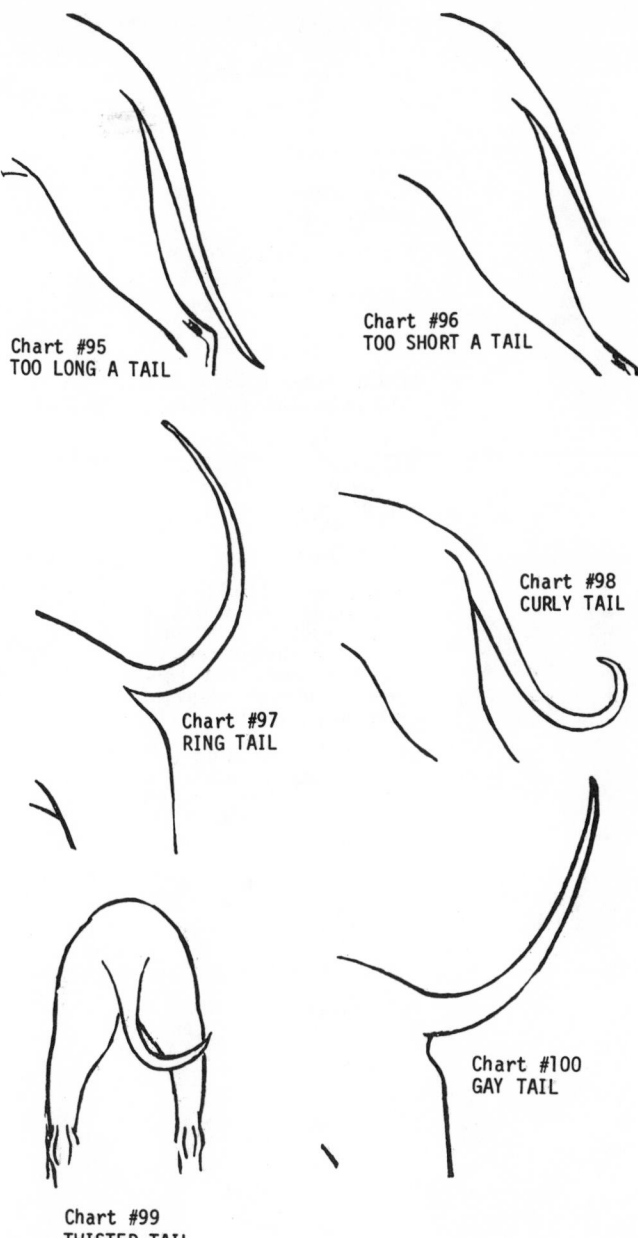

Chart #95
TOO LONG A TAIL

Chart #96
TOO SHORT A TAIL

Chart #98
CURLY TAIL

Chart #97
RING TAIL

Chart #100
GAY TAIL

Chart #99
TWISTED TAIL

129

FAULTS OF THE GREAT DANE

Disqualification Faults

Deaf Danes

Danes under minimum height

Without visible scrotom

Spayed bitches

Monorchids

White Danes without any black marks (albinos)

Merles (a solid mouse-gray color or a mouse-gray base with black or white or both color spots or white base with mouse-gray spots

Harlequins and solid-colored Danes in which a large spot extends coat-like over the entire body so that only the legs, neck and the point of the tail are white

Brindle, Fawn, Blue and Black Danes with white forehead line, white collars, high white stockings and white bellies

Danes with predominantly blue, gray, yellow or also brindled spots

Docked tails

Split noses

The faults below are important according to their grouping (very serious, serious, minor) and not according to their sequence as placed in each grouping:

Very Serious	Serious	Minor
Lack of Unity	Out of condition	Doggy bitches
Poor Bone Development	Coarseness	Small white marks on chest and toes—Blues, Blacks, Brindles and Fawns
Poor Musculature	Any deviation from the standard on all coloration	
Rickets		
Timidity	Deviation from parallel planes of skull and foreface	Few gray spots and pointings on Harlequins
Bitchy dog		In Harlequins, black spotted nose
Sway back	Wedgehead	
Roach back	Poorly defined stop	White tipped tail except on Harlequins
Cowhocks	Narrow nose bridge	
Pitching gait	Snipey muzzle	Excessively long hair
Short steps	Any color but dark eyes in fawns and brindles	Excessively dull hair
Undershot teeth		Apple head
Lightweight, Whippety Danes	Mongolian eyes	Small stop
	Missing teeth	Fluttering lips
	Overshot teeth	Eyes too far apart
	Heavy neck	Drooping lower eyelids
	Short neck	Haws
	Dew laps	Any color but dark eyes in blacks, blues and harlequins
	Narrow chest	
	Narrow rib cage	Discolored teeth
	Round rib cage	Even bite
	Shallow rib cage	Pigeon breast
	Loose shoulders	Loaded shoulders
	Steep shoulders	Elbows turned outwards
	Elbows turned inward	Paws turned inward
	Chair legs (Front)	Splay foot
	Knotty bulge in pastern joint (adult dog)	Excessively long toe nails
	Weak pastern roots	Light nails (except in harlequins)
	Receding back	Low-set tail
	Too long a back	Too long a tail
	Back high in rear	Too short a tail
	In harlequin, a pink nose	Gay tail
	Poor tuckup (except in bitches that have been bred)	Curled tail
		Twisted tail
	Too straight croup	Brush tail
	Too sloping croup	
	Too narrow croup	
	Overangulation	
	Steep rear	
	Too long rear legs	
	Poorly muscled thighs	
	Barrel legs	
	Paws turned outward	
	Rabbit paws	
	Wolf's claw	
	Hackney gait	

This is an historic picture of three of the superlative dogs of the past. The place, the Morris and Essex Show, 1939, American bred dogs and bitches. Dogs pictured as placed: 1. Ch. Kurt von Loheland with breeder, Wm. J. Gilbert; 2. Ch. Jansen of Brae Tarn, bred by R. P. Stevens with handler, the late James McGhie; 3. Ch. the Duke of Roxdane with owner, Wm. A. Ehmling.

The Great Dane in the East

PEGGY SEITZ

T is generally conceded that, until a few years ago, the consistently fine Great Danes in this country were bred in the relatively small area of New York, New Jersey, and Connecticut. At the present time, good specimens are being bred and shown from coast to coast. This is a healthy sign, manifesting a constructive factor; more and more breeders are striving to produce the nearly perfect Great Dane, as described and illustrated in our Standard.

Latterly in breeding, the comment has been made by many knowledgeable persons in the fancy, that current breeders have been placing too much emphasis on height, head, and neck. The croups and rears have suffered accordingly. Since the Great Dane is a working dog, a faulty rear, with the accompanying bad movement, is a matter of much concern. The remedy is an obvious one. Champion stud dogs, no matter how excellent otherwise, having bad rears, or coming from this defect, should not be used. The same drastic program if followed with the bitches, would, in a few generations produce a Great Dane with balance: a good front and a correspondingly good rear.

For this desired balance, or "over-all" conformation, which we had to a greater degree in the past, we turn back to a few of the outstanding examples: father, son, and grandson, Ch. Peer Gynt's Erl King, Ch. Steinbacher's King,

CH. STEINBACHER'S KING
Sire: Ch. Peer Gynt's Erl King. Dam: Germana v. Freigericht
Breeder: Jacob Steinbacher. Owner: Mrs. A. M. Hirsch

Amer. and Can. CH. GILBERT'S NANCY OF BRAE TARN
and VASSAL OF CAIRNDANIA with owner, Mrs. Betty Hyslop

Ch. the Duke of Roxdane; Ch. Gilbert's Marching Peter, Ch. Kurt von Loheland, Ch. Gilbert's Nancy of Brae Tarn, and even further back to the Saalburgs, Birkenhofs, etc.

The picture today is not all black, of course. We have some almost perfect Great Danes being shown currently in the ring. (Never forget, the flawless one has yet to be whelped!) Pictures of our top Eastern specimens are used as illustrations for this chapter. By reason of lack of space, or inability to secure photographs, all of the fine dogs in this section are not presented. We hope this is understandable.

To go back fifteen years, the top flight breeders were: Brae Tarn Kennels, owned by R. P. Stevens; Carliss Kennels, owned by Ada Carliss; Gilbert's Kennels, owned by William J. Gilbert; Roxdane Kennels, owned by William Ehmling; Steinbacher's Kennels, owned by the late Jacob Steinbacher; and Warrendane Kennels, owned by Harry Warren. From these kennels came the Winners Dog, Winners Bitch, and on up to Best of Breed, at the largest Dane entries—Morris and Essex, the Westminster Show, or the Specialty Shows in 1939, 1940, and 1941.

Some of the *great* Great Danes at this time, according to their show records, were: Ch. Kurt von Loheland, bred by William J. Gilbert; Ch. Dolf von Schloss Dellwig, bred by Fritz Hirsh; Ch. Blitz von Schloss Staufeneck of Warrendane, bred by Carl Maurer; Ch. Czardus von Eppelein-sprung Norris, bred by Hans Hofman; Ch. Steinbacher's King, bred by Jacob Steinbacher, Ch. the Duke of Roxdane, bred by Ewald Scheutze. Also, four of the outstanding specimens bred by R. P. Stevens: Ch. Jansen of Brae Tarn, Ch. Heide of Brae Tarn, Ch. Afra of Brae Tarn, and Ch. Juno of Brae Tarn. (Ch. Jansen of Brae Tarn died, with the record, then unmatched, of winning Best of Breed 68 times.)

All of these fine dogs and bitches from Brae Tarn, Carliss, Ehmling, Gilbert, Steinbacher, and Warrendane are the ancestors of our current good ones. Of the six kennels listed, three are inactive. Those still breeding are Mrs. Carliss, Mr. Ehmling, and Mr. Gilbert.

In the early nineteen-forties, the Daynemouth Great

135

CH. DEACON OF MARYDANE
Sire: Ch. Gerhardt of Marydane
Dam: Ch. Marshmellow of Marydene
Breeder-owner: Mary K. Johnston,
Wilton, Conn.

CH. SUITOR OF BRAE TARN
Sire: Brucie 2nd of Brae Tarn. Dam: Ch. Olivia of Brae Tarn
Breeder: Mrs. James McGhie. Owners: Mr. and Mrs. Charles Staiger

Danes came into prominence. Blood lines, Brae Tarn and Send. This kennel, now active, bred many Champions. Ch. Olga of Brae Tarn was Best of Breed at the Westminster Show in 1943. Same win at the same show in 1944 went to another Dane from this kennel—Ch. Fergus of Daynemouth.

From 1945 to 1950, the outstanding Great Danes, proven by their consistent wins in large entries, came from the following breedings: Brae Tarn, Carliss, Duysters, Ehmling, (Roxdane) Gilbert, and the Johnstons (Marydane).

Starting with the Brae Tarn line, the dominant stud dog, sire of many Champions, Ch. Ajax Telamon of Brae Tarn, is an example. Ch. (American and Canadian) Gilbert's Nancy of Brae Tarn was a sensational winner in the largest entries—Best of Breed at the Westminster Show in 1945, and a consistent B.O.B. winner at subsequent shows. At the Westchester Specialty Show in 1946, Nancy was B.O.B., while her litter brother, Ch. Suitor of Brae Tarn, was Best of Opposite Sex—keeping the top awards in the same family, Brae Tarn. Ch. Ona of Brae Tarn, dam of Ch. Senta, is another excellent example of the worth of this blood line.

The Carlisses have been showing for about ten years, although they have been breeding Great Danes for the past thirty-five. One of the first dogs they exhibited was Thor von Thaden, litter brother to Ch. the Duke of Roxdane. Thor had a superlative head in addition to his other fine qualities. A leg injury stopped his show career. However, Thor sired some very good ones. (It was quite a thrill to the Carlisses to attend a show a couple of years ago—seven of the Specials were by Thor.)

Those exquisite bitches, Ch. Lady Lu, Ch. Carliss Dawn, Ch. Winged Victory, Ch. Carliss Bright Star, and Carliss Portia (13 points) are compliments to this kennel. Another adornment is Ch. Lady Vicky (bred by Winifred Duysters), out of the Carliss Champion, Winged Victory, by Ch. Ajax Telamon of Brae Tarn. Third, the Duysters breedings. Mrs. Duysters began with show Great Danes when she purchased from Mrs. Carliss a beautiful brindle puppy bitch, Winged Victory. With good luck (and all breeders know we have to have it), Mrs. Duysters chose this puppy. She had no idea

137

of showing—had never been to a dog show in her life.

When "Vicky" was nine or ten months old, Mr. Gilbert saw her, with her owner, at the Carliss home. This veteran breeder was so extremely enthusiastic with the magnificence of the young bitch, he convinced Mrs. Duysters that it would be a shame not to show Vicky and subsequently breed her. This was good advice, and it was acted upon by the owner. Mr. Gilbert was right. Vicky finished her Championship easily and has been bred twice to Ch. Ajax Telamon of Brae Tarn. Both breedings produced magnificent specimens: Ch. Ajax Cinderella, Ch. Gilbert's Star Dust, Ch. Carliss Lady Vicky, Ch. Duysters' Linda Mia, Ch. Duysters' Cherokee Chief. Duysters' Lord Jim had 12 points toward the title, and there were two more from this second litter coming out in 1950: Honey Girl and Duysters' Dorian von Seitzen.

Again, with luck, Mrs. Duysters was able to sell her beautiful puppies to "show-minded" people. In preparing this chapter, I have been told by the experienced top breeders again and again: "We *lost* this or that litter—don't know whatever became of the dogs, and some of them were such promising puppies." Or, to quote Mrs. Carliss: "We sold one of the most beautiful bitches we ever bred. The owner subsequently had her spayed!" (That is, literally and figuratively, "the most unkindest cut of all.")

The Ehmlings of Roxdane owned Ch. the Duke of Roxdane, one of the outstanding sires in this section. He was a dominant stud that passed on his remarkable head, superlative neck carriage, and excellent body conformation to his offspring. The Duke was Best of Breed at the Westminster Show in 1940. This was a magnificent animal. At maturity, and as a proven sire of superior puppies, Mr. Ehmling had a standing offer of $5000 for the dog. This Great Dane did not have a price, to the owners.

How Mr. Ehmling got the Duke is an interesting tale. Mr. Jacob Steinbacher called on the telephone to ask Mr. Ehmling if he had a very good four-months-old puppy dog. A regular customer wanted one in a hurry and Mr. Steinbacher had nothing to offer. If Mr. Ehmling could produce

138

CH. THE DUKE OF ROXDANE

Sire: Steinbacher's King.   Dam: Rino von Bremen
Breeder-Owner: Mr. and Mrs. Wm. A. Ehmling, Roxdane Kennels

139

CH. KERMIT OF ROXDANE
Sire: Schnetze's King. Dam: Freia of Roxdane
Breeder-Owner: Mr. and Mrs. W. A. Ehmling, Westfield, N. J.

CH. WANDA OF ROXDANE
Owners: Roxdane Kennels, Mr. and Mrs. Wm. A. Ehmling, Westfield, N. J.

one, at once, he could have the Steinbacher stud puppy-pick of the litter—from a mating of Ch. Steinbacher's King and Rino von Bremen.

Mr. Ehmling *did* have a four-months-old puppy dog, a very promising one he was keeping for himself. However, Mr. Steinbacher, his friend, was in a jam. So, Mr. Ehmling gambled and won! The stud puppy became Ch. the Duke of Roxdane.

Of the Roxdane breeding came Ch. Heidi of Roxdane, Ch. Kermit of Roxdane, Ch. Paulette of Roxdane, Ch. Molla of Roxdane, Ch. Wanda of Roxdane, Ch. Steinbacher's Thyla of Roxdane, and Ch. Roxanna of Roxdane.

The top Eastern breeder of fawns and brindles today, by reason of the number of Champions bred, is Mr. William J. Gilbert, who got into the Dane business by accident. He needed a large watch dog; bought one for five dollars. The animal, unknown to Mr. Gilbert at the time, was a Great Dane. Both Mr. and Mrs. Gilbert fell in love with "Pat," and decided to go to the dogs, entirely. They did, with spectacular results.

The start of this Kennel was that remarkable brood bitch, Fay. She was a dominant bitch, regardless of sire. She consistently dropped her exquisite parallels of head, body conformation, and excellent rear. Fay's progeny included Ch. Kurt von Loheland, Ch. Gilbert's Marching Peter, Ch. Gilbert's Thorden von Eric, Ch. Gilbert's Bjorn Herwolfson, Ch. Gilbert's Diana and Ch. Gilbert's Streamline Tiger. Grand progeny: Ch. Eric of Shadow Knoll, Ch. Carliss Dawn, Ch. Diana's Gabrielle, and Ch. Gilbert Thor, 2nd. The consistent excellency of Fay's puppies was proven at the Westminster Show, 1941. Winners Dog, Winners Bitch, and Reserve Winners Dog were out of this brood matron, with three different sires.

More Gilbert Champions include: (Canadian and American) Ch. Gilbert's Nancy of Brae Tarn, Ch. Ona of Brae Tarn, Ch. Gilbert's Butch, Ch. Dolf Crusader, Ch. Senta, Ch. Gilbert's Glory Adele, Ch. Duke of Gilberts, Ch. Gilbert's Thor of Kalmar, Ch. Gilbert's Bruce of Broadacre, and Ch. Gilbert's Olga. Of the twenty Champions listed, only two

141

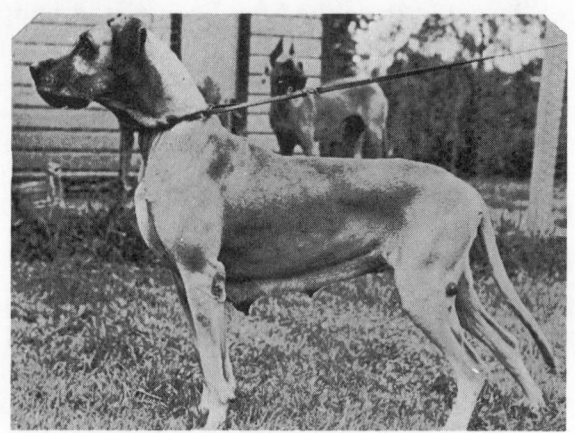

FAY (whelped 1934)
Foundation bitch of the Gilbert Kennels.
Dam of 6 champions.

Bill Gilbert setting up three nearly perfect Great Danes. Left to right:
Ch. Senta; granddaughter, Bianka; and daughter, Ch. Senta's Astrid.

142

March 1950. Bill Gilbert was presented with a scroll of citation, a wrist watch, and a B.O.B. placing by the Great Dane Club of America (left, Bob Seitz; right, Chalmers Burns).

Bill and Nell Gilbert relaxing at home with Great Dane, of course!

143

The Gilbert Kennel, Whitehouse, New Jersey
Owners: Nell and Bill Gilbert

CH. GILBERT'S KING II
Sire: Ch. Duke of Gilberts   Dam: Ch. Gilbert's Glory's Adele
Breeder: William J. Gilbert   Owners: Grace and Joe Cornell

were bought by Mr. Gilbert and subsequently finished by him, to their titles.

The outstanding Great Dane bitch of the past ten years is Ch. Senta (Gilbert bred)—a remarkable credit to her breeder. Senta is the *only one of her breed, dog or bitch,* to win more than one Best of Breed at the Westminster Show. Three times this magnificent specimen has taken the honor—1947, 1949, and 1950. Also at the 1950 Show, Senta placed third in the Working Group, first such win for a Dane in fifteen years.

Senta has other spectacular wins: Best in Show, Brooklyn Kennel Club, 1949; Best of Breed, Morris and Essex, 1948; Chicago International Show, Best of Breed, 1949. Forty-five times Senta has won Best of Breed—always with large entries. She also has many group wins or placings to her credit.

For those who have not had the pleasure of watching Ch. Senta in the ring, "see" her, through the eyes of Berthe Soubeyrand Gauthier: "Senta has a superbly feminine head, more mask desirable, yes. But with her tremendous size, a mask of depth might make her look masculine. Senta·has a magnificent front, spring of rib, deep brisket, denoting plenty of heart and lung room—all that could be desired in body. The croup and tail set is excellent and hindquarters absolutely correct. From within, there is a style and flash seldom seen in the show ring, regardless of breed.

"From the betterment of the breed angle, the owner of Senta, Mrs. Walter Schroeder, bred her Champion twice to Ch. Dolf Crusader. From the first litter came Ch. Senta's Astrid—also a constant Best of Breed winner. Astrid is very like her dam but lacks the Senta showmanship. To see this pair in the ring, the dam and her get, is a sight the discerning Great Dane lover will never forget."

Another consistent contributor to the show ring is Marydane Kennels, owned by Mr. and Mrs. Gerard Johnston. Ch. Molla of Roxdane was the foundation of their breeding. From the beginning, as of today, quality has been the watchword.

Molla was a very fine specimen, excellent in head and

145

BOHRER'S BREDOR (whelped 1935)
The first of 14 generations of Harlequins for the Chalburn Kennels.

OTHELLO VON DER DOGGENBURG
Sire: Eric von Bankenberg.   Dam: Justine von der Doggenburg
Bred and owned by Mr. Gustav Kley

146

beautiful in body. She was, in addition, a magnificent brood matron, passing to her offspring the best of Roxdane, Steinbacher, and Brae Tarn blood lines.

Bred to Ch. Neil of Brae Tarn, Ch. Molla dropped the favorite stud dog of the breeders, Ch. Gerhardt of Marydane, a dominant brindle sire. Also in this litter was Ch. Marshmellow of Marydane, a very lovely black-masked fawn.

In visiting the Marydane Kennels, a completely modern building, one is struck with the condition, friendly manners, and, a little unusual, the dark eyes of every dog or bitch there.

Marydane is not a commercial kennel, rather a labor of love. Hard work and great discrimination in breeding have brought gratifying results. The Johnstons have five Champions to their credit, and three more lacking a few points to the title.

So far, we have covered the fawns and brindles of our breed. Some outstanding Harlequins have been bred in the East by the Chalburn Kennels, owned by Mr. William Chalmers Burns. The material presented for this chapter was so complete, written with such clarity, that it was given exactly as sent by Mr. Burns.

CHALBURN HARLEQUIN GREAT DANES

"When asked why we chose to breed Harlequin Great Danes our reply is that it was prompted mainly by two things:

"First, we had a very nice Harlequin male (Bohrer's Bredor), a house pet, who had a grand disposition and good conformation, although we knew little about conformation until we conceived the idea of breeding.

"Secondly, perhaps the 'stubborn' trait inherited from Scotch ancestry was forced to the front when we felt that our dog did not receive as much recognition in the showring as he deserved.

"In our search for a Harlequin bitch with Harlequin coloration, conformation, and head, the best we could find in the East at that time was Alva Schatzie, owned by

147

Miss Ella Millbank. We leased Alva Schatzie for one breeding. From this breeding we kept three with outstanding Harlequin coloration, two of which turned out to be Ch. Pierrot of Chalburn and Ch. Pierrette of Chalburn.

"We next bred Pierrette back to her father, Bredor. From this breeding we kept Miss Patches of Chalborn and Mister Punch of Chalburn. Miss Patches developed into a very sound bitch with a good head, but we felt that she was not quite large enough to show. She later proved to be our best brood bitch. Patches' size may have been the result of close breeding. We sometimes wonder if this could be the cause of the too numerous small Harlequin Danes that we see in the ring today. While Mister Punch was a large, strong dog with good coloration, his head was the old fashioned Harlequin type that could not win these days. He had terrific strength. We entered him in the K-9 Corps of the Army at Fort Meyer, Va., but heard nothing about him after his training was completed at Parris Island.

"In order to maintain the standard of Harlequin coloration that we had set for ourselves and bring a new bloodline into our kennel, our search next led us to the purchase of Kentucky Colonel of Vakeck. His first breeding to Miss Patches of Chalburn gave us an outstanding litter of four Harlequins, one of which we kept in our kennel—Major Chips of Chalburn—who received his first point, a major, on March 26, 1944, and finished with seventeen points, including three majors, on June 4, 1944, at the age of seventeen months.

"Othello v.d. Doggenburg (sire of Ch. X Beau Jack) died before finishing his championship with twelve accredited points. We feel that Othello was an outstanding Harlequin Great Dane and, had he been campaigned at the shows more frequently, we believe that he would have finished his championship very easily. It is our feeling that he was one of the best of all the Harlequins ever bred by Mr. Gustav Kley, whose serious breeding of Harlequin Great Danes has been a real contribution to those of us who are partial to the Harlequin.

"We figure this gives us ten generations of pure Harlequin coloration."

148

We quote further, from a recent critique written by Mr. Burns for *Dane Digest,* the only national magazine devoted exclusively to the Great Dane. In this article, subject, the Harlequin, Mr. Burns used his own dogs, pictured in this book—all magnificent specimens—for comments.

"The best way for me to say anything about Harlequin Danes is to quote from our own experience. I will take 'Big Koger' first. Consider his coloration. In my opinion, if the coloration is not in accordance with our Standard, it isn't a Harlequin. The white background is perfect, as are the white neck, chest, and forelegs; with the torn black patches well distributed over the balance of the body. The facial markings are excellent. The one criticism I make of these markings is that the black patches should be larger.

"While many breeders and exhibitors consider the head of great importance, I consider soundness, which includes everything but the head, more important—the way the body is put together. To me this means bone structure that allows the legs to move properly, and the musculature that causes the whole structure proper movement. The original photograph of Koger showed his muscular gear. I hope the reproduction carries this point. In my opinion, this was one of the best moving Great Danes I have ever seen in the ring. Notice in the picture the terrific strength of the hindquarters. In actual movement, every step showed power and push and it appeared that the long strides of the forelegs were necessary to balance the body.

"My criticism of the body: it is possibly two inches too long for the height. Koger was 33″ at the withers. Plainly seen is the croup which goes with proper rear end structure, very necessary if the movement is to be powerful; at least I have never seen a dog with a steep croup move correctly. Back line straight. Toes short and arched.

"The head is a pleasant picture—forehead and bridge of nose, level planes with a distinct stop. Muzzle deep and square. However, you will notice that the foreface is about ½″ shorter than the forehead, although the head does not have the appearance of being skully, as was prevalent in most Harlequins a few years ago.

149

CHALBURN BRIDE BROOK PIERROT
Sire: Ch. Major Chips of Chalburn.   Dam: Bride Brook of Elco
Owners: Mr. and Mrs. W. Chalmers Burns, Chalburn Kennels

CH. PIERRETTE OF CHALBURN
Sire: Bohrer's Bredor.   Dam: Alva Schatzie
Owners: Mr. and Mrs. W. Chalmers Burns, Chalburn Kennels

150

"Ch. Pierrette of Chalburn. In my opinion this bitch was the nearest in conformation to our Standard that I have had the opportunity to go over. Proportion of length to height of 32″ at the withers, by measurement, absolutely square. Bone structure ideal and put together with proper angulation. Head as good as anyone could hope for, with an eye expression that showed just a little devilment, brisket and tuck up in right proportion, proper croup, back line and arched neck. As to coloration, with the exception of a few spots on the back of the neck and on one elbow, the black patches are properly distributed on white background. 'Rette' was powerful—she could cover more ground *faster* than any Great Dane I've ever seen in action!

"Ch. Pierrot of Chalburn. 'Rot' was one of the most striking Harlequins I have ever seen. In coloration, the whitest white, and the blackest black torn patches in variable sizes. He had a pure white neck, chest, and forelegs. His head was as long as could be desired and was comparable to any good fawn or brindle head, in my opinion. 'Rot' was 35½″ at the shoulder; brisket, tuck up, back line, and croup all that could be asked for in a Great Dane.

"Major Chips of Chalburn. I hope I can supply a new picture of Chips before this goes to press, as it doesn't do the dog justice, having been taken when Chips completed his Championship at the age of seventeen months. He was still undeveloped, and has matured beautifully since that time. While the coloration is pure white and the black torn patches are properly distributed, white neck, chest and forelegs, noticeable is a merle spot attached to the black on his side. I do not consider a merle spot of this size, even though there may be two or three, a fault. It is not desirable, but we disregard a small white chest blaze, commonly seen in the fawn and brindle coloration, also listed in the Standard as undesirable. Chips is another very powerful specimen—a true Harlequin. Notice even at the early age: the brisket, tuck up, feet, back line, and croup.

"Pierrot 2nd of Chalburn. Pierrot is a young dog in our kennel today which we expect to start showing this spring. He is sired by Ch. Major Chips of Chalburn."

151

Erna Heidere of Greenwood Lake, New Jersey, has bred such beautiful Great Dane Champions. They are: Champion Heidere's Alexi (Duke of Awosting ex Blondie of Sunningdane); Ch. Heidere's Brandi of Lidgerwood (Gibor of Greglon ex Heidere's Bonna); Ch. Sunningdane Heidere—a litter brother of Alexi; Ch. Heidere's Zita (Ch. Dinro Aslan ex Heidere's Mati Paras); The Champions from this kennel are Fawn and Harlequin; Ch. Heidere's Theda Bara (Ch. Dinro Aelric ex Ch. Heidere's Alexi); and Ch. Heidere's Heide, out of Ch. Heidere's Alexi by Ch. Dinro Aelric.

All of these lovely creatures are a credit to their breeder, but perhaps two of the most outstanding Great Danes are the Harlequin, Ch. Brandi, now owned by Ben Shalom, Elizabeth, New Jersey, and the fawn, Ch. Alexi. Alexi was the dam of three Champions, and three more of her offspring have ten points (all majors) toward the title. Erna Heidere was proudest when Alexi's son, Ch. HyCrest Prince, was a Best in Show winner.

The Champions and the point-getting young Great Danes of the past five years were well represented by the top winners at the classic Westminster Shows. Let's "review the bidding."

1950: Dogs in competition, 71. Judge, Harry M. Warren. B.O.B., Ch. Senta—also third in the Group (breeder, William J. Gilbert; owner, Herta Schroeder). B.O.S. and B.O.W., Lord Creston of Bauertown (breeder and owner, Naomi N. Bauer). Reserve Winners Dog, Deacon of Marydane (breeder and owner, Mary K. Johnston). Winners Bitch, Gilbert's Adele Cinderella (breeder and owner, William J. Gilbert). Reserve Winners Bitch, Lady Michelle of Elmhaven (owner, Betty Hyslop).

1951: Dogs in competition, 63. Judge, K. C. Tiffin. B.O.B,. Ch. Oakdane's Blitzen (owner, R. M. Findlay). B.O.S., Ch. Senta's Astrid (breeder and owner, Herta Schroeder). W.D. and B.O.W., Shir Van's Mark (owner, Mrs. R. E. Boyle). R.W., Ajax of Zeunges (breeder and owner, V. M. Zeunges). Winners Bitch, Heidere's Alexi (breeder and owner, Mrs. E. Heidere). Reserve Winners Bitch, Gilbert's Braemar Blossomtime (breeder, William J. Gilbert; owner, Mrs. F. Neuwirth).

CH. MAJOR CHIPS OF CHALBURN
Sire: Kentucky Colonel of Vakeck.   Dam: Miss Patches of Chalburn
Breeder-Owner: Mr. and Mrs. W. Chalmers Burns, Chalburn Kennels

CH. HEIDERE'S BRANDI OF LIDGERWOOD
Sire: Gibor of Greglon.   Dam: Heidere's Bonna.
Breeder: Erna Heidere.   Owner: Ben Shalom.

153

1952: Dogs in competition, 75. Judge, Rose Sabetti. B.O.B., Autopilot of Kanedane (breeder, L. T. Cayce; owner, Mary K. Johnston). B.O.S., Ch. Foray's Antoinette (breeders, Auds and Al Litchfield; owners, Alice and Lester Sawyer). W.D. and B.O.W., Autopilot of Kanedane. R. W., Foray's Bismark (breeders, the Litchfields; owners, the Sawyers). Winners Bitch, Evanger's Tigress of Regnave (breeders and owners, Mr. and Mrs. F. W. Evanger). Reserve, Gilbert's Leading Lady (breeder, William J. Gilbert; owner, R. B. Hull).

1953; Dogs in competition, 82. Judge, Charlie Kapp. B.O.B., Ch. Dion of Kent (breeder, Mrs. M. Rankin; owner, Lee Garnett·Day). B.O.S., Ch. Heidere's of Lidgerwood (owner, Ben Shalom). W.D., Lane's Turn Burgundy (breeder and owner, Ruth Allen). R.W., Sirbir (owners, E. O. and G. L. Baxter). Winners Bitch and Best of Winners, Medina of Evanger (breeders and owners, Mr. and Mrs. Evanger). Reserve Winners, Thordis of Shaland (breeder and owner, Mrs. M. M. Kurth).

1954: Dogs in competition, 63. Judge, J. P. Wagner. B.O.B., Ch. Lane's Turn Burgundy (breeder and owner, Ruth Allen). B.O.S. and B.O.W., Gilbert's Jersey Queen (breeder, William J. Gilbert; owners, Mr. and Mrs. McCrumb). W.D., Eaglevalley Crescendo (breeder and owner, Dorothy Montgomery). Reserve, Jo-Art's Jac (breeders, the Cornell's; owner, G. R. Phillips). Reserve Winners Bitch, Alldanes Urania (owners, Alldanes Kennels and C. Grana).

1955: Dogs in competition, 65. Judge, J. Bremner Proctor. B.O.B., Ch. HyCrest Prince (breeder, Erna Heidere; owners, Alice and Lester Sawyer). B.O.S., B.O.W., and W.B., Jo-Art's Heather (breeders, Grace and Joseph Cornell; owner, Mrs. Dorothy Merrill). W.D., Kenda's Dolphin (breeder and owner, Mrs. Kenneth C. Host). R.W.D., Rienzi of Marydane (breeder and owner, Mary K. Johnston). R.W.B., Lisa of Marydane (breeder and owner, Mary K. Johnston). The Brace Class was won by Ch. Heidere's Brandi of Lidgerwood (bred by Erna Heidere) and Shalom's Honey (bred by Frieda L. Hall). Both these Harlequin beauties are owned by Ben Shalom.

CH. SUNNINGDANE HEIDERE
Breeder: Erna Heidere.   Owners: Marie and Charlie Staiger.

CH. MOE v. EDELHERZ
Sire: Ben Hecktor v. Edelherz   Dam: Victory Hergunbar
Breeder-owner: W. J. Mackensen, Jr.

155

CH. DION OF KENT

Breeder: Marion Rankin. Owner: Lee Garnett Day.

The 1953 Best of Breed winner at the Garden, Ch. Dion of Kent, was purchased late the same year by the Days for their kennel. No living Great Dane had a comparable show record. This included: 6 Best in Show, 36 Groups, 98 Best of Breed, 3 Best American-bred, and Best at 4 Specialty Shows.

Bred by the Rankins, Dion is out of Ch. Cassandra of Kent, by Ch. Xerxes of Twin Cedars. (Xerxes relationship to Dion was the reason the Days bought the dog. Xerxes was sired by Ch. King Kong of Daynemouth). By using Dion at stud, Garnett Day thinks he will make a terrific contribution to the Daynemouth line-breeding. Dion has been bred to Ch. Teckla of Daynemouth and Garnett was extremely pleased with the promise he saw in a litter of eight puppies.

Nell, Bill, and the Gilbert Great Danes are now living at Whitehouse, New Jersey. Their kennel (designed by Bill) is right up to the minute in conveniences for man and Dane. The large building is divided in the middle by an office, sleeping facilities, a bathroom, and a kitchen. By this arrangement, the older dogs are partitioned off from the maternity department and puppy stalls.

In recognition of Bill Gilbert's ability as a breeder (and his worth as a *very* nice gentleman), the Great Dane Club of America honored him in March 1950. Bill was presented with three gifts. One was a parchment scroll, inscribed in illuminated Old English script: "A citation to William J. Gilbert, for his consistent contribution to the betterment of our favorite breed, the Great Dane." Bill also received a gold Movado wrist watch and a Best of Breed envelope containing a new fifty dollar bill. Appropriate speeches of presentation were made by Chalmers Burns and Bob Seitz.

Bill considers Senta the nearest to perfection of any of the Champions he has bred. Senta (owned by Herta Schroeder) retired with this spectacular show record: 1 Best in Show, 58 Best of Breed, 9 Groups, and 25 Group placings.

The Gilbert name is still synonymous with the word Champion. In the original Eastern Dane chapter, eighteen title holders from this kennel are listed. From 1950 until

CH. CHAUCER OF MARYDANE
Sire: Ch. Gerhardt of Marydane. Dam: Ch. Marshmellow of Marydane
Owners: Mr. and Mrs. Gerard Johnston, Ridgefield, Conn.

CH. GERHARDT OF MARYDANE
Sire: Ch. Neil of Brae Tarn. Dam: Ch. Molla of Roxdane
Owned by Mr. and Mrs. Gerard Johnston, Ridgefield, Conn.

1954, Bill has bred thirteen more. They are: Ch. Gilbert's Glory Adele's Cricket, Ch. Gilbert's Glory Dixie, Ch. Gilbert's Adele's Cleo, Ch. Gilbert's Braemar Blossomtime, Ch. Gilbert's King, Ch. Gilbert's Meadow Lane Kinsman, Ch. Gilbert's Leading Lady, Ch. Gilbert's Jersey Girl, Ch. Gilbert's Adele's Cinderella, Ch. Gilbert's Braemar Dolly, Ch. Gilbert's Braemar Eric, Ch. Gilbert's Ensign, and Ch. Gilbert's Jersey Queen. Gilbert's Adele's Copilot has fourteen points and Gilbert's Braemar Dolfina has twelve toward the title.

Bringing the record of Marydane Kennels up to date was fun—a continuing success story is nice to report. Ch. Gerhardt of Marydane and Ch. Marshmellow of Marydane became the basic stock out of which the Marydane bloodline has developed. To date, this kennel has bred or owned thirteen Champions and has several more close to the title. Their studs have sired many additional Champions throughout the country.

Mary and Jerry Johnston are interested primarily in breeding quality and not quantity. Since the kennel was started in 1942, the dogs have been carefully line bred, conforming to a long-range, studiously planned breeding program. The results speak for themselves. Marydane has four generations of Champions now, and many in the fifth generation already have points.

A list of the Champions of Marydane include: Ch. Molla of Roxdane, Ch. Gerhardt of Marydane, Ch. Marshmellow of Marydane, Ch. Chaucer of Marydane, Ch. Canute of Marydane, Ch. Deacon of Marydane, Ch. Brenda of Marydane, Ch. Lucky Adolph of Marydane, Ch. It's Mellow of Marydane, Ch. Illiance of Marydane, Ch. Bornholm's Cyanara, Ch. Autopilot of Kanedane, and Ch. Kenellen's Kadeen.

As the records show, Marydane Kennels have also been consistently contributing to the betterment of the breed. That is the true test of a bloodline. As examples, Gerhardt sired nine Champions; Marshmellow was the dam of four; Deacon sired four; Brenda was the dam of Lucky Adolph,

159

who sired the Best in Show winner of the 1953 Sweepstakes, Pudding of Marydane; Chaucer sired Autopilot, the winner of fifty B.O.B. and three firsts in Group.

Dorothy Montgomery, owner of Eaglevalley Kennels, has received many compliments on her first two Champions. Brindles, they are a litter brother and sister—Crescendo and Sonata—out of Eaglevale Gale by Ch. Deacon of Marydane. After acquiring the American title, Sonata went to Canada and quickly collected the points for a Championship of a second country. Crescendo finished in a blaze of glory, too. He specialized in being Winners Dog at Specialty Shows in 1954. These wins include Westminster, Baltimore, Boston, and the Great Dane Club of Canada.

Bred to Ch. Autopilot of Kanedane, Sonata produced Eaglevalley Moonlight. At the Westchester Show (1954), this beautiful fawn youngster went from Winners Bitch to Best of Winners in an entry of 95.

Another puppy in this litter, Eaglevalley Pilotlight, was Best Puppy in Show and Best of Opposite Sex to Best in Show at the 1953 Sweepstakes held by the Great Dane Club of America. Pilotlight is owned by that connoisseur of Great Danes, Rose Sabetti.

Betty Hyslop, creator of Cairndania Kennels at Brockville, Canada, continues to breed and show prize-winning Danes. The current stars of this establishment are: Canadian Ch. Lettie of Cairndania; American and Canadian Ch. Lady of Elm-Haven; Canadian Ch. Sabre of Cairndania; and American Ch. Zen von Zordane.

Zen, a handsome fawn dog, started his show career at the age of thirteen months. In large Dane entries, and with the stiffest Eastern competition present, Zen did some pretty fancy winning. He was Winners Dog at Morris and Essex in 1952. The next day, at Plainfield, Zen went from Winners Dog up to Best of Breed. Also in 1952, this dog delighted his owner with Best in Show at Ottawa, Canada.

For many years, the Ehmlings of Roxdane have bred fawns, brindles, and the most difficult of Dane breeding for correct coloration, Harlequins. In 1950, Bill and Marion

160

CH. AUTOPILOT OF KANEDANE
Sire: Ch. Chaucer of Marydane.   Dam: Ch. Bonnholm's Cynara.
Breeders: Jane and L. M. Cayce.   Owner: Mary K. Johnston.

CH. ITS MELLOW OF MARYDANE
Sire: Ch. Gerhardt of Marydane
Dam: Ch. Marshmellow of Marydane
Breeder-owner: Mary K. Johnston, Wilton, Conn.

Mrs. Dorothy Montgomery, Eaglevalley Kennels, New Milford Connecticut
with (left) Eaglevalley Moonlight, (center) Ch. Eaglevalley Crescendo, and
(right) Int. Ch. Eaglevalley Sonata.

Peggy, Bob, and the little Seitzes—Eaglevale Gale and
Ch. Duyster's Dorian von Seitzen.

bought a very beautiful black and white, Canadian Champion to use as a stud dog in their kennel. Graf's Dane Hurricane lived up to his call name of "Hurry" in acquiring his American Championship. He romped to Winners in five successive shows. The merit of a dog never defeated in the classes is obvious.

Hurry has been a source of pride to his owners. He has not only been a star in the show ring, but also has earned his meals in the kennel by siring good Roxdane Harlequin puppies.

The Lane's Turn Kennel, owned by Ruth and Leo Allen of suburban Boston, has produced some very nice fawn Great Danes in the past five years. The foundation bitch was Astrid of Marydane. Bred twice to Rose Tong's Ch. Dinro Aslan, "Trid" was the dam of four Champions. They are Ch. Lane's Turn Asgard, Ch. Lane's Turn Aurora, Ch. Lane's Turn Burgundy, and Ch. Lane's Turn Banner. (Astrid died, unfortunately, of a heart attack at a fairly young age. She had eleven points toward her Championship.)

Ch. Burgundy has really done the Allens proud! The big blond boy completed his Championship in 1953 by going Winners at Westminster. At the same show in 1954, Burgundy was Best of Breed.

The Allen's Kennel, a compact building constructed of log siding, looks like a log cabin. Inside, there are stalls for eight Danes, and a kitchen. The dogs have the benefit of thermostatically controlled heat. For exercise, there are forty-foot asphalt-base runs leading from the kennel to a large area of rough ground. Many trees provide shade from summer heat.

We asked Ruth when she started with Great Danes. She told us that she bought a brindle bitch twenty-one years ago —the only brindle she has ever owned. Quoting Ruth, "This Dane instilled in me a permanent affection for the breed because of such an outpouring of love and loyalty to all of us in the family."

Bill Mackensen, Jr., Yardley, Pennsylvania, is a veteran breeder and exhibitor of fawns, brindles, and Harlequins. In the past five years, he has finished six Champions of his

163

breeding. They are: Ch. Moe von Edelherz (Harlequin); Ch. Waldo von Edelherz (brindle); Ch. Tiger von Edelherz III (brindle); Ch. Baldur von Edelherz (brindle); Ch. Freya von Edelherz (fawn); and Ch. Frieda von Edelherz (fawn). Bill also finished to the title the dam of Tiger, Gilbert's Glory Dixie, bred by Bill Gilbert. Freya and Frieda (the latter owned by Norman and Leona Cappel) are litter sisters. In fact, they were the whole litter—two puppies. At the time they were whelped, Bill was annoyed with the dam, Tania von Edelherz. Now he thinks she did all right!

The von Edelherz Great Danes have the physical conformation to win at Specialty Shows (Westchester, Baltimore, Philadelphia, and the Great Dane Club of Pennsylvania). In addition, they are the steadiest dogs. We *know*. Some years ago, Bob was walking our entry down the Dane aisle at the Westchester Show. Bang! An unattended Dane on a slack bench chain leaped out and fastened his jaws on our bitch's flank. It took a few seconds for the other exhibitors to see what was going on and come to the rescue. Bob was pulling as hard as he could to release the girl when the offending biter was grabbed and yanked off. The sudden release of tension on the lead caused Bob to lose his balance, and he fell backward on five Mackensen Great Danes. What happened? Nothing. Those lovely creatures just shook their heads as a strange man was helped off their bench.

HyCrest LaDane Kennels are located in Sterling, Massachusetts. The owners are Alice and Lester Sawyer. They breed fawn Great Danes, exclusively. This coloration is complimentary to the Sawyer home-bred herd of registered Brown Swiss cattle. Alice describes their nice kennel as follows:

"We started breeding Great Danes in 1949 and have found this breed very interesting. To be sure, we have spent many hours analyzing factors important to the rapid growth of the Dane, but this sort of work has always intrigued us both. We might add this is not a new venture for us. After the many years we have bred cattle, we can conscientiously say we have had a real schooling for breed-

CH. HYCREST PRINCE
Sire: Ch. Foray's Bismark.   Dam: Ch. Heidere's Alexi.
Breeders-owners: Alice and Lester Sawyer, Leominster, Mass.

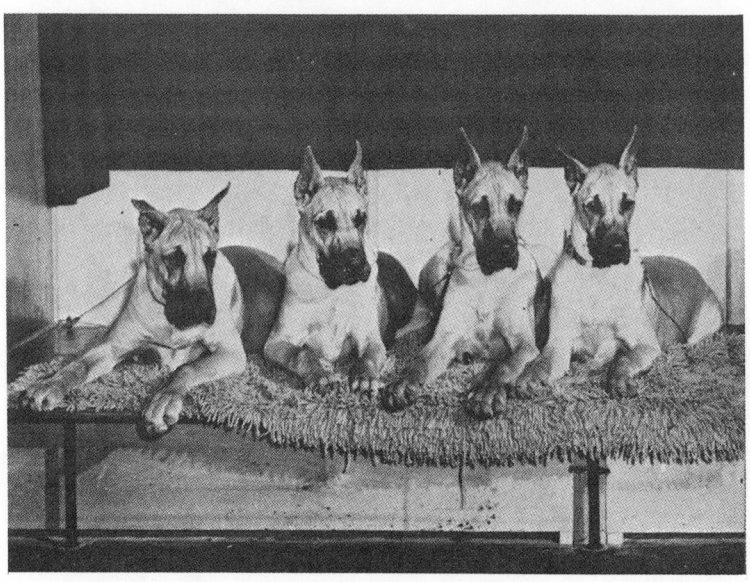

Puppies sired by Ch. Hycrest Prince
Breeders-owners: Alice and Lester Sawyer, Leominster, Mass.

165

CH. HYCREST DEWEY
Sire: Hycrest Baron.   Dam: Ch. Foray's Fancy.
Breeders-owners: Alice and Lester Sawyer, Leominster, Mass.

Ch. Foray's Antoinette "taken for a ride" by the Sawyer-bred Brown Swiss steers, Hi and Low.   (In the foreground, not a champion—not even registered—but a good little cat.)

166

ing dogs. We found, however, that it takes many more years to develop top cow families, as cows have only one calf each year providing your breeding program runs smoothly, whereas dogs average eight pups per litter.

"Our kennel consists of a two-story building, having fourteen pens; each pen has adequate space for two Danes. The walls are asbestos board, the grills solid aluminum, the feed and water racks adjustable; each pen has indoor windbreaks, preventing drafts; and the outdoor sunporches provide shade in the summer and protection in the winter. The floors are asphalt, which has some resiliency. At the end of the sixty-foot runs, a gate is provided, which allows the dogs to run in a three-acre field daily. One can well imagine that there are days when they return to the kennel a little battered from too much play. However, the risk of major injuries has to be considered on a percentage basis, and we feel this does not warrant our confining the dogs or depriving them of their natural instinct to run and play and occasionally chase and kill one of the great pests of any farm, woodchucks!

"Our medical room, bathing facilities, and office occupy one section of the kennel. The kitchen, we feel, is the hub of the kennel and is located about midway. Here we keep daily charts on the amounts of food given each dog, as well as any medication given. Each Dane has 1½ quarts of Brown Swiss milk daily, in addition to their other rations, after they are six months of age. This will seem shocking to some dog fanciers, but Brown Swiss milk has more nutrients than any other milk, a deciding factor in feeding this quantity of milk to our dogs. (We hope that some day, some dog-food manufacturer will put out a dog food that will contain all of the elements, traced minerals, amino acids, etc., thus eliminating the addition of the many things we now add to our present-day food in order to have a dog in top condition. Some day this will come to pass, and from there on, some of the prevalent ailments and troubles of dog owners today will be a thing of the past.)

"The second floor of our kennel consists of a large training room plus quarters for the kennel attendants. We have

167

Mr. and Mrs. Leo Allen with (left) Ch. Lane's Turn Asgard, (center) Lane's Turn Frappe, and (right) Asgard's young daughter, Lane's Turn Eggnog.

CH. LANE'S TURN AURORA
Sire: Ch: Dinro Aslan.   Dam: Astrid of Marydane.
Breeder: Mrs. Leo Allen, Chestnut Hill, Mass.
Owner: Miss Nielsen, Holliston, Mass.

equipped this training room with benches, thus giving our dogs a real dog-show setting, which we find particularly helpful in training puppies to learn the routine of being tied and benched.

"In 1949, we started the HyCrest Kennels with three Great Danes (two females and one male), and in 1955 we find ourselves with twenty-five HyCrest Danes ranging from one month to six months of age (including our foundation stock, Ch. Foray's Antoinette, Ch. Timberlane Suzanne, Ch. Foray's Bismark)."

In her modest way, Alice did not mention the brightest star of the kennel—Ch. HyCrest Prince. Out of Ch. Heidere's Alexi by Ch. Foray's Bismark, Prince finished to the title at the age of one year and ten months. His show record to December 1954 includes: 1 Best in Show, 17 Best of Breeds, 3 Groups, and 12 Group placings.

Because of the difficulty in breeding black and white Danes with the correct coloration, not too many are seen at the shows. One very good bitch being shown now is the lovely (Harlequin) Ch. Heidere's Brandi of Lidgerwood. Brandi, according to information supplied by her owner, Ben Shalom, had the greatest number of show wins of any Great Dane bitch in the United States (regardless of color) in 1954. On January 30, 1955, Brandi was Best of Breed at the Baltimore show and placed third in the Group. The show record for this Harlequin beauty is twenty-nine Best of Breed wins and twenty-five Best of Opposite Sex ribbons.

Brandi's daughter, Ch. All's Brandy of Lidgerwood, is owned by Al Jensen of Detroit. Sired by Ch. St. Magn Obertraubling, All's Brandy thrilled her breeder, Ben Shalom, at the Dane Specialty Show, May 16, at Buffalo, where she was Winners and Best of Winners. Going into Specials, All's Brandy had to compete against her dam. Brandi dropped the youngster—she was Best of Breed. All's Brandy has won six Best of Breed honors and one Group.

We mentioned briefly the 1953 Junior Sweepstakes and the two top winners: Best Adult in Show, Pudding of Marydane, and Best Puppy in Show, Eaglevalley Pilotlight. There were other winners! All, in the opinion of the judge, Phil

169

Marsh, were a credit to their breeders. This show, with an entry of eighty, was the largest Sweepstakes ever held by the Great Dane Club of America.

First in their classes were the following: Six- to nine-months puppy dog, Eaglevalley Pilotlight (breeder, Dorothy Montgomery; owner, Rose Sabetti). Nine- to twelve-months puppy dog, Gessel's Master of the Range (breeder and owner, Charles Gessel). Novice dogs, Hi Ville's Dennis (breeder and owner, Viola T. Brenner). Open dogs, Kolyer's Cygni von Adonis (breeder and owner, Catherine Kolyer).

First in the six- to nine-months puppy bitch class, Gilbert's Cleo (breeder, Bill Gilbert; owner, Mrs. Augusta White). Puppy bitches, nine- to twelve-months old, Cairndania's Zen's Zebar (breeder, J. B. McLean; owner, Betty Hyslop). Novice bitch, Chasnell Cleo (breeder and owner, C. Gunold Williams). Open bitch, Pudding of Marydane (breeder and owner, Mary K. Johnston). Reserve Best Adult in Show, Chasnell Cleo. Reserve Best Puppy in Show, Cairndania's Zen's Zebar. (Cleo became a Champion in 1954.)

Again in 1954, Rose Tong was Chairman of the Sweepstakes Show Committee, and she repeated the same brilliant job she did in 1953. The entry was down to sixty—due to the arrival of hurricane Edna, a most unwelcome guest. The brave breeders, exhibitors, and their Danes sat out the wind, the rain, and the collapse of two tents last October at Westchester, New York. By two-thirty in the afternoon, the skies cleared and a mass exodus from the station wagons began.

From a beautiful crowd of young Danes, Judge Lena Ludwig made the following top placings: Best Adult in Show, Jo-Art's Jac (breeders, Jo-Art's Kennel; owner, George R. Phillips). Reserve Best Adult, Canadian Ch. Zen's Zebar (breeder, J. B. McLean; owner, Betty Hyslop). Best Puppy in Show, Glad Pink Confetti (breeder and owner, Mrs. Hubert Lee). (This breeder of superlative Danes also won the President's trophy for the highest point score.) Reserve to Best Puppy, Danelagh's Fergus (breeder and owner,

CH. LANE'S TURN BURGUNDY
Sire: Ch. Dinro Aslan.   Dam: Astrid of Marydane.
Breeder-owner: Mrs. Leo Allen, Chestnut Hill, Mass.

CH. LANE'S TURN ASGARD
Sire: Ch. Dinro Aslan.   Dam: Astrid of Marydane.
Breeder-owner: Mrs. Leo Allen, Chestnut Hill, Mass.

171

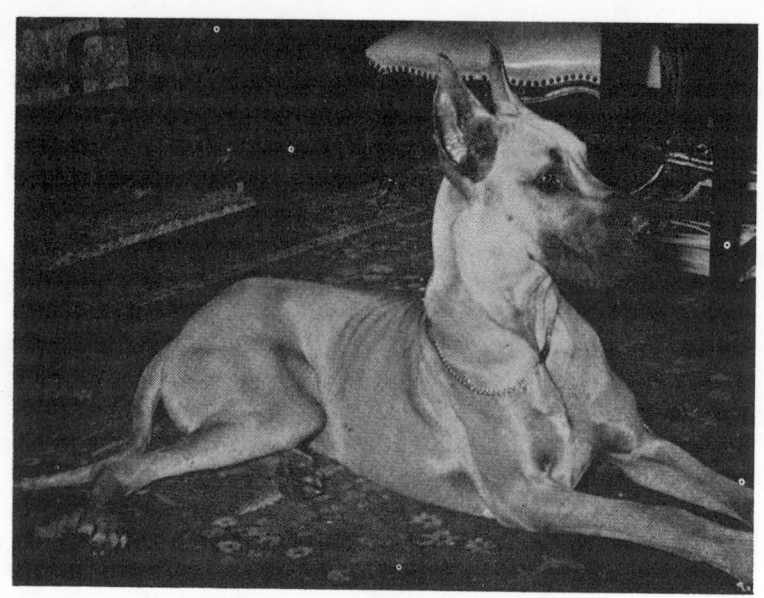

A BEAUTIFUL DOG OF YESTERDAY
Ch. Gail's Dolf of Evangers (Primas of Brae Tarn ex Reitzes Woglinde)
Owner: Gail Schuster

Gail Schuster, Skokie, Illinois, with litter of twelve blues

Nancy Draper). Best Sire and Get, Ch. Autopilot (owner of the sire, Mary Johnston). Best Dam and Get, Ch. Tekla of Daynemouth (breeders and owners of the dam, Mr. and Mrs. Lee Garnett Day).

The Eastern breeders prefer fawn, brindle, and Harlequin Great Danes in that order of coloration. While blue is accepted by the Standard, Danes with this coat color are not shown in our section of the country.

The breeders of Blue Danes nearest to the Atlantic seaboard (as far as we know) are Frieda Schuster and her daughter Gail of Skokie, Illinois. They bought their brood bitch, Rungmook's Rosette, from those veteran blue breeders of Western Canada, Mr. and Mrs. Cowan.

"Rosie's first blue litter was a "doozy" of a whelping initiation for the Schuster ladies. They literally and figuratively had *Blues in the Night*(s). In no hurry at all, the dam whelped a puppy periodically for forty-eight hours. It was a litter of sixteen. With supplementary feeding, the breeders raised twelve of that number to a saleable age. Fortunately, the Schusters have had less suspense and less labor with subsequent litters.

In conclusion, a hearty thank you to the owners of Great Danes for being so generous in contributing your material and beautiful pictures. The revision of this chapter, with your help, was a pleasure. Unfortunately—as in the first chapter—it was impossible to get information and pictures of all the fine Danes in the East. For this we are sorry, for we love them all—fawns, brindles, and Harlequins.

Ch. Dane Eden's Samson with twelve of his get in the stud dog class at the Los Angeles Kennel Club Specialty Show, December 1953.

The Great Dane in California

JOHN G. McEDWARD

(With supplemental information furnished by the
Great Dane Clubs of California)

REAT Dane owners throughout
the country are alert to the fact that California-bred Danes
are contributing their share for the improvement of the
breed without the expense and uncertainty encountered by
the early fanciers in seeking from Germany the stock necessary to accomplish their aims in respect to bloodlines and
strong, showy, healthy progeny. Moreover, the influence of
California Danes is not confined to this country but extends
to England, Canada, South America, Cuba, Mexico, the
Philippines, in fact, to all lands accessible by air freight.

The roster of the charter members of the Great Dane
Club of California, organized in 1931, is composed of the
names of many, a few of whom are still active breeders and
fanciers, whose contributions to the breed will continue to
exert an influence for all time. An informal organizational
meeting was held in Balboa on the first of August of that
year. Present, in alphabetical order, were the following:
Mary A. Davis, Ernest E. Ferguson, Albert B. Gardner, Hazel
L. Gardner, Margaret B. Hostetter, D. Herbert Hostetter, Jr.,
Donald Hostetter, James Lawrence, Donald Luckham, Edward and Harold McNulty, Laura O'Day, Sterling O'Day,
Bertha B. Torrence, J. Findley Torrence, E. Wills Watkins,
and H. Wills Watkins. The group chose Mrs. Hostetter to
serve as the Club's first President; Mr. Lawrence, Vice-
President; and Mr. Gardner, Secretary-Treasurer. The Club

175

CH. NANDA von LOHELAND
Sire: Champion Dolf v.d. Saalburg.   Dam: Ch. Ferguni v. Loheland
Owned by Planetree Kennels

REICHSIEGER RIESE v. LOHELAND, center,
with his younger brother and sister, VASSALL and VACCA v. LOHELAND

176

thus founded has enjoyed a sound and steady growth, numbering today close to seventy-five active members, and October of 1949 marked the twenty-second Specialty Show it has held. Officers for 1949 were Budrick Schindler, Great Dane Judge and owner of the Wonred Danes, President; Roy Marlin, Vice-President; Mrs. Gerie Coombs, Secretary; and Dr. Jack Wooding, Treasurer. For the past several years it has been the practice of the Club to sponsor two Specialty Shows a year, one in June at the nationally important Harbor Cities Kennel Club Show at Long Beach, and the other in October at the combined California Associated Specialty Clubs' Show in Los Angeles. For the past three years at Long Beach the Great Dane entries have approached or exceeded one hundred dogs—99 in 1947, 105 in 1948 and 110 in 1949. The honors won by Danes in the years mentioned, against the toughest competition, have had far-reaching significance for all owners of the breed. Each year a California-bred Great Dane bitch has topped the Group—Ch. Duchess of Zel-Thor over 609 working dogs in 1947; her daughter, Dane Eden's Delilah, over 754 in 1948; and Ch. An Gleann Planetree-Gael over 740 in 1949, winning also the coveted spot of Best Dog in Show. The last Great Dane to achieve this honor at Harbor Cities was Mr. Vincent Garrity's Ch. Hansi of Garricrest in 1941. Also, in 1948 and 1949, Best Team in Show honors went to Great Danes, the champion Dane Eden Team handled in spectacular fashion on four separate leads by the one handler, Russell Zimmerman. When Danes can win Groups and Best in Shows it helps the breed, and other achievements of California dogs in this field will be mentioned later on. For the moment it will be worth while to review somewhat the part played in breeding and importations by some of the founders of the Great Dane Club of California and by other breeders over a period of years.

Foremost, in the opinion of many breeders and from the point of view of definite nation-wide influence, stands the name of Margaret Hostetter of Ridgerest Kennels. From Mr. Josef Eigenbauer, who still has Danes in Mexico City, Mrs. Hostetter purchased the great fawn bitch, German and

American Ch. Etfa v.d. Saalburg, in December of 1928. Ben Brown, well-known professional handler, has made it a point often to ask a judge what dog, of any breed, has most impressed him and the answers have usually been, "Etfa." Etfa was whelped May 17, 1925, and was German Champion in 1927. She was a full sister to Ch. Dolf v.d. Saalburg (Ch. Bosko v.d. Saalburg ex Fauna Moguntia). The first time exhibited for her new owner, at Westminster in 1929, Etfa was Best Great Dane and her subsequent show career included seven Best in Shows. Mrs. Hostetter also acquired two fine sisters, bred by Mr. Eigenbauer out of Etfa by Harold Lloyd's Ch. Lloyd's Titan Boy, a brindle, Princess Barba and Betty of Ridgerest. More will be said later on about Ch. Princess Barba and her quality as a producer. Betty completed her championship before eighteen months old, was also Best Great Dane at Westminster and won several Best in Shows. Mrs. Hostetter's son, Donald, still in his teens, shared her enthusiasm for the breed and learned to handle them so adroitly that as a general rule all the Ridgerest dogs were handled by him. It was Mrs. Hostetter who called together the group mentioned earlier which formed the Great Dane Club of California, and since then she has filled every office in the club and in 1948 was its Vice-President. In 1931 she took Etfa and Betty to Germany, breeding Etfa to Helios Hexengold. She purchased Irmin v. Odenwald and later bred Betty to him. Donald spent a year or longer in Germany, visiting and studying all the leading kennels of the country. Little Sister of Ridgerest, also out of Etfa by Titan Boy, was bred in Germany to Elch Edler v.d. Saalburg. Ozelot v. Birkenhof, mother of Oerlang v. Loheland by Halfdan v.d. Rhon, Dolf grandson, was a product of this mating. Ch. Igor of Ridgerest, son of Etfa and Irmin, Ridgerest outcrossed to Mancusi's Lada, seeking substance and soundness. Merry M of Ridgerest, a daughter from this mating, was bred to a sire of great distinction in the Ridgerest Kennels, Ch. August of Brae Tarn, brindle son of Ch. Randolph Hexengold and Dixi v. Schloss Dellwig. It is interesting to know that August never sired a fawn, but always beautiful dark brindles with lovely bodies and top lines. A splendid ex-

178

CH. DANE EDEN'S GOLDEN BARON
Sire: Ch. Dane Eden's Samson.   Dam: Duchess of Farmers Hope.
Breeder: Phillip T. Ries.   Owners: Gerald C. and Mary P. McKinnon.

Litter of puppies out of OAKDANE'S BARBEE BELLE
by CH. DANE EDEN'S SAMSON
Breeder-Owner: Leroy S. and Barbara J. Marlin, Glendale, Calif.

179

ample is Mrs. Hostetter's Ch. Voro of Ridgerest who reached the dignified age of ten on April 18, 1949, and is still, as this is written, in excellent health and condition.

Among the many outstanding champions sired by Ch. Voro of Ridgerest, which include Mrs. Florence Lary Wasson's Ch. Faecarl's Voro, Oakdane's Ch. Faecarl's Brenda Aloho, Ch. Valor of Ridgerest who died of pneumonia in 1946, Taneric Kennels' Ch. Faecarl's Brenda's Boy, is the important fawn stud, Ch. Faecarl's Brendo, owned now by Dollymount Kennels, Tacoma, Washington. Here the Eastern influence shows itself, for Brendo's mother was Ch. Brenda of Brae Tarn, brought to California by Planetree Kennels and acquired from Planetree by the Faecarl Kennels of Dr. and Mrs. McPheeters of Fresno. Brenda was a fawn daughter of that prepotent sire, Ch. Czardas von Eppeleinsprung-Noris. Czardas was personally selected in Germany in 1936 by the owners of Brae Tarn, Mr. and Mrs. R. P. Stevens of Greenwich, Conn. Her mother was Ch. Quia of Brae Tarn, Brae Tarn's greatest producing matron of that time. Brendo, unfortunately for the breed in California, has not been easily accessible to many owners of good bitches who might otherwise have availed themselves of his excellent potency and direct father to son lineage from Ch. Dolf v.d. Saalburg. In the short time Brendo stood at stud in Southern California, then under Planetree Kennels' ownership, he was bred to three champion bitches, Ariel of Taneric, Rinni of Planetree, and Duchess of Zel-Thor, and to Berta de Or, owned by Joseph and Pauline Walmsley, of Van Nuys, more about whom will appear later. Out of these matings have come nine champions: Victor of Taneric from Ariel, An Gleann Planetree-Targe and Gael from Rinni, Felix de Or from Berta, and the five Dane Eden champions: Lorelei, Sunny, Duchess of Malibu, Samson, and Delilah out of the Duchess of Zel-Thor mating. All, with the exception of Victor and Targe who have not been actively competing, are group winners and four have won Best in Shows, All Breeds: Gael at the 1949 Harbor Cities Show, Dollymount Kennels' Lorelei with a total of five and the 1949 Fall Specialty, Samson at San Mateo, and Delilah at San Diego. This

180

record, in respect to group and finals competition and the number of litters involved, is exceptional. What influence Brendo will exert on the breed in the years to come rests in the ability of Victor, Targe, Felix, and Samson to carry on, and in the foresight of owners of good brood matrons to take advantage of the potentialities of these young studs.

Returning again to the period of Margaret Hostetter's activity in the breed, Ridgerest was by no means the only kennels of importance during those years in respect to imports, breeding and the show ring. Apart from the heavy Eastern Competition in imports on the part of the Stevens of Brae Tarn, the Warrens of Warrendane and Charles Kapp, later of Canidom Kennels, Harkness Edwards of Walnut Hall, Mrs. G. W. Hyslop of Canada, Dr. Henry Celaya of San Antonio, to mention a few, there were others in California equally able to afford the expense and interested enough in the breed and competition to make the game interesting. In the San Francisco area there was Vincent J. Garrity of Garricrest who owned Ch. Count Felix v. Luckner, the last Great Dane to win Best in Show, in 1937, at the Los Angeles Kennel Club until Ch. Duchess of Zel-Thor annexed that honor over a decade later, fresh from her win of Best Great Dane at Westminster in 1948. Previous Great Danes to win Best in Show at the Los Angeles event were: in 1926, Francis X. Bushman's Zampa von Wilhelmstrand; in 1928, Etfa v.d. Saalburg, owned then by Mr. J. Eigenbauer; in 1931 D. Herbert Hostetter, Jr.'s Ch. Betty of Ridgerest; and in 1936 Mrs. Mary A. Davis' Ch. Etfa v.d. Saalburg's Boy Brion. The memory of Mr. Garrity's great Hansi, mentioned previously for his Best in Show win at Harbor Cities in 1941, still brings a glow to the eyes of the noted dog photographer, William Deo Paul. There was Dr. L. C. Spangard, owner of many Great Danes, whose Int. Ch. Riese v. Loheland and Ch. Cyrus v.d. Pissa were two very dominant fawn male German imports and both exerted a definite influence for the improvement of the breed on the Coast. There was Mr. E. E. Ferguson, who imported Champions Ozelot v. Birkenhof, Zelia v. Loheland, and Oerlang v. Loheland. According to Mr. Ferguson, the mating of

181

August to Ziele and also the offspring sired by Oerlang have had a decided influence on the breed in California. Zelia had one litter, the "Z" litter, by Ch. August of Brae Tarn, of which Ch. Estid Zilch is the best remembered. A "Z" daughter, Zola, strayed into a mistake mating with her brother, Zilch, while a Specialty Show was in progress. This resulted in a litter of nine but all were lost by the ravages of distemper. Zola also died of the disease. Ozelot was bred to Ch. Etfa v.d. Saalburg's Boy Brion but died two weeks before the litter was due, an aftermath of a nail injury from the crate on the voyage over. Zelia, it is interesting to know, made her American championship with three Best in Show wins, the Specialty Show, Santa Monica and Santa Barbara. Mr. Ferguson had also made arrangements to bring another great German dog to California, Ziskow Kadow, but unfortunately the dog died in Greenland where Frau von Rhoden used to take the von Loheland Great Danes for conditioning.

What has just been said about Ch. Oerlang v. Loheland and the high estimation as a sire accorded him by his importer, Ernest Ferguson, recalls an interesting anecdote related by a breeder of distinction in California, Mrs. William J. Clark, about Oerlang's first stud service upon reaching his new home. First, however, a few words are in keeping on Mrs. Clark's activities in Great Danes, for her Dane Lair dogs are to be found in the pedigrees of today's finest specimens. Mrs. Clark acquired her first Great Dane in 1931 and the following year joined the newly formed Great Dane Club through her friendship with Mrs. Mary A. Davis, owner of Ch. Etfa v.d. Saalburg's Boy Brion. Mrs. Clark was so impressed by Boy Brion at the Ambassador Dog Show that year that she acquired the bitch Yabut Loheland Pfaff and mated her to Boy Brion. The resulting litter of five was the foundation of the Dane Lair Kennels. Anemone of Dane Lair, from this mating, produced so many champions that she was awarded a Certificate of Honor from the American Kennel Club for the champions she produced which brings us to the story about Oerlang. The scene is Dane Lair, the telephone is ringing: Mrs. Clark (Alverda, to her friends)

182

Ch. Boy Brion   Ch. Chien D'Ore

Owner: Mrs. Mary A. Davis, South Pasadena, California

PROVAN'S QUEST
(Am. and Can. Ch. Dollymount's Balthazar ex Alexis Von Essen)

DeOR's D'ARTAGNAN (left) and dam, TANERIC'S LADY DANA (right)
Breeder: Virginia McDonald, Burbank, Calif.
Owners: Mr. and Mrs. E. Benson, Sun Valley, Calif.

CH. DeOr's LADY LeMELLE OF WONRED
Sire: Ch: Felix DeOr.   Dam: Claudia of Wonred.
Breeders: Maryon and Bud Schindler, Van Nuys, Calif.
Owners: Mr. and Mrs. Harry C. LeMelle, Los Angeles, Calif.

hears Ernie Ferguson's voice on the wire. His great import, Oerlang, has arrived but is gravely ill with pneumonia contracted on the Bremen on the voyage over and is not expected to survive. Has Alverda any bitch ready for a mating? Yes, Anemone of Dane Lair was ready to breed. Would she meet them at the veterinarian's and undertake the slim chance of salvaging something from the considerable investment and trouble involved in Oerlang's acquisition. Alverda and Anemone were quick to cooperate and with the help of the veterinarian and despite his pessimistic predictions that nothing worth while could possibly result from a mating with a sire in so desperate a condition, the breeding was accomplished. How wrong he was, the results determined. Four champions came from this eleventh hour emergency breeding: Orell, Ora, Ocelot, and Ortrud of Dane Lair. Ortrud, Alverda sold later to Dr. Spangard. Ocelot completed her championship with twenty points before reaching her first birthday. Many picture stars became the owners of Dane Lair dogs—Don Ameche, Janet Gaynor, and Hedy Lamar to mention three—and many were shipped out of the country. From Mrs. Hostetter she acquired Herta of Ridgerest, beautiful brindle daughter of Ch. Phobe v. Birkenhof of Ridgerest and Ch. Benoni of Ridgerest. Herta won her championship in five shows, wins that included three group wins. She acquired Dane Lair's Herma from Laura O'Day out of Mrs. O'Day's Ch. Sandra of Ridgerest by Dr. Spangard's Int. Ch. Riese v. Loheland. Her Ch. Ocelot of Dane Lair, from the Oerlang and Anemone hurry-call mating, she bred to Riese, and Runa of Dane Lair, sire of Margaret Shave's Carla of Zel-Thor, was a product of this mating. Mrs. Shave bred Carla to Ernie Ferguson's Ch. Estid Zilch (Ch. August of Brae Tarn ex Int. Ch. Zelia v. Loheland) which produced Ariel of Dane Lair, mother of Ch. Duchess of Zel-Thor. Ariel was owned by Edward S. Todd, who also owned Bandit of Dane Crest, Duchess' sire, and here is where Oerlang, given up for lost upon his arrival in California, again comes into the picture in his relationship to Bandit. Bandit, although bearing the suffix of Dane Crest, the kennels owned by Katherine Retting, now

185

CH. ARIEL OF BLUE OAKS
Sire: Ch. Pirate of Caldane.   Dam: Athena of Twin Cedars.
Owners: Crockerly Kennels, Sacramento, Calif.

Left: Peter's Big Boy.   Right: Kay-Rio's Kitanya of Taneric.

Katherine Hyde, of Castaic, was by no manner of means Dane Crest bred as is the current misconception, but was bred by John S. Chichester, then living in San Fernando, California. Oerlang's part in the story comes about in the following manner. Contrary to everyone's expectations, Oerlang did not die from the pneumonia attack from which he was suffering when bred to Anemone of Dane Lair, but lived to sire several other excellent litters. He was bred to Ch. Flamme of Willow Run and to Firefly of Willow Run. Willow Run was the kennels of Albert B. Gardner, author of the very excellent book *Dane Data*. This book truly contains very valuable data and fortunate is the Dane owner who has a copy in his possession. It is illustrated by photographs of many outstanding specimens, by drawings by the author and cartoons by Walter Lantz, owner of Estid Biggs (Ch. Estid Zilch ex Pamela of Dane Lair.) Ridgerest, too, used Oerlang, mating him to Ch. Gretchen of Ridgerest, one of three spectacular group and best in show winners, the others being Champions Guardian and Grizelda of Ridgerest. Gretchen was sired by Ch. Irmin v. Odenwald of Ridgerest out of the bitch previously mentioned bred by Joseph Eigenbauer, Ch. Princess Barba (Ch. Lloyd's Titan boy ex Int. Ch. Etfa v.d. Saalburg). It was the mating to Gretchen that put Oerlang's blood in Bandit's veins. A daughter from the litter, Arla of Ridgerest, was bred to Dr. Spangard's Int. Ch. Riese v. Loheland, and Mr. Chichester acquired a male from the litter, Brian v. Riesen, a fawn, which he bred to his golden fawn bitch, Tanya of Granada, the breeding which produced Bandit. Tanya's sire was Ch. Sunswept Alecto, a fawn owned and bred by Mr. Albert A. Hilton of North Hollywood, by Lief of Ridgerest out of Sunswept Jemba. In the August, 1939, issue of *Dog World,* there is an imposing picture taken by Paul Ladin at the Long Beach show the month before, showing Judge Charles Williams selecting his Best of Breed from the 25 champions entered for Specials only and the BW winner of an all-time high in Great Dane entries of 138. Quoting from *Dog World*: "Here is the arresting list of Danes competing for BB: Chs. Count Felix v. Luckner, Joan v. Luckner of Garricrest,

PROVAN'S QUINTESSENCE

ALEXIS von ESSEN

CH. TONIA OF RUHAVEN

CH. LIL OF GUILERDANE

CH. PIRATE OF CALDANE

CH. SWANDANE'S ALLURE

188

Flamme of Willow Run, Ilse of Ridgerest, San Marino Gruenwald, Achim's Freund of Planetree, Kuno of Warrendane, Jaga of Warrendane, Planetree's Cyrus of Riviera, Hulda of Planetree, Glory of El Rancho, Blumen of Adow, Mancusi's Toby, Orell of Dane Lair, Riese v. Loheland, Asta of Brae Tarn, Guardian of Ridgerest, Igor of Ridgerest, August of Brae Tarn, Grizelda of Ridgerest, Haida of Ridgerest, Ocelot of Dane Lair, Riddles Hamlet, and Medwin of Ridgerest. The coveted purple and gold went to Albert A. Hilton's special male, Ch. Sunswept Alecto." Many of the dogs competing in this spectacular array have been mentioned already in this chapter or will be in the pages to follow. The beautiful fawn Ch. Flamme of Willow Run, for instance, was owned by William McCann, president of the Great Dane Club of California in 1947 and 1948. Flamme was by Ch. Baron of Ridgerest out of Ch. Fleeta of Willow Run and lived to the really ripe age for a Dane of eleven and a half years. She died at the Aviation Cadet Center in San Antonio, Texas, where Capt. McCann was Commander of the B-29 Flight Engineer Officers Training School. Champions Guardian and Grizelda of Ridgerest were by Ch. Irmin v. Odenwald of Ridgerest out of Ch. Princess Barba. Mention of Ch. Princess Barba brings us to some interesting recollections on California Great Danes, past and present, as related by a lady whose experience and importance in breeding extends over a period of many, many years, Laura O'Day, for it was in 1928 that she acquired her first Great Dane, Princess Barba.

One of the founder-members of the Great Dane Club of California, Secretary of the Club in 1948, Mrs. O'Day's activities have done a great deal for the breed, and her knowledge and advice have helped many breeders. She relates that since 1927 there have been but four German Reichssieger and Reichssiegerin in California: Etfa v.d. Saalburg, Remus v.d. Reinschanze, Cyrus v.d. Pissa, and Riese v. Loheland. It has already been told how Etfa v.d. Saalburg was brought over by Josef Eigenbauer and later sold to Ridgerest Kennels and how, before selling her, Mr. Eigenbauer bred her to Harold Lloyd's Ch. Titan Boy, a grandson

189

of Dolf v.d. Saalburg. Out of this litter of eight, three became champions: Ch. Etfa v.d. Saalburg's Boy Brion owned by Mrs. Mary A. Davis, Ch. Betty of Ridgerest owned by Ridgerest Kennels, and Ch. Princess Barba owned by Mrs. O'Day and later by Ridgerest Kennels. Princess Barba produced some of the best Danes and the best litter Ridgerest ever had, three champions out of a litter of three. Guardian and Grizelda were group and Best in Show winners for many years. Ch. Gretchen, a temperamental shower, Mrs. O'Day acquired on breeding terms, mating her to Ernest Ferguson's Ch. Oerlang v. Loheland, which resulted in three puppies. One was put to sleep because of an injury. Adonis was poisoned when he had fourteen points towards his championship. Arla had many reserve wins to her credit but did not like dog shows and usually sulked. It has already been told how Arla was bred to Riese v. Loheland. The breeding produced four puppies. One was given to Dr. Spangard for breeding and was injured, one was shipped to Oregon and Mrs. O'Day never heard from him again. The only female was sold and she heard she died. Brian, father of Bandit and grandfather of Ch. Duchess of Zel-Thor, she sold to one of her neighbors, John S. Chichester. Later Princess Barba was bred to Ch. August of Brae Tarn, out of which litter Mrs. O'Day picked Sandra of Ridgerest who finished her championship at eighteen months, a great showgirl, thoroughly sound with the most perfect head one could imagine. In the latter part of 1939 Riese v. Loheland, who had been brought from Germany at a reputedly very high price, was given to Mrs. O'Day by the importer, Dr. Spangard, because he had always been a house dog. Riese lived until 1943, which, at ten years, made him the oldest imported Dane thereabouts. It is noteworthy that in addition to Riese, there were five other American champions from the same litter: Reh, Raan, Rista, Rungnir, and Ratastok. Laura O'Day tells how another German Reichssieger, Remus v.d. Rheinschanze, was imported by Ridgerest Kennels and looked as though he could have been the greatest of the imported males if in good condition, but due to having been horribly neglected on board ship he arrived in a condition

CH. DANE EDEN'S SAMSON
Sire: Ch. Faecarl's Brendo.   Dam: Ch. Duchess of Zel-Thor
Breeder-Owner: John G. McEdward, Dane Eden Kennels

Guilerdane litter at four weeks
(Ch. Dane Eden's Samson ex Ch. Cliza of Caldane)

191

from which he never recovered and died soon afterward. The fourth German Reichssieger, and champion in two other countries, Cyrus v.d. Pizza, was bought by Dr. Spangard at about eight years of age, around the time he imported Riese. Mrs. O'Day also bred her Sandra to Riese and she whelped six brindle puppies. Two were born dead, one died soon thereafter of the four remaining which were bought by Dane Lair. Two were sold for pets and never cropped and the fourth was Herma of Dane Lair, which Mrs. Clark kept for five years, for although she had bred hundreds of Danes of her own, even giving away champions, she held on to Herma in the hope that when the war was over she could start again with Herma as the foundation. However, war work and war conditions prevented her realizing her plans, and at the age of five years Herma was sold to Mrs. Phebe D. Long of Dollymount Kennels. Herma was bred to Canyon Crest's Ingo and had two Caesarian daughters, Ch. Dollymount's Hilda and Dollymount's Heidi. Both were bred to Ch. Faecarl's Brendo. Never a woman to be long without a Great Dane, Mrs. O'Day now has a promising young fawn male whelped in June, 1948, out of the mating of Heidi to Brendo. Mrs. O'Day remembers Champions August of Brae Tarn and Brenda of Brae Tarn as very large Danes and sound, almost pure Saalburg strain.

Because of the significant part she had played in the breeding back of Ch. Duchess of Zel-Thor, through Arla of Ridgerest and Brian v. Riesen, a close friendship developed between Laura O'Day and the owners of Dane Eden Kennels, and she was given her pick of the puppies remaining in Duchess' first litter. She selected a promising-looking fawn bitch, ears still in rolls, named her Lorelei for the German blood that flows in her own veins, and presented her to her daughter Margaret. She raised and trained Lorelei for show, but, lacking the time to give her the show career she felt she deserved, following the Harbor Cities Show in 1948 where Lorelei's sister Delilah had just won the Working Group, she placed Lorelei in the hands of her friends, the Longs, of Dollymount. From then on, her show career was spectacular. She quickly finished her American cham-

Head Study of CH. KUNO OF WARRENDANE, C.D.
Sire: Ch. Rungnir v. Loheland. Dam: Ch. Nanda v. Loheland
Breeder: Warrendane Kennels. Owner: Planetree Kennels

Four champions of the Dane Eden litter from Ch. Faecarl's Brendo, Dolly-
mount Kennels, out of Ch. Duchess of Zel-Thor, Dane Eden Kennels
L. to R.: Int. Ch. Lorelei, owned by Dollymount Kennels, Ch. Sunny of Dane
Eden, owned by A. Forbes Foster (handling), Ch. Dane Eden's Delilah and
Ch. Dane Eden's Samson, owned by John G. McEdward, Dane Eden Kennels

pionship showing the same distinction as a group winner as her brother and three sisters, went on to annex the Canadian title and four Best in Shows, the 1949 Olympia show in Renton, Washington, and the Los Angeles 1949 Fall Specialty show. Mrs. O'Day takes great pride in Lorelei's achievements and hopes to do as well with the present object of her care and affection, Dollymount's Balthazar, the young son of Brendo and Heidi.

A kennel that has exerted a profound influence on the breed on the West Coast, from the competitive standpoint and that of bloodlines, is Planetree, mentioned heretofore as the owners of Ch. Faecarl's Brendo during the short time Brendo stood at stud in Southern California. Planetree Kennels, Reg., received its American Kennel Club license in 1934, and was then located in Encino, California. It was started by two University of California College of Agriculture students who had come south two years before to complete their degrees at U.C.L.A. In their own words the owners of Planetree, Ruth Martin and Suzanne Daniel Hawkins, review their experiences in Great Danes as follows:

"We happened to stop in at one of the old Los Angeles Kennel Club shows then held at the Ambassador Hotel Auditorium in Los Angeles, and watched the Dane judging. As youngsters, our families had owned a Dane or two (harlequins and blues) and we were very much impressed with the beauty, elegance, and comparative refinement of the top specimens shown. Margaret Hostetter's Ridgerest Kennels topped the breed that day and we obtained their kennel address and set out some days later to buy one of their dogs, simply for the pleasure of owning one and with no thought then of later starting our own kennels. We emerged from Ridgerest with a brindle bitch known as Diana of Ridgerest by imported Ch. Irmin v. Odenwald ex Ch. Princess Barba. She was well bred, but frankly we chose her not for her breeding, brains, or beauty, but because she was the only dog in the kennels we could afford to buy at the time.

"Later, we bred her, and were subsequently forced to move, due to neighborhood feelings, with bitch and litter to a small and very dilapidated farm in Encino. With no

194

CH. DANE EDEN'S DUCHESS OF MALIBU
Finished her championship in ten days—four shows
Breeder-Owner: John G. McEdward, Dane Eden Kennels

L. to R: Owner-handler, John G. McEdward with Best Team in Show,
Ch. Dane Eden's Samson, Ch. Dane Eden's Delilah, Ch. Duchess of Malibu
and Ch. Duchess of Zel-thor (Dam of the four) and Caesar of Dane Eden,
owned by Rodney H. Davis, Long Beach, Calif. Judge: Mrs. Eva Hill

195

adequate housing, not even heat or hot water for either ourselves or our dogs, we lost the entire litter with distemper. However, out of this experience we met Dr. E. J. Bonneville, then veterinarian to Harold Lloyd's kennels of some fifty or sixty Danes and a member of the Great Dane Club which we later joined. Subsequent visits to shows and kennels increased the great appeal the breed already had for us—we were already interested in breeding, raising, and judging livestock and had had considerable experience in this line both in our animal husbandry courses and on our family ranches before going to college—so the logical outcome was to enter the breeding field in Danes.

"Studies of pedigrees, particularly when we knew many of the individuals in the immediate vicinity, either by picture or direct contact, convinced us that the Saalburg strain evidenced more beauty, nobility, refinement, and true Dane character than any other, but we did feel that some individuals of this strain lacked soundness, constitutional vigor, and soundness of temperament. We decided, therefore, while looking around for the dogs we wanted to found our line, to try an experiment—a complete outcross, motivated by the stockman's code of outcross vigor. We bred Diana to Albert Gardner's Ch. Canis Major of Willow Run, a big-boned, stolid brindle dog of the 'old-fashioned' type, and got what we sought in increased size, stamina, and soundness. However, there was too much variation in type in the litter to recommend this practice if we wished to establish a strain and type of our own.

"Being unable at the time to afford the purchase price of an imported dog of the strain we wanted, we decided to look over the Eastern kennel imports and select puppies from the dogs or bitches that we liked best, or to purchase an older import, past its show peak but still able to turn out one or two litters. We found what we wanted in Ch. Nanda v. Loheland, daughter of the great Dolf ex Ferguni v. Loheland, also a Dolf daughter. We purchased Nanda only after the Warrens ascertained they could replace her with her sister, Nepa, dam of the great litter containing Rungnir, Reh, Riese, Rista, Raan, etc. We also purchased a three-

DeOR'S SIR ROBIN
Sire: Ch. Felix DeOr.   Dam: Claudia of Wonred.
Breeders: Maryon and Bud Schindler, Van Nuys, Calif.
Owner: Adrienne Dawn, Hollywood, Calif.

CH. CZAR OF WONRED
Sire: Ingo of Canyon Crest.   Dam: Wonred Echo of Canyon Crest.
Breeders-owners: Maryon and Bud Schindler, Van Nuys, Calif.

INFANTA OF TANERIC

CH. KAY-RIO'S PAN

198

weeks-old puppy of Nanda's by Rungnir named Kuno of Warrendane, who later became our principal stud. Kuno, used on the bitch Mancusi's Toby, an outcross on the dam's side, produced many champions, Hulda, Karla, etc., of Planetree, who, bred to our other important stud, Ch. Planetree's Cyrus of Riviera, son of imported Ch. Cyrus v.d. Pissa, 'set' the type we wanted."

A fine example of the type Planetree was striving for is Mr. and Mrs. Griffith McKeeby's An Gleann Kennel's Ch. Rinni of Planetree, by Ch. Planetree's Cyrus of Riviera out of Ch. Hulda of Planetree. Rinni has already been referred to as the mother, by Brendo, of Champions An Gleann Planetree's-Targe and Gael. In 1946, at the Harbor Cities show Judge Alva Rosenberg took this strikingly sound fawn bitch from the open class to Best of Breed over a very imposing array of specials, which completed her championship. That Judge Rosenberg recognized type when confronted with it was demonstrated three years later when he selected Rinni's daughter, Gael, for his Best of Breed and took her on to Best in Show, as has already been told, at the same show in 1949.

Another striking example of the type achieved by Planetree is Christian Knudsen's Ch. Winki of Planetree. Winki was the first Great Dane to win a Best in Show in 1948, in March, at White Plains, N. Y., which afforded great pleasure to the many California admirers and friends of the Knudsens who live in Cranford, N. J. They had been in California the year before, judging at Harbor Cities. Miss Hilda Knudsen did the breed and placed Ch. Duchess of Zel-Thor best and Mr. Knudsen thought so well of her selection that for the first time in his judging career he placed a Dane first in the Working Group. Mr. Knudsen judged again on the West Coast in 1949 at San Jose and one of his assignments was Danes. His Best of Breed was a Northern entry, Mr. and Mrs. J. E. Shapro's Lady Buffe of Bettwood.

A lady very active in Southern California breeding circles, whose activities have lately included judging Danes and Boxers, is Mary G. Hungerford, Secretary of the Club in 1947, and owner of Taneric Kennels. Ever anxious to

199

improve the breed and encourage new breeders and exhibitors, there are a very great many who can attribute their success in breeding, in the avoidance of pitfalls and in the show ring, to the help and encouragement they have obtained from Mary Hungerford. Her interesting and instructive articles in *The Tailwagger, Leash and Collar,* and other dog publications are written from a knowledge derived from practical experience and study of breeding principles. Her Ch. Ariel of Taneric (Ch. Voro of Ridgerest ex Tanya of Dane Lair), dam of Ch. Victor of Taneric by Brendo, is the true Saalburg type and was ever a great show lady. Her Ch. Faecarl's Brenda's Boy, full brother to Brendo and one of the tallest Danes competing today, finished his championship at three straight five-point Specialty Shows, Best of Breed at the 1947 Fall Specialty under Judge Russell Zimmerman, Winners Dog at Harbor Cities in 1948 under Arthur Zane of Honolulu, and Winners Dog in the 1948 Fall Specialty under Mrs. Eva Hill. What is most important, his offspring are showing considerable promise.

In somewhat the same category as Mary Hungerford are the Walmsleys, Joseph and Pauline, of Van Nuys. Their first Great Dane was a fawn bitch bred in 1936 by Mrs. Mary A. Davis out of Ch. Chien d'ore Loheland Saalburg by Ch. Etfa v.d. Saalburg's Boy Brion. Mr. Walmsley's cork-covered scrapbook contains priceless pictures of many of California's great ones. There is a Ladin photo of Vincent Garrity's Hansi winning his first Best in Show on his first birthday, and another by Romaine where the caption reads: "Ch. Hansi of Garricrest. Best in Show Marin-North Bay Kennel Club, August 17th (1941). Shown seven times this year, Hansi has been consecutively seven times best in show all breeds and is undefeated by any dog of any breed. This brings his total of best in shows to thirteen. Hansi celebrated his third birthday this August 13th. Owned, bred, and shown by Vincent J. Garrity, Los Altos, California." Turning the page, there is another shot of Hansi after his eighth consecutive best in show in 1941 at Portland. There is a picture of Ruth Martin, of Planetree, with Mrs. S. Daniel Wall and their Ch. Brenda of Brae Tarn who was

200

AM. and CAN. CH. LADY MICHELLE OF ELM-HAVEN
Owner: Betty Hyslop, Brockville, Canada

CH. ZEN VON ZORDANE
Owner: Betty Hyslop, Brockville, Canada

best in show at both the 1940 Beverly Hills Club and Great
Dane Club Specialty Shows, and one showing Mrs. Wall
with Ch. Brenda receiving the best in show trophy at
Riviera from Judge G. R. Perkins the year before. Judge
Ernie Ferguson is shown in a Ludwig photo presenting the
best Working Group trophy at Pomona to Mrs. D. H. Hostetter showing her homebred Ch. Voro of Ridgerest, and
there is a clipping showing Josef Eigenbauer and the im-
mortal Etfa. In 1947, the Walmsleys acquired Buckaroo of
Lyn Dee, bred by Mr. and Mrs. Jernigan of Jefferson, Ontario, in 1941. Russell Zimmerman took "Buck," a fine
brindle grandson of Czardas by Ace of Lyn Dee out of
Paloma of Kittyglade, to a few local shows where he quickly
piled up points, and at the 1948 Los Angeles Kennel Club
show, judged by Budrick Schindler, President of the Dane
Club, he went Winners Dog to finish for the title. Another
male, a fawn, in which the Walmsley's take pride for he is
their breeding out of Berta de Or by Ch. Faecarl's Brendo,
is Mr. and Mrs. Jimmy Roche's group-winning Ch. Felix
de Or. Some of his experiences and reminiscences Mr.
Walmsley has passed on to other Dane fanciers in articles
he has written from time to time for *The Tailwagger*. His
scrapbook and articles, and also those of Maryon Schindler
written by her for the *Kennel Review* Dane Section, have
been of considerable value in compiling the data for this
chapter and their permission to refer to them has been
greatly appreciated.

In addition to the sources of material already mentioned,
and apart from the American Kennel Club Stud Books and
Gazettes, a great deal of assistance has been generously
furnished by a breeder of distinction and editor of the most
popular magazine, *Dane Digest,* Stanley K. Coates and his
wife and co-editor, Rissa Intha Coates. Under the kennel
name "Oakdane," the Coates' Great Danes are exerting a
strong and desirable influence on the breed. Before the
responsibilities and work of publishing *Dane Digest* took up
all their spare time, for it really started as a hobby, they
were very active in the show ring and in breeding. Their
champion bitches, Venni of Planetree and Faecarl's Brenda

TANSY OF CANYON CREST
at ten weeks

TANSY
at three months of age

CH. TANSY OF CANYON CREST, C.D.X.
Sire: Ingo of Canyon Crest. Dam: Katrina of Canyon Crest
Breeder: Canyon Crest Kennels. Owner: Jean Shapiro, Los Angeles, Calif.

CH. SANDRA OF RIDGEREST
Sire: Ch. August of Brae Tarn. Dam: Princess Barba
Breeder-Owner: Mrs. Laura O'Day

Margaret O'Day with INT. CH. LORELIE
Sire: Ch. Faecarl's Brendo. Dam: Ch. Duchess of Zel-Thor
Owner: Dollymount Kennels, Tacoma, Wash.

Aloha, have done well, not only in the ring, but as brood matrons, and their pedigrees contain many of the dogs previously mentioned. The pedigree of their stud dog, Ch. Damocles of Hazelcrest, is particularly interesting, since the great Dolf v.d. Saalburg appears therein almost within stroking distance. Ch. Damocles, or "Sword" as he is called by his friends, is out of Dawn of Hazelcrest by Ch. Danhalf of Brae Tarn. Dawn, his mother, is out of a mating of Achimreine of Hazelcrest to her own sire, Ch. Achim v. Odenwald of Erindane, son of a mating of Dolf to his first cousin, Ilse v.d. Rhon. Both Ilse and Dolf were sired by Bosko v.d. Saalburg, Dolf out of Fauna Moguntia and Ilse out of Ilse v.d. Alteburg. This makes "Sword" a great-grandson of Dolf's on his mother's side. Moreover, he is but one more generation removed from Dolf on his sire's side, for Ch. Nepa v. Loheland, out of Ch. Ferguni v. Loheland by Dolf, was mated to Oerlang to produce Ch. Voro v. Loheland of Brae Tarn, sire of Ch. Danhalf of Brae Tarn, "Sword's" father. To know that there is a sound, potent sire alive today, only three generations from Dolf on his mother's side and four on his father's is a point to remember by all breeders while the opportunity exists. Dane Eden has taken advantage of it in a double-barrelled fashion, by breeding "Sword" to a daughter of the Duchess, and by breeding Samson to a daughter of "Sword's." It was a puppy from the first of these matings who has already made a name for himself in South America. Oakdane's Brenda Holly, whelped Christmas Day, 1948, and owned by Commander Escodedo of the Chilean Navy, won best in show, all breeds, for dogs under one year of age. Another male from the same litter, Oakdane's Donder, owned by Mr. and Mrs. John Button of La Canada, at six months defeated dogs up to a year of age, going best Dane under Porter Washington at the Orange Empire all breeds puppy match. Both puppies were from the mating of Samson to Oakdane Kennel's Ch. Venni of Planetree.

The names of Canyon Crest Kennels and Mrs. William O. Bagshaw, experienced judge and president of the Los Angeles Kennel Club, are very widely known and play an

Best Team in Show, 1948 and 1949, Russell Zimmerman handling
L. to R.:   Ch. Dane Eden's Samson, Ch. Dane Eden's Delilah, Ch. Dane
Eden's Duchess of Malibu, Ch. Duchess of Zel-Thor (dam of the three)
Owner: John G. McEdward, Dane Eden Kennels, N. Hollywood, Calif.

important part contemporary with Planetree and others since mentioned. Russell Zimmerman handled Mrs. Bagshaw's Warrendane bred Ch. Fabian of Warrendane to six best in shows, all breeds, and the 1941 Great Dane of America and Morris and Essex Specialty shows. Fabian's name figures in the pedigrees of many of today's winning dogs. He was by Ch. Blitz v. Schloss Staufeneck of Warrendane ex Ch. Gretchen of Warrendane. Canyon Crest also acquired the stately brindle, Ch. Muldoon, from his breeder, Lee C. Hagerty. Muldoon, also a best in show winner, was best Dane at Westminster in 1942, Zimmerman handling. A granddaughter, Muldoon's Gilda, is owned by John G. Reichl, Jr., of Reseda, California, who bred her to Ch. Dane Eden's Samson, and pups from a very promising litter of fawns and brindles have gone to Long Island, Nebraska, Oklahoma, and Northern California. Never shown before whelping her litter Gilda won her class both times shown thereafter, at the Fall Specialty show under Earl Kruger and the Palm Springs show under Suzanne Hawkins. Another best in show brindle, Ch. Honey's Lady out of Ch. Honey by Ch. Jansen of Brae Tarn and bred by Robert A. Cavanaugh, was acquired by Canyon Crest in 1946 and accounted for herself well in the show ring. The stud, Ingo of Canyon Crest, although handicapped by injury from showing, has none-the-less been noteworthy as a sire of excellent stock. Tansy of Canyon Crest, owned by Jean Louise Shapiro, a fawn bitch who recently finished her championship and one of the few CDX champions in California today, is an Ingo daughter, as is Ch. Ursula of Canyon Crest and Ch. Cliza of Caldane, owned by Mr. and Mrs. John A. Guiler of Arcadia. Cliza, Winners Bitch at Harbor Cities in 1949 under Alva Rosenberg, finished her championship at the Fall Specialty show with the same win under Earl Kruger. She is by Ingo out of Clyde and Wiljoe Morgan's best in show Ch. Tonia of Ruhaven. Another fawn bitch by Ingo out of Ernflo's Sandra, Lady Lucretia owned by John J. Oppenheimer of Van Nuys, is doing her share of winning and is on her way to finish. Czar of Wonred, owned by Budrick and Maryon Schindler, whose Best of Winners under Earl Kruger at the

207

1949 Fall Specialty show finished him for the title, is also an Ingo sired fawn out of Wonred's Echo of Canyon Crest. In May, 1948, Mrs. Bagshaw judged Great Danes at Morris and Essex, selecting as Best of Breed the beautiful fawn bitch she had put up the year before at Camden and Judge John P. Wagner's choice the preceding day at Philadelphia, Mrs. Herta Schroeder's Ch. Senta, Best Great Dane at Westminster in 1947 and 1949. Mrs. Bagshaw must share the joy of all California Dane owners in hearing that Ch. Senta has fulfilled the hope of her owner by adding an all breeds Best in Show to her grand record with her win at Brooklyn in December of 1949.

On July 30, 1949, Mrs. Bagshaw judged the first annual Specialty Show of the Great Dane Club of Northern California, at Redwood City, preceding the San Mateo show there the day following. Her Winners Bitch, Best of Winners, and Best of Breed went to the Northern entry of Evelyne Asther, Vida's Belvora (Ch. Voro of Ridgerest ex Belga de Or Phyllis), and Edgar Harvey Vincent's bitch, Beach Belle of Surfside, was Reserve. Best Opposite went to the Roche's Ch. Felix de Or, and Winners Dog to Mrs. G. M. Jewell's Ladymeade Hyawatha II, out of her Ladymeade Flamanda of Billil by her celebrated Hyperion of Ladymeade. Reserve Dog was Robert and Gwyneth Hind's promising large male, Avenger v. Hidane. The following day at the San Mateo K.C. all breed show, with Mrs. Lena Ludwig judging the breed, her placings were the same for Winners Dog, Reserve Dog, Winners Bitch, and Best of Winners. Reserve Bitch went to C'Bonnet of Caldane, owned by Roy Taylor, and Best Opposite Sex to Ch. Dane Eden's Delilah, who did not compete the day before, nor her brother Samson who was Mrs. Ludwig's choice for Best of Breed. Samson went on to win the group under Mr. Isadore Schoenberg of Texas, and capped the day with Best in Show under Mrs. Geraldine R. Dodge. This win more than made up for the defeats suffered by the Southern California entries the day before and in the classes both days.

The last statement indicates what is very true, that there is close rivalry between the Northern and Southern sections of California, but it is also true and very important that it is a rivalry of a friendly nature. Some three or four years ago the Northern breeders and exhibitors felt that because of the four hundred odd miles separating the two sections, it would be to the interests of all to have a Great Dane Club of their own. In order to secure American Kennel Club approval, consent of the Great Dane Club of California was required. This was given without a dissenting vote and the charter club in the South has continued to manifest a great spirit of cooperation in respect to entries at Northern shows and trophy donations. It has worked out for the best in both ways and dogs from the North are appearing in more and more frequency in the Southern shows and are doing a share of winning which is bound to increase in the years ahead. The Great Dane Club of Northern California was organized and licensed in 1947 and held their first meeting at the Serenade Restaurant in San Francisco on November 8th with an enthusiastic turnout of over forty Dane owners in attendance. The following officers were elected: President, E. A. Chopson; Vice-President, Harold Abraham; Secretary, Gwyneth Hind; and Treasurer, Carol Tuohy.

In Northern California the Eastern influence, particularly Vakeck, is much more strongly felt than in the Southern section of the state. Sky's Pamela, a fine sound fawn who has done considerable winning at the Northern shows, is by Ch. Vakeck's Gallant Cavalier ex Ch. Gilded Lady of Hageo. She is owned by Phyllis and Edgar H. Vincent of Davenport, California, and is the dam of their promising puppy, Beach Bell of Surfside, Reserve Winners at the Northern Specialty Show. By the same great sire out of Valencia of Vakeck, is Barbara and Jack Rieser's Vakeck's Mary Quite Contrary, a brindle, and also by Ch. Vakeck's Gallant Cavalier out of Vakeck's Romance is Dr. and Mrs. J. H. O. Clayton's fawn male, Desmond of Vakeck, best opposite to Sunny of Dane Eden at the 1949 Golden Gate Show in San Francisco. Reserve at that show was taken by a young brindle male, now owned by Mrs. G. M. Jewell of Ladymeade Kennels, who finished his championship at eighteen months, Vakeck's Constant Companion, by Ch.

Vakeck's Dennis out of Vakeck's Woodlar. Another Northern champion, bred by Vakeck, who finished at Santa Cruz in May, 1948, is Ch. Vakeck's Varo, owned by Mr. and Mrs. Lawrence McKinley of Oakland. He is a fawn son of the famous Ch. Wasdan v. Loheland of Vakeck out of Ch. Odette of Brae Tarn. Robert M. and Gwyneth Hinds, of Redwood City, own a very promising young male, Avenger v. Hidane by Vakeck's Mechain out of Angell's Cleo of Kalmar. Avenger was bred by his owners and was judged best of breed by Major Godsol and placed fourth in the group at the San Joaquin Show in August, 1949. The Shapro's Lady Buffe of Bettwood, best of breed at San Jose in April of 1949 and best opposite at San Joaquin, is by Vakeck's Gay Commander ex Queenie of Bettwood, and by the same sire out of Nini of Willcrest is Henry C. Crouser's Willcrest's Flicka, shown for the first time at San Jose. Ch. Sunny of Dane Eden, already mentioned as the fifth to finish out of the Brendo-Duchess litter, is owned by Phyllis and A. Forbes Foster of San Jose. She completed her title at the Contra Costa Show June 19th, 1949, Mrs. B. H. Godsol judging, and went on to win the Working Group under Judge Jack Leitch. The showy brindle bitch already mentioned as winner of the first Northern Specialty Show, Vida's Belvora owned by Evelyn Asther of Burlingame, has a good start on her title. At Santa Cruz in May, 1949, she was best of breed, owner handled, under Mrs. Blythe Williams. The brindle male, General Sans Souci (Ch. Eric of Shadow Knoll ex Gilbert's Gloria of Stirling) was best opposite and is owned by Mr. William Kuster of San Francisco. Vakeck's Gay Commander is the sire of another promising Northern male of excellent size and type, Viking of Lewhaven, owned by Barbara Ann Lewis of Lafayette, California, and bred by Mrs. Clifford G. Lewis out of Naka v. Birkenhoff. Viking went from senior puppy class at San Jose under Judge Christian Knudsen to winners dog and best opposite. Since that show he has taken at least two best of breeds, Marin-North Bay K.C. in July, 1949, under Judge D. G. Rayne, and Vallejo two weeks later under Judge Isadore Schoenberg, who placed Samson first in the Working Group at San Mateo on July 31.

Col. and Mrs. Frank Grimwood of Fairfax, California, are the owners of the lovely brindle bitch, Ch. Dana of El Rancho Sinaloa, CD. In addition to her achievements in the obedience ring, Dana has always done her share of winning at the Northern shows. In August, 1949, she was best of breed at the Richmond Show under Judge Dr. H. Fremont and repeated at Reno in October under Judge E. L. Pickhardt. Best Opposite and Best of Winners was C.'Zander of Caldane, and Winners Bitch, C.'Bonnet of Caldane, owned by two very active and popular members of the Northern Club, Bettie and Roy Taylor of Redwood City. Litter brother and sister, they were bred in December, 1946, by Clyde and Wiljoe Morgan of Arcadia, California, owners of Caldane Kennels, and are out of the Morgan's best in show Ch. Tonia of Ruhaven, sired by Ingo of Canyon Crest. These two fawns of the Taylors always look good in the ring and two of the few examples of Danes showing in the northern part of the state, bred by breeders in the southern section. Mr. E. A. Chopson, first President of the Northern Club when it was formed, bred his Athena of Twin Oaks to Mr. Morgan's Ch. Pirate of Caldane. Athena's bloodlines come from the East, as she is by Ch. King Kong of Daynemouth out of Ch. Duchess of Twin Cedars and was bred by John W. Zawacki. Other Danes owned and shown by Mr. Chopson from Eastern stock include Hedwig of Bremendale, bred by Florence O. Proctor by Ch. Gautier's Talisman out of Ch. Flora of Canidom, and his Ch. Steinbacher's Tigress, bred by Helen Steinbacher, also by Talisman out of Steinbacher's Hilda. Some of the other officers and members of the new club usually to be found in the entry and premium lists of the Northern shows include Mr. and Mrs. Maurice T. Trotter of San Mateo with their Lady Liebchen and Topsy of Surfside, Thomas M. Tuohy with Carry on Kay of Lestomuir and Salty Sal of Surfside, Mr. and Mrs. Lester T. Longton with their Lestomuir entries, and Carmen D. Moss, who owned Commodore of Surfside bred by the Vincents.

Mrs. G. M. Jewell has already been mentioned as the owner of the winners dog at the Specialty Show, Ladymeade

211

Hyawatha II, and Ch. Vakeck's Constant Companion. A most active member of the Northern club and a frequent exhibitor at the Southern shows as well, Mrs. Jewell has made California her home following the war and her Ladymeade Kennels are now located at Mountain View near San Mateo. Formerly of Chew Stoke, England, she operated Ladymeade there for years. Carrying on her breeding in spite of the war she was awarded a bronze statuette of Dolf v.d. Saalburg in recognition of having done the most for the breed. Long a member of the Great Dane Club of England, Mrs. Jewell was made life president of the Great Dane Club of Ireland before sailing aboard the Queen Elizabeth with her Danes to the United States. The North is bound to benefit greatly by Mrs. Jewell's presence in their breeding circle. Unfortunately, her pride and joy, the 37½" Hyperion, died soon after coming to California. His granddaughter, Tosca of Ladymeade, was winners bitch at the Club's sanction match at San Mateo in January of 1949, and has had promising litters by Ch. Faecarl's Brendo and by the Taylors' C'Zander of Caldane, winners dog at San Mateo. Tosca is by Irish Ch. Hyawatha of Ladymeade out of Boadicea of Barvae. Barvae Kennels is owned by another prominent English breeder and exhibiter, Mrs. G. M. Clayton, Barrow-on-Humber, Lincolnshire, owner of Ch. Bon Adventure of Barvae. A picture of this striking first postwar Champion Bitch appeared in the February, 1949, issue of *Dane Digest*. In the October, 1948, issue there is a picture of Mrs. Jewell's Hyperion and an interesting article about her background from which some of the above was obtained.

Having covered as thoroughly as space permits the activities of Great Dane breeders in Southern California over a period of some twenty years and, to a lesser extent, activities in Northern California since the formation of the new Club, there is one important subject left which should be touched upon in order to give a true picture of the Great Dane in California, Obedience Trials. The vital part played in popularizing the breed for the show-going public by training the Dane for the obedience ring, which always draws a great gallery, is becoming more and more recognized by breeders. Too great a majority of breeders find the competitive task of making champions of their dogs difficult enough in itself, and the thrill of seeing their dog walk off with a group or Best in Show ample reward without striving for Obedience honors. However, recognition is certainly due the Great Dane owners who can train their dogs to win CD's and CDX's. The Grimwood's Ch. Dana of El Rancho Sinaloa, CD, and Jean Louise Shapiro's Ch. Tansy of Canyon Crest are two fine examples previously mentioned. Another fine obedience trained dog and an equally good showboy with several points towards his title is Ernflo's Count Geoffry, CD (Ch. Pirate of Caldane ex Lady Jean Macbeth), owned by R. T. Yankie of San Marino. Rodney Davis of Long Beach, owner of Caesar of Dane Eden, has a splendid black, Skipper of Dane Crest, CD, who also looks good in the show ring. There was a young fawn puppy in the 9 to 12 months class at the San Diego show in August 1949, who got more applause than any dog competing by attaining almost a perfect score the first time ever in an obedience ring, D. G. Fleming's Great Tawny Bruno. Two other Great Dane owners from San Diego who frequently have their dogs competing for obedience are Mr. and Mrs. Kenneth V. Campbell who enter their Eric and Dana von Kesselhut, and Helen L. Smiley, owner of Sonny Boy from Berge. At the December, 1949, Glendale K. C. Show, there was a sensational newcomer, named Treseder's Fritha, CDX, who placed first in the Utility Class with a score of 199 out of a possible 200 against competition from C.D.X. dogs of other breeds. Fritha is by Dinro Jamas out of Countess Cornelia Hexengold and won her C.D. and C.D.X. in Westchester County and Connecticut. Her owner is Florence Treseder who lived in Dobbs Ferry before moving to Hollywood. On the November cover of *Dane Digest*, 1948, and also on page 114 of Mrs. Keckler's new book, *The Great Dane*, are pictures by Joan Ludwig of a truly grand obedience-trained Great Dane, the Harlequin Lady Hilda of Charlene, C.D.X., owned by the Rosclun Kennels, Los Angeles, and usually handled by her very young little owner,

213

Miss Gay Ross-Clunis. Lady Hilda can also give competition in the ring. In July, 1948, at the Orange Empire Show she took Best of Breed and placed fourth in the group under Judge G. Staines.

Mrs. Laura O'Day's hopes were achieved with young Balthazar, who completed his championship when he was approximately two years old and then went on to win the same title in Canada, thus giving him the right to use both American and Canadian Champion before his name. Ch. Balthazar sired Kay-Rio's Pan (now a champion), and there are, today, some promising youngsters of his started in the show ring, among them, Kay-Rio's Pandora (Pan's litter sister), who is again in the capable hands of Mrs. O'Day and, although late in starting, making her points toward the title. Among others which show promise are: Gillean's An Gleann Entente and Gillean's An Gleann Alliance (both ex Gillean's Lass of Gairloch); Anadane's Idol (ex Anadane's Heartthrob) and Anadane's Impetuous, Idol's litter sister; Provan's Quay and Provan's Quest (ex Alexis Von Essen).

Mary Hungerford, although not active at the present time, is keeping her Taneric Kennel name alive through a co-ownership which was brought about like this: Some five years ago a newcomer to Southern California's Dane circles made her appearance—a Britisher, Kay Kinosita, who, after twenty-five years of living in Japan, brought with her a Great Dane from that country. The most noteworthy episodes in the history of that particular Dane are the difficulty experienced by her owner in bringing her into this country, and Mrs. Kinosita's, now amusing, reactions when she learned that the young bitch was far from a top specimen. So, with nothing but determination, Mrs. Kinosita began her search for a Great Dane good enough to become a champion. She bought several and in turn gave each away. It was during those days of searching that Mrs. Kinosita became acquainted with Mary Hungerford. Their association developed into a friendship, then into a verbal partnership in 1952, and finally in August 1954, The American Kennel Club renewed the registration of Taneric Ken-

214

nels under the two names. Meanwhile, Mrs. Kinosita has acquired Gillean's Lass of Gairloch, a brindle bitch of An Gleann-Planetree breeding, who was bred to American and Canadian Ch. Dollymount's Balthazar. The resulting litter consisted of two puppies, Kay-Rio's Pan and Kay-Rio's Pandora. Young Pan started his show career at the age of six months, winning in his class over seven youngsters at the San Francisco Specialty Show. He continued to romp through, taking his puppy classes and going Best of Breed at the San Fernando Sanction Match that year. Pan gathered his first points at the age of ten months and became an accredited champion at the age of twenty-six months. Competition was keen, with some excellent young males taking their share of the honors. Mary and Gerald McKinnon's handsome Golden Baron, a youngster extremely hard to fault (now a champion), and the Duke Von Bahmueller, C.D., who died with only three points to go, were among the regular contenders in the ring. Pan now has four Best of Breed wins and a third in Group and, still a young dog, is proving himself as a sire. Of the thirty-six puppies he has sired to date, Kay-Rio's Kendrick of Taneric and Kay-Rio's Kim of Taneric (ex Infanta of Taneric) are probably the outstanding examples. It would almost seem that Pan and Golden Baron (sired by Dane Eden's renowned Samson) are the outstanding young studs at the present time. It is to be hoped that the excellent and very similar line-breeding behind these two will be used advantageously for the future of California's Great Danes.

Clyde and Wiljoe Morgan's Ch. Tonia of Ruhaven produced two fine Danes (from different breeding), Ch. Cliza of Caldane (sired by Ingo of Canyon Crest), of whom more will be said later, and Ch. Pirate of Caldane (sired by Estrid Zilch). Pirate in turn sired seven champions, two of which are Swandane's Allure and Brigadier of Swandane, full brother and sister out of breedings to Vakeck's Mistress Mary, a granddaughter of Ch. Heide of Brae Tarn. Allure and Brigadier acquired their championships before they were two and a half, both being owner handled and both being shown at the same time. Allure has eleven Best of

Breed wins and nine Group placements to her credit, and Brigadier has five Best of Breed wins with four Group placements to his.

Going back to Ch. Cliza of Caldane, there is no doubt that she will leave a lasting mark on Dane history. John and Ruth Guiler, using her as brood matron for the new registered kennel Guilderdane, chose to breed her and subsequent daughters selectively, going out to the best available studs, including Dane Eden's great Samson, and have kept those bitches which were considered most desirable for base stock. A program of some eight years of such breeding has given them a fine kennel of young bitches, including Ch. Lil of Guilderdane and Ch. Duchess Zel Thor II (both sired by Samson). Duchess is now owned by Mrs. Lee Bordner, President of the Dane Club of California. Guilderdane's present formulative plan seems to be based on a majority of good brood matrons and uses as sires the fine male specimens here in California. With this program, so strongly enforced, it would seem that the name Guilderdane is to be noteworthy in the breeding field in the future.

Last to be mentioned is Southern California's own Dane heroine, Alexis Von Essen, so recognized by the National Dog Welfare Guild when she was given an award in September 1953 for notifying her owners of a fire in a back bedroom in the house. She removed her very young master, age three, from the completely enflamed clothes closet and guarded him until the adults in the family arrived. Then, roaring through the house, she took her own litter of seven to the safety of the garage, tucked them under a car parked there, and returned in time to meet the firemen at the front door, not quite sure she should let them in. With her alert perception and commanding bark, Alexis prevented what might have been a costly and heartbreaking tragedy for her human family.

In every breed there is a need for newcomers as well as more experienced breeders. When the newcomers combine willingness to learn, sportsmanship, and a genuine love and desire to work toward improving their breed, it may well be predicted that they will make their mark sooner or later.

216

Mr. and Mrs. James A. Blood may be an exemplification of those in this category.

Five years ago, after always having lived in San Francisco, business moved the Bloods to Sacramento. Having left children and grandchildren behind, Jim Blood decided to fill the void by presenting to Helen the Dane pup she had long yearned for, little realizing that he was starting the raising of a second family. Bred by Mr. and Mrs. C. R. Haak, this fawn male is one of the largest on the West Coast, a handsome pet but not a show dog. The Bloods attended a Dane gathering not long after acquiring the dog, and heard several members being asked if they could find room for Ariel of Blue Oaks (bred by E. W. Chopson), a three-year-old who needed a new home very quickly. Pricking up their ears when they realized this was their young pup's mother, Mr. and Mrs. Blood listened to the following story: Ariel, still owned by the Haaks, had traveled with them to a site near Friant Dam, where Ray Haak was an engineer. Ariel, without an adequate place to be kenneled, was having a gay old time and was getting out at intervals to run the cattle in the area. On being warned that Ariel would be shot if found engaging in this exciting pastime in the future, the Haaks sadly realized it was necessary to find a new home for her. Sight unseen, the Bloods volunteered to take her, and this fortunate gesture surprisingly repaid them with a future champion and a brood matron with fine bloodlines.

Ariel is a large sturdy brindle and has the dominant characteristic of passing on to her offspring her lovely strong head and excellent disposition. Ariel's sire, Ch. Pirate of Caldane, has a number of champions to his credit. He was bred by Clyde and Wiljoe Morgan out of their Best in Show winner Ch. Tonia of Ruhaven by Ingo of Canyon Crest. Ch. Tonia's dam was Athena of Twin Cedars, bred by John W. Zawacki, by Ch. King Kong of Daynemouth ex Ch. Duchess of Twin Cedars. Athena was a litter sister of Xerxes of Twin Cedars, who has sired many champions, among which is the Best in Show winner Ch. Dion of Kent.

Still unaware that Ariel would have a show career ahead,

the Bloods decided to raise their first litter and bred her to Royal Danes Tell of San Souci, owned by William Kuster. Tell was bred by Forbes Foster, sired by General of San Souci ex Foster's Ch. Sunny of Dane Eden. Sunny was one of the well-known litter of champions sired by Brendo ex Ch. Duchess of Zel Thor.

Shortly after Ariel's litter was whelped, Ben Brown, the well-known handler, saw Ariel and predicted some show wins for her, so in her fourth year she was entered in the 1952 Great Dane Club of Northern California, Inc., Specialty. Mary Hungerford judged the entry of fifty-three Danes and put Ariel up for Best of Winners and her first points. Finishing her championship in Northern California in that year, she added some Best of Breed wins and Group placements to her laurels. When nearly six, she retired from the ring with a day as Best of Breed at her last specialty, a Group placement, and the title of Best Local at the Allbreed Show. Winning ribbons in the classes that day were four of her progeny and two of her grand-progeny, a combination of placements which is always a pleasant sight.

In her fifth year Ariel had her third litter, boosting the number of her puppies to twenty-four. This time, Ch. Bismarck of Royal Dane, owned by Howard Rogers, was the sire. Ch. Bismarck, a half-brother of Tell, was also bred by Forbes Foster out of Ch. Sunny of Dane Eden by Luke of Forbesdale. This litter of Ariel's, now eighteen-months old, is being watched with interest.

Again heeding the advice of their handler, Ben Brown, the Bloods kept Crockerly's April for their third bitch. She is a pretty golden fawn, who made her debut in the ring with a reserve specialty win at six months, and won her first points at Reno under Derek Rayne. A few weeks later, she went Winners Bitch and B.O.S. under Budrick Schindler at the Northern California Specialty. Her brother, Crockerly's Aabenraa, a large fawn, owned by Mr. and Mrs. C. R. Haak, acquired a major at nine months under Mrs. Milton Erlanger at Golden Gate K. C. at San Francisco. Crockerly's Arden, owned by the Norman Wilsons, also has her points. These youngsters, with their good backgrounds, and Crockerly Kennels may have the opportunity to do some interesting future breeding.

With their love for their Danes and their interest in acquiring knowledge of the breed, Helen and Jim Blood have also taken an active part in the activities of the Great Dane Club of California, Inc. He is a past President of the Club and current Secretary, and she was Secretary and is now Vice President. Carrying their interest for dogs further, Mr. Blood now serves as President for the Sacramento Dog Fanciers Association and has recently accepted a directorship in the Sacramento Kennel Club.

Moving into a new home a few years ago, they combined lovely surroundings with a practical working plan for Crockerly Kennels, Reg. The result could serve as an inspiration to the small, selective breeder. Ariel, Tia, April, and Brew are well-trained, careful house pets that grace the lovely rooms of the home. One looks from the living and dining rooms past the patio and over the Bloods' own grassed and bedded garden, to the Danes' section of the property. Unadorned steel fencing allows one to enjoy the beauty of the Danes at play. On one side and along the back of the property is one long playground about thirty feet wide. On the other side, a separate steel-fenced play-yard leads off the patio. Off a breezeway from the kitchen is a large square puppy yard and the puppy room. The latter, insulated and paneled in shiny linoleum simulating grained wood, is easy to keep clean and attractive. This room houses two raised whelping boxes. What a happy life is provided for the puppies! All are given affection individually and gradually graduate into the home so they may be ready to be trained as pets by their future owners.

Any newcomers combining a pleasurable hobby with the sincere desire to reap the benefits of experienced breeders are an asset to the Dane fancy and should be encouraged. The return on this investment will be a great deal of pleasure, rewarding work, and many new friends with mutual interests.

Ch. Kalmar's Excalibur and J. Wen Lundeen III, grandson of the Lundeens, at Kalmar, Stone Mountain, Ga.

CH. KALMAR'S DINRO AJAX

Owned by Mr. and Mrs. J. Wen Lundeen, Kalmar, Stone Mountain, Ga., Ajax is notable for having a badly' broken leg in an auto accident early in his show career, but recovering completely to finish his championship.

Great Danes of the South

By J. Wen Lundeen

HARLIE MEYERS, a professional handler, tells a story about a Northern exhibitor who had a Great Dane with 18 points but needing two major shows (3 points or better) to finish his championship. This exhibitor figured it would be as easy as falling off a log to send the dog on a Southern circuit and pick up the needed points.

But what a shock was in store. Out of six shows, the dog wound up with three third place and two fourth place class ribbons. The quality of Great Danes in Southern shows has improved by leaps and bounds, and the days of picking up easy points in the South are over. In reverse, many Southern Danes are invading the Northern shows and grabbing off top honors.

The famous Champion Dion of Kent, jointly bred by the Rankins of Knoxville, Tennessee, and Kalmar of Stone Mountain, Georgia, has perhaps made as spectacular a show record as any Dane in the past quarter of a century, and its great number of Best of Breed, Best Working Group, and Best in Show winnings will be hard to top. Going Best of Breed both at Morris and Essex and Madison Square Garden is not an easy achievement, but Dion did it.

Just to mention a few, Southern champions with good show records are Rebel Inn's Hoe-down, Kalmar's Xerxes of

221

Twin Cedars, Chintz of Roxdane, Diana of Kent, Waleshire's Golden Boy, Madamazelle of Readane, Kalmar's Princess Vesta, B & B's Beauty, and Kolyer's Cygni v Adonis, owned by Rebel Inn Kennels, still a young Dane but credited with two Best in Show placings.

Until recent years Great Danes were not commonly seen in the South and to drive up with one and park in a small town would usually result in a crowd of from fifty to one hundred and fifty people around the car. The comments were usually true to pattern, such as:

Don't they eat you out of house and home?

Why don't you put a saddle on him and ride him?

What are they good for? etc., etc., etc.

In one North Carolina town we had a large black and white harlequin Dane in the rumble seat, and a young fellow posing as a real canine expert remarked that it was the biggest "Dalamatitian" he had ever seen.

Sometimes one's patience is strained in answering all the nonsensical questions, and it's easy to drift into sarcastic answers. One Major Hoople type gentleman asked us if they were good for hunting, and we told him they were excellent for hunting wild boar. "But," we added jokingly, "they never have been known to bother a sow," and he said, "Isn't that amazing?"

At a dog show in Knoxville, Weston Booth, a professional handler and a very soft-spoken and genteel person, had about reached the end of his patience in answering questions about a Great Dane he was preparing to show. One of the know-it-all, talkative types started firing questions at him, and among dozens of others, he asked, "How much does he weigh?" Weston had stood all he could and said, "Last time we weighed him he weighed 476 pounds," and the fellow said, "That's just about what I figured."

So there it goes, on and on, and we never know when someone is coming up with a new question, but you can be sure he is going to get an answer, right or wrong.

Great Danes continue to grow in popularity in the South, and we hope the day will come when we won't have to tell people what kind of dog he is and what he is good for.

Here is one of our pet peeves: there are two subjects that every comedian, cartoonist, and humorous writer seem to pick on without justification—one is the lowly "mother-in-law," the other is a "Great Dane's appetite." Most mothers-in-law are fine people, and we contend and can prove that an average grown Great Dane can be kept in prime condition with the same amount of food as a regular Hound or any of the medium-sized popular working breeds. Of course it is easy to understand how some people can love a Dane so much they want to feed him porterhouse steaks, but don't blame the Great Dane for that.

The Great Dane seems to be well suited to the Southern climate, and the problem of worms, fleas, and ticks is apparently no more serious in this warmer zone than elsewhere. The new chemicals and drugs seem to cope well with these pests.

New Orleans boasts one of the largest Great Dane Specialty Clubs in the country, with a half dozen sizeable Dane kennels. This enthusiastic group has already had three successful specialty shows in New Orleans.

The Great Dane Club of the Mid-South comprises as its show-giving territory the States of Georgia, Tennessee, and Alabama with members in seven States. It has held three Great Dane Specialty Shows in Atlanta, one in Knoxville, and one in Birmingham.

Several Southern kennels are specializing in harlequins and blacks, so some good ones should be forthcoming.

The Great Dane of the South is taking his place in the fastest company, and in years to come, exhibitors everywhere had better not sell the South short, for they may expect worthy competition from below the Mason and Dixon Line.

Dance stars Marge and Gower Champion with Ch. Big Kim of Bella Dane, handled by Marge's sister, Lina Basquette.

Character and Temperament of the Great Dane

GERDA M. UMLAUFF

THE transformation of the character of the Great Dane, during the course of his life history, is fully as remarkable as the obvious changes made in his external appearance. His ancestors, which had been members of hunting packs, were clumsy and coarse in body and mind. Not only had they been successfully used for the hunting of wild animals, but they had also been trained as fighters and as ferocious dogs of war. Tremendous strength and courage were required of them, rather than a refined appearance, hence they were dogs with rough coats, stocky heads, and short muzzles. Sometimes their noses were split, and, in general, their dispositions were mean and sulky. As a consequence it was only in exceptional cases that the dogs were permitted to accompany their masters on walks.

The many changes in the Great Dane should be credited exclusively to patient German breeders. The metamorphosis of this originally uncouth looking animal into a dog of beauty and intelligence was the result of long and tedious experimentation. Unavoidable relapses were frequent in the beginning, but gradually the breeders were disappointed less and less often until success crowned their efforts. The welcome news of the transformation of this breed spread, and soon the dogs were in demand, not only because of their handsome appearance, but because of their excellent dispositions. The Great Dane had become suitable for his modern role of house dog and trusted companion.

At the end of the nineteenth century we find in print many diversified and contradictory opinions about the character of the Great Dane. One authority said, "This dog is good-natured in his youth, but as he becomes older and reaches a certain age, he develops an evil disposition, and is no longer a true and faithful friend." Another expert declared, "The Great Dane possesses a peaceful disposition, is handsome and agreeable as a companion, and a good watch dog of unquestioned faithfulness and devotion. The love of the Great Dane for his master is boundless. He is fearless in danger, has a noble character, and is gay and friendly in the company of other dogs." An old breeder of Great Danes once said, "I have sometimes kept forty or fifty Great Danes together, and never had an ill-natured one among them."

It has always been the aim of the German breeders to create a Great Dane which would produce a very favorable impression through his size, power, and beauty. In order that the dog may develop in this manner, never manifesting cowardice, nervousness, or anxiety, he must have the best of care. If his needs are not met adequately he loses his good looks, his noble bearing, and proud, self-confident character. He becomes stiff and awkward, his coat loses its sheen, and the fine lines of the body are effaced. Boils caused by long hours of continuous lying down may appear on the legs, and his disposition becomes sullen, irritable, and angry.

The Great Dane requires large quantities of meat in his diet, a clean bed with plenty of room in order to avoid tail injuries, and much daily exercise. If he is to develop strong muscles and joints he must have vigorous exercise, such as playing with other dogs, or following his master on long bicycle or horseback rides. The Great Dane should not be kept on a chain, as he needs freedom to maintain his self-confidence. He also needs assurance of his master's love, and craves his company. If these principles are observed

226

he will become a healthy, happy dog, and, with training, a valuable watchdog.

In 1938 at a championship contest for working dogs a harlequin Great Dane gave the best performance. Out of one hundred points he received ninety-four in competition with seven Shepherds, one Doberman, one Boxer, and one Giant Schnauzer. He was five years old, and excellent in the obedience class, the trailing test, and leaped over hurdles. When his master was under attack he furiously defended him. The training of this dog had begun at the age of six months, and by the time he was fourteen months old he was awarded the highest rating of "excellent" in the trial for dogs whose duty it is to protect.

In spite of this record we seldom find Great Danes at training centers. The chief of the most famous German police dog school declares "We don't want Great Danes for police dog work, because it is too dangerous to train and use them. Every dog jumps at the time he attacks and bites. According to their size the German Shepherd, the Doberman Pinscher, the Boxer, etc., can jump to the height of a man's arm, but the Great Dane can easily reach his face." It is to be hoped this prejudicial attitude will be altered in time, perhaps by stories such as those which so well illustrate the highly developed intelligence of the Great Dane.

The Great Dane has been characterized by one dog fancier as "the most good-natured of all breeds." It has been proven that the Great Dane is very fond of children, playing gently with them, and preferring their society to that of their elders.

We cannot finish this chapter about the Great Dane's character and temperament without reporting on an interview with Mr. Hagenbeck of circus fame. He gave us a detailed account of his experiences with contemporary Great Danes whom he has very often exhibited among the trained beasts of prey in his circus performances. They were used primarily because they made a good appearance, and, in a moment of danger, might give the impression that they were protecting their master. As a matter of fact, a lion could very easily kill a Great Dane with one sweep of his sharp claws, and the dogs seemed to know that. So, far from enjoying the company of the lions, the Great Danes were frequently apprehensive, and often were actually ill when forced to remain with them for some time. There were, of course, individual differences in the dogs, and while some were very shy of the lions, others could be trained to jump over them. Mr. Hagenbeck found it preferable, however, to show the Great Danes with bears, because in the company of these animals the dogs behaved much more fearlessly. This was a real satisfaction to their trainer who was responsible for their conduct.

In connection with the Great Dane's behavior with wild animals, two extraordinary incidents must be related. Mr. Hagenbeck tells a story which his father related to him, and which occurred several decades ago. A gentleman living in Africa bought a Great Dane from Mr. Hagenbeck, Sr. This dog had worked for some time in the circus with lions and other wild animals. One day his new master rode into the bush accompanied by the dog. Suddenly a leopard leaped out and attacked the Great Dane, but he defended himself so violently the leopard actually ran away.

Once upon a time a Danish king visited France, where he met a lady who owned a huge Great Dane. During their conversation the dog put his heavy head on the ruler's knee and looked truly in his eyes. "Isn't he nice?" asked the lady. "Indeed, he is one of your truest subjects!"

The king answered that he liked the dog very much, but then he asked: "To which breed does the dog belong?" Whereupon she replied: "His Majesty is joking? You won't say that you don't know a Great Dane?" The king wondered and answered: "Very funny indeed! Never have I seen in my country a Danish dog!"

228

Bismarck and His Great Danes

RINCE OTTO von BISMARCK, who founded the new empire and became chancellor in 1871, was not only the greatest statesman Germany ever had, but also a great lover of dogs. From his childhood he was especially fond of Great Danes, and dogs of this breed accompanied him throughout his lifetime for an even longer period than did his wife. When he was a student at Göttingen, his yellow male dog, Ariel, was his constant companion, and he was always regretful that it was impossible to take the dog into the university.

In Bismarck's dialogues and diaries .his dogs are mentioned repeatedly. One author has referred to these dogs as resembling their master in many ways, for like him they were of gigantic stature, nervous, bold, and dangerous. Prince Otto was always accompanied by his "Empire-dogs," as they were called, and they kept a constant, alert watch beside their master. Bismarck mistrusted anyone who behaved indifferently towards his dogs. It was always an impressive sight to observe this giant man walking along with two enormous Danes flanking him.

It is said Bismarck had more patience with dogs than with men, for they desired nothing from him and were never in opposition to him. They were silent, obedient, and faithful, yet seemed to understand everything. When the young female Rebecca was disobedient he laughed about her intelligence, and when "Flora was running through the rooms like crazy" or Sultan disturbed the conversation he never reprimanded them. When Bismarck's wife complained that the curtains had been made too long, he praised the upholsterer because his dogs could squat down on them! Aesthetic aristocrats were disgusted at dinner when he ordered large pieces of meat and then threw them across the room to the dogs.

When it was necessary to decide whether Bismarck should go to Gastein for his summer vacation, Sultan's state of health was the determining factor. The beloved male Sultan was not well and could not stand the difficulties of the long journey, so Bismarck did not go. Sultan, a big blue Dane, had been the gift of a Moroccan prince, and was a beautiful dog with a proud and unruly disposition. Once when Bismarck intended to engage a new administrator, Sultan sniffed at the man, then put his enormous head on his knee. At that moment the case was decided because Bismarck said, "I respect my dog's opinion because he apparently has more knowledge of human nature and a clearer mind than I."

On one occasion after a meeting with his master, Sultan was chained by him. He felt so offended that he tore his chain, gnawed through two inches of wood on whose splinters blood was observed, and ran off into the woods. For a time he lived in the forests and lived on young game, but, after a long search instituted by Bismarck, he was returned to his master. He lived with Bismarck for five years after his return, but one day he vanished again because of a love affair in a neighboring village. Bismarck became very angry and said he would punish the dog himself, but when Sultan returned during the night it was only to die. The prince sat near him on the floor, keeping the dog's head in his hands. Bismarck was disconsolate, blaming himself for the previous punishment, in spite of the fact that the dog's death was caused by palpitation of the heart. He accused himself, however, for twenty years, speaking of Sultan even on his own deathbed.

One day when the princess was grieving over the death

of the female Dane Freia, a dog who had been most devoted to her, she remarked that she believed she would meet Freia again in the hereafter. Surely animals with so much soul must have the same fate as men. The prince replied, "I believe the same as you do, for if there is a heaven it must be for animals too. How could one imagine that any other arrangement could be possible? At any rate I firmly believe that I shall see my dogs and horses again in heaven."

Of his beloved Tyras, Bismarck has written in his memoirs: "When I went to the Parliament I took the path through the garden behind the Reichskanzlerpalais. There I opened the door to the Königsgrätzerstrasse, and turning to Tyras, who had accompanied me as always in a very jolly manner, I said 'Parliament.' At once the dog put his head and tail down, and seemed very depressed. Once I put my walking stick against the garden wall before I entered the gate because, being in uniform, I was not allowed to carry it. After four hours I returned home but Tyras was not there to give me his usual welcome, so I asked the guard, 'Where is the dog?" He replied, 'He has been near the garden wall for many hours and will permit no one to touch the walking stick of your Highness!' "

When Bismarck grew older and more misanthropic, his love for his dogs became greater and greater. In his park by the side of his favorite horses his dogs are buried in a long line. When Tyras II died because of old age, Bismarck, then eighty years old, did not take another dog because he could not bear to bury another canine friend.

Alexander Pope and his dog Bounce. From the portrait by Jonathan Richardson
(about 1718).

BOUNCE

Alexander Pope's Great Dane That Saved His Master's Life

SOMEONE once said that no man could be really bad if he had room in his heart for the love of a dog. If that is true, then the great English poet, Alexander Pope, who lived over two hundred years ago, was a pretty good person in spite of his faults. He was miserable and unhappy most of his life. During a period of about five years, however, his misery was somewhat mitigated by his love for the best and truest friend he ever had. That friend was Bounce, his Great Dane, who worshipped his master. He thought Pope was the kindest man in the world —and he was to Bounce. He also thought Pope was the most attractive man in all the world—and that took a tremendous amount of imagination on Bounce's part; for the poet was a deformed dwarf of a man. Since he was a chronic invalid, he could not rise from his bed or chair without assistance and he was obliged to have a servant to dress and undress him. When he stood up, he was not much taller than Bounce and he sat at the table in a specially made high chair.

Like most invalids of his type, he was extremely sensitive to the cold and wore a tight-fitting fur vest under his heavy shirt and over all this a heavy flannel waistcoat. His short, thin legs were so slender that he wore three pairs of stockings to make them appear normal size. When he was alone and not expecting company, he wore over his bald head a

233

heavy velvet cap, which was replaced by a wig at other times.

Even if Pope had been able, for one single moment, to forget his ailments and idiosyncrasies, his ruthless enemies were always ready to remind him by writing sarcastic and venomous satires about him. But they, of course, did not know him as Bounce did. To Bounce he was a perfect specimen of everything a real gentleman should be. It was the others who were cross, irritable, and deformed. There was that soft voice of his master, still as gentle and pleasing, at times, as it had been when he was a small child— a voice which had won for him, then, the name of "the little nightingale."

But all mildness of voice vanished when Pope was suffering from wracking, splitting headaches and again when he found himself the helpless victim of some contemporary critic. At such times he ranted and stormed in a loud, angry voice at his cruel destiny and at all who had maliciously condemned him; following which spells he slumped down in his chair, weak, exhausted, and dejected. After he calmed down, he frequently was ashamed and contrite. When he wrote the line, "To err is human; to forgive, divine," he was sure, always, about the first part, but he had little hope that his friends would live up to the latter. Most of them were not divine enough to forgive; a few were, the most forgiving of whom was Bounce.

There were some people, however, who were willing to overlook Pope's peculiarities, for the moment at least, just to be near the great poet and to enjoy his hospitality at his large estate at Twickenham on the Thames, not far from London. In the summer months, Pope entertained his celebrated guests in his beautiful garden, landscaped according to the formal style of his day. But the spot dearest to his heart was his grotto, which was considered the most famous architectural achievement in all Middlesex. It was really only a glorified tunnel under the main highway connecting his house and lawn. Although admired by most of his friends, it was viewed askance by others, one of whom remarked that it was better fitted for frogs than for philoso-

234

phers with rheumatic pains. Its sides and roof were lined with many different kinds and colors of marble, crystals, spar, and granite, all of which reflected beautiful iridescent lights. The soft and subdued glimmer from the thin alabaster lamp hanging from the middle of the ceiling gave the interior a fantastic and fairylike appearance. It was a perfect retreat for a disturbed poet when he longed for solitude, and a unique and unusual place in which to entertain when he recovered and again craved friends about him.

Here the most distinguished men and women of England flocked to enjoy the hospitality of the greatest poet of the day, whom they flattered one moment and bitterly criticized the next. In the midst of all these festivities Bounce was the center of attention, basking in the reflected glory of his famous master. It was well he could not understand all the cryptic remarks tossed about by the guests. It was, as you know, an age of criticism when at every word a reputation died, and often it was Pope's that suffered. Of all the guests —which included poets, philosophers, society belles, and even royalty—Prince Frederick, the Prince of Wales, was the favorite one, as far as Bounce was concerned. In fact, the admiration was mutual. The two exchanged courtesies as one royal person to another. The Prince was so much impressed by the good manners and handsome appearance of Bounce that he expressed a wish to own a dog just like him. Pope, naturally quite flattered—as who wouldn't be? —made Prince Frederick a promise in Bounce's name, which, in due time, was fulfilled. In the spring the Prince of Wales carried home with him one of Bounce's puppies and placed him in the royal kennel at Kew, the summer residence of the royal family. For fear the puppy might stray away, Pope wrote a rhyming couplet to be engraved on his royal collar.

"I am his Highness' dog, at Kew.
Pray tell me, sir, whose dog are you?"

There was one guest who frequented Twickenham to whom Bounce took a violent dislike. That was Jonathan Swift, the famous author of *Gulliver's Travels*. Bounce had a feeling that his master, too, was not always pleased to

235

have the author around—and judging by the unhappiness of Swift during his stay in the Twickenham house, he had a pretty strong conviction that the guest was as miserable as the rest of the household, if not more so. Bounce's otherwise quiet evenings spent with his master were turned into a veritable madhouse during the sojurn of this eccentric man. Swift, who was about sixty years old at this time, was quite deaf, causing the invalid Pope to shriek and bellow in an effort to make himself heard, all of which made Bounce extremely nervous and almost wrecked his master. The dog would stand this stormy banter just so long as he could; then he would retreat to the far end of the garden, to get out of earshot of the voices. He had another excellent reason for remaining outside. He did not dare risk getting in the pathway of Swift, for the latter's fits of dizziness made him tottery and dangerously unsteady on his feet. He had a nervous habit of pacing silently back and forth across the room like a caged animal; while Pope, unable to rise from his chair without help, had to sit and wait until his guest grew too dizzy and too fatigued to walk any longer; then they began their screaming conversation.

Both Pope and Bounce, completely worn-out and exhausted, were relieved and happy when Swift finally took his departure, after which they spent their well-earned freedom recuperating out in the cool, quiet, shadowy grotto. Pope gave orders to the servants to admit absolutely no one, not even his best friends. It was probably at this time that he composed those two lines found in one of his satires:
"Shut, shut the door, good John!
Tie up the knocker! say I'm sick, say I'm dead."
Pope's ill-humor and frequent tantrums could not always be attributed to an unpleasant house guest, however. Sometimes it was only a very little thing that would put him into a towering rage. Often, in the throes of writing a poem, he became disgusted because he could not find another old envelope on which to finish out a line. He was so stingy that he would not buy regular writing paper, but used old envelopes. Imagine his utter frenzy when he had a fine poetic line in mind, and no more old envelopes—and no servants

236

near to help him to rise from his chair to search for one! Then sometimes, when he had whole stacks of old envelopes lying before him, he lacked inspiration and could not express himself as poetically as he wished! Now the average person whose mind refuses to work when he needs it most, just raves in strong language; but a poet raves in poetic couplets.

Bounce was wakened from a sound slumber one day to find his master in one of his poetic rages—and this is what he heard:

"You beat your pate, and fancy wit will come:
Knock as you please, there's nobody at home."

You can well imagine what a hard life Pope's servants had in the employ of such a temperamental master. As a result, he was always hiring and firing valets. If he had turned the business of hiring servants over to Bounce, it might have simplified matters. In fact, if most people would let their dogs do the choosing of maids and butlers, there would be fewer help-wanted ads in the daily papers.

Once when a new butler arrived to take over his duties, Bounce took one look and one sniff—then began plotting. He knew that his master could not understand what he had discovered; so all he could do was to bide his time.

That night the new valet lifted his dwarfed master from the large, cushioned chair and carried him into the bedroom, where he assisted him to undress for the night. After placing him gently on the big canopied bed, he pulled the heavy curtains together to shut out the moonlight, which came in through the long French windows, and to prevent drafts from reaching the invalid while he slept. Then he quietly slipped out of the room.

Along about midnight, Pope thought he heard a noise. He lay quiet and listened. What he saw completely paralyzed him for the moment. A figure of a man was stealthily approaching the bed, carrying in his hand a large knife that glittered in the moonlight. The poor invalid, helpless to rise and protect himself, could only scream for his valet, not knowing it was he who was creeping toward him at that very moment. The cry brought Bounce, who dashed into

237

Pope's Shell Temple at Twickenham. Note the dog in foreground. Drawing by William Kent.

the room, and throwing his huge body against that of the man, toppled him over and held him down until the other servants came to the rescue. Nobody ever knew the purpose of the valet in his attempt to kill Pope. As for Bounce, he was just thankful that he had been able to save his master's life.

When Bounce died, Pope buried him at one end of the garden, placing at the head of the grave a plain stone. He really wished to inscribe on it the words, "O rare Bounce," but refrained because he might seem to be ridiculing "O rare Ben Jonson." However, any number of quotations from his own great poetic works would have made fitting epitaphs for his beloved dog. This one from his translation of the *Odyssey* seems particularly appropriate.

"Mirror of constant faith, rever'd and mourn'd."

GREGORY OF KENT
Sire of 18 champions 1955-1961

The Leading Great Dane Sires, Dams and Winners

T IS interesting to study what correlation there might be between top winning at the shows and the production of champions.

In the October 1968 issue of *Pure-Bred Dogs—American Kennel Gazette* (official publication of the American Kennel Club) Mrs. Gerri Kelly, breed columnist for the Great Dane Club of America, presented three lists. The first named all the dogs that had won one or more Bests in Show (all breeds) in the period reported in the Gazettes of August 1958 through July 1968. The second listed all the studs that had sired ten or more champions in this period, and the third identified the dams that had produced five or more champions.

In presenting them here, we have updated the list of Best in Show winners to include all reported as of July 1972 Gazette, and have added note of developments from August 1968 to July 1972 to the lists of the sires and dams.

The wise breeder will keep in mind that sheer numbers of champions produced are not the only criterion of a great sire or dam. Frequency of matings, outstanding show records, accessibility to certain sires and dams—all these, and other factors, have to be taken into account. A sire or dam may produce several champions from only one litter and never produce another champion. Or, it may "nick" successfully with one mate, but not others. The *quality* of champions, preferably from more than one mate, is the best measure of a stud or dam.

GREAT DANE
BEST IN SHOW WINNERS

(As listed in the Gazette, August 1958 - July 1972)

Ch. Abner Lowell Davis
Ch. Amor v Meistersinger
Ch. Aqua Vista's Mighty Thor
Ch. Bart Spanish of Bella Dane
Ch. Big Kim of Bella Dane
Ch. Blaise O'Gold
Ch. Brookmohr's Royal Fury
Ch. Brus Zingaling of Shijo
Ch. Cleo of Hi-Flight
Ch. Cloudland's Inquisitive Baron, C.D.
Ch. Conny Rux von St. Magnobertraubling
Ch. Crockerly's Folly
Ch. Crockerly's Harmony Siers
Ch. Crockerly's Primrose
Ch. Daneridge Caliban
Ch. Deacon's Golden Fury v Geordon
Ch. Dixie's Dirk of Kallish
Ch. Edvinrock's Cande Cane
Ch. Gretchen's Khan of Mountdania
Geurin El Tigre de Orou Saxony
Ch. Heather's Hrothgar
Ch. Heidere's Devil D of Marydane
Ch. Heidere's Kolyer Kimbayh
Ch. Highfield's Buchanan
Ch. Honey Bun of Marydane
Ch. Honeygold von Overcup
Ch. Honey Hollow Great Donner
Ch. Honey Hollow Stormi Rudio
Ch. Imperial Js Jubilant Apollo
Ch. Jocopa's Beeri Bina of Wildane
Ch. Kolyers Kowton Kim v Hedgerow
Ch. Lane's Turn Gunnar
Ch. Laurado's Prince Rebel

Ch. Leslie's Thumper v Barnhardt
Ch. Long Crest March Wind
Ch. Maximilian v Meistersinger
Ch. Michael of Kent
Ch. Nandane's El Tigre of Robmar
Ch. Old Fitz Herrscher v d Wilhelmshohe
Ch. Reggens Madas-L of Marydane
Saxony's Miss Jeni of Barclay
Ch. Sheela's Scheherazade
Ch. Starlight's King
Thunderdane's Classic Major
Ch. Tivoli's Newt v Harmony Hill
Ch. Tozer's Golden Rex
Ch. Wacos D' King Solomon v Prin-zel

TOP SIRES

(As reported in Gazettes from August 1958–July 1968. Number in parentheses indicates champion offspring.)

Ch. Heidere's Devil D of Marydane (29)
Ch. Deacon's Golden Fury v Geordon (23)
Ch. Nandane's Tamanaco (19)
Ch. Dinro Taboo (19)
Ch. Mountdania's Yancy (18)
Ch. I. W. Harper v d Stadt Hamburg (14)
Ch. Lillard's Deacon of Vizier (14)
Ch. Paethan of Mountdania (12)
Ch. Astrid's Bodo (10)
Ch. Gideon of Guilerdane (10)
Ch. Honey Hollow Great Dion (10)

TOP SIRES: Supplementary

(As reported in Gazettes from August 1968–July 1972)

11 more champions sired by Ch. Nandane's Tamanaco finished in this period to bring his total to 30
3 more champions sired by Ch. Deacon's Golden Fury v Geordon finished in this period to bring his total to 26
2 more champions sired by Ch. Mountdania's Yancy finished in this period to bring his total to 20
Ch. Big Kim of Bella Dane (20)
Ch. Sham's Sacerdotes (17)
Ch. Taboo Again (13)
Ch. Kent's Brandt (11)

TOP DAMS

(As reported in Gazettes from August 1958–July 1968.
Number in parentheses identifies champion offspring.)

Ch. Heming's Heide-Ho (8)
Ch. Meyer's Dane Holly (8)
Mountdania's Mimi (8)
Ch. Thendara Henriette Keppen (8)
Ch. Heidi of Thorn Run (7)
Cayenne v Riesenhof (5)
Ch. Geordon v Riesenhof (5)
Ch. Geordon's Rozie (5)
Gypsy Lane's Nanette of Kaleen (5)
Honey Hollow Dion's April (5)
Kolyer's Fire of Holland Brook (5)
Ch. Laurado's Czarina (5)
Ch. Ross' Sheela of Guilderdane (5)
Sabrina of Mountdania (5)

TOP DAMS: Supplementary

(As reported in Gazettes from August 1968–July 1972)

7 more champion offspring of Ch. Thendara Henriette
Keppen finished in this period to bring her total to 15
Ch. Kolyer's Heidere Heidee (7)

WINNERS AT THE SPECIALTY SHOWS OF THE GREAT DANE CLUB OF AMERICA, 1950-1971

The winning of a major award at the breed's parent club Specialty carries a special meaning for the dog fancier. The competition is usually keen at Specialties, and a high placing at such an event often means more to the winning dog's owner than a Breed or Group win at other shows.

In the tabulation below the Best of Breed is shown in the top line of the fourth column, with the Best of Opposite Sex under it, for each show. Similarly, in the fifth column, the top line identifies the Winners Dog, and the line below it the Winners Bitch.

The abbreviation (BW) identifies the Best of Winners.

The annual Specialty of the Great Dane Club of America is held with the Westchester Kennel Club all-breed show each September. For the period from 1957 to 1966 the club held an additional Specialty at the International Kennel Club of Chicago show, but since 1967 there has been just one Specialty each year—at Westchester.

Year	Judge - Show	Entry	Best of Breed Best of Opposite Sex	Winners Dog Winners Bitch
1950	Mrs. Ludwig	74	Ch. Senta's Astrid Ch. Deacon of Marydane	Sunningdane Heidere (BW) Gilbert's Glory's Dixie
1951	Charles Kapp	99	Ch. Graf Dane's Hurricane Ch. Senta's Astrid	Kingcourt's Gustav (BW) Vakeck's Belle of Machune
1952	C. G. Williams	74	Ch. Foray's Antoinette Ch. Dion of Kent	Clodo v Meistersingersburg An Gleann Planetree Ailis (BW)
1953	Mrs. Ehmling	80	Ch. HyCrest Prince Mathilde of Balney Hinch	Oh Me of Marydane Mathilde of Balney Hinch (BW)
1954	B. Schondler	95	Ch. Hi Ville's Dennis Ch. An Gleann Planetree Ailis	Tiper v Edelherz Eaglevalley Moonlight (BW)
1955	Owens	82	Ch. Lillard's Sir Galahad Ch. Kenellen's Kadeen	Sunningdane's Tony Glad Pink Confetti
1956	K. Tiffin	61	Ch. HyCrest Prince Chasnell Eadie v Ralmar	Kim of Carlsdane Chasnell Eadie v Ralmar

Year	Judge - Show	Entry	Best of Breed / Best of Opposite Sex	Winners Dog / Winners' Bitch
1957	Mrs. Baiter *International*	96	Conny-Rux v St Magn Obertraubling Golden Girl v Riesenhof	Conny-Rux v St Magn Obertraubling (BW) Golden Girl v Riesenhof
	Burns *Westchester*	66	Royal Master of Breezydane Gloria v Alten Peter	Royal Master of Breezydane (BW) Gloria v Alten Peter
1958	Staiger *International*	100	Ch. Lillian's Mr. President Ch. Erikke v Riesenhof	Radcliffe's Matador Asta vd Grossen Geist (BW)
	Mrs. O'Day *Westchester*	78	Ch. Bolo's Magnificent Ch. Gilbert's Braeview Lady	Highfield's Apollo Zita of Marydane
1959	Weaver *International*	75	I. W. Harper v d Stadt Hamburg	I. W. Harper v d Stadt Hamburg (BW) Rheba Zebra v Riesenhof
	Staiger *Westchester*	60	Ch. Herold v St Magn Obertraubling Ch. Heidere's Cinnamon Cindy	Old Sock from Rockdale (BW) Highfield's Bittersweet
1960	H. D. Cozier *International*	77	Dinro Taboo Ch. Long's Kandi v Lee	Dinro Taboo (BW) Honey Hollow Linda Mia Again
	Charles Kapp *Westchester*	75	Ch. I. W. Harper v d Stadt Hamburg Ch. Turkadana Nini of Wynridge	Highfield's Alexander Trogalana's Bridey Murphy (BW)
1961	Sabetti *International*	66	Ch. Rori of Noblebrook Ch. Gypsy Lane's Golden Doll	Nandane's El Tigre of Robmar (BW) Nandane's Gypsy of Waymar
	Mrs. Hyslop *Westchester*	87	Ch. Dinro Taboo Hilldane's La Chapelle	Lane's Turn Tonto of White Oaks Hilldane's La Chapelle (BW)
1962	Mrs. Warren *International*	91	Ch. Deacon's Golden Fury v Geordon Agylla of Chenoweth	Taboo v Riesenhof Agylla of Chenoweth (BW)
	K. O. Peterson *Westchester*	60	Ch. Gretchen's Khan of Mountdania Ch. Valeska v Meistersinger	Maximilian of Evergreen (BW) Kent's Angel of Northcliff
1963	Mrs. Williams *International*	73	Ch. Deacon's Golden Fury v Geordon Tig Mers Tiger Lilly	Gamboa's Guss of Mountdania Tig Mers Tiger Lilly (BW)
	A. F. Jensen *Westchester*	98	Ch. Amor v Meistersinger Laricas Bernadette	Frefin's Clown Laricas Bernadette (BW)
1964	H. A. Hodges *International*	78	Ch. Deacon's Golden Fury v Geordon Ch. Tig Mers Tiger Lilly	Wacos Pecos Pete Serafino's Sophia (BW)
	J. W. Lundeen *Westchester*	90	Ch. Gretchen's Khan of Mountdania Ch. Khan's Kim of Mountdania	Harpie v Meistersinger (BW) Mountdania's Glamor Girl

247

Year	Judge - Show	Entry	Best of Breed / Best of Opposite Sex	Winners Dog / Winners' Bitch
1965	Mrs. Johnston	79	Ch. Tig Mers Tiger Lilly Ch. Charbos Regenbogen	Bart Spanish of Bella Dane Golden Leto of DuKay (BW)
	F. S. Cartwright	109	Tars Dusty Dane v Birchwood Ch. Kolyer's Fireball Hellery	Tars Dusty Dane v Birchwood (BW) Cedardane's Royal Belenda
1966	K. O. Peterson	121	Ch. Big Kim of Bella Dane Ch. C'est Si Bon v Meistersinger	Jumpin Ken of Marydane Wacos Butterscotch
	L. Allen.	109	Ch. Laricas Ernesto Ch. Khan's Kim of Mountdania	Turkadana Strathspey (BW) Craig's Saar of Greenbriar
1967	J. D. Cozier	151	Ch. Reggens Madas L of Marydane Ch. Big Kim of Bella Dane	Jupiter's Apollo (BW) Eaglevalley Hex v Doggenhof
1968	Robt. E. Gregory	164	Ch. Reggens Madas L of Marydane Ch. Jupiter's Apollo	Kolyer's Jeff of Urban Zatarae von Zordane (BW)
1969	A. E. Jensen	161	Ch. Olympia Ch. Mountdania's Timber	Von Riesenhof's Valkyrie Kolyer's Ou La La of Sapphire (BW)
1970	W. J. Gilbert	197	Ch. Brandt's Barrister of Dane Oak Ch. Heidere's Hamborger Deem	Dinro Strictly Taboo Brentwood's My Fair Lady v Rex
1971	I. A. Baskind	144	Ch. Tiara Terry's Shanee of Caesar Ch. Heidere's Kolyer Kimbayh	Major the Melancholy Dane Knajar's Balletina (BW)

THE Great Dane Club of America, INC.

May 23, 1972

Dear Member:

The Great Dane Club of America, Inc. has been appealed to by many breeders and members from all over the country for a clarification of its code. It has become apparent that breeding practices show a marked retrogression to a situation that has not existed in the United States since the early 1900's or in Germany since the 1800's.

As a result of the examples and report of the Color Research Committee, the Board of Directors of the Great Dane Club of America, Inc. has set forth a solution in its revised Code of Ethics. It shows an awareness of the existing situation in the country today.

Therefore, pedigrees of Fawns and Brindles shall, at the moment, be required to carry a minimum of four (4) generations pure color breeding. With regard to Harlequins, Blacks and Blues, the Parent Club realizes that the current situation calls for considerations in an attempt to aid these breeders in clarifying their color lines.

However, at a future date, the four (4) generation pure color pedigree will be extended as a further requirement.

The breeder truly interested in establishing a pure color line must use the revised Code of Ethics.

Sincerely,
The GREAT DANE CLUB OF AMERICA, INC.

Bette Lasky

Mrs. Bette Lasky, Secretary

249

BREEDERS CODE OF ETHICS

as endorsed by

THE GREAT DANE CLUB OF AMERICA

There are only five recognized colors; all these basically fall into four color strains: 1. FAWN and BRINDLE, 2. HARLEQUIN and HARLEQUIN BRED BLACK, 3. BLUE and BLUE BRED BLACK, 4. BLACK. Color classifications being well founded, the Great Dane Club of America, Inc. considers it an inadvisable practice to mix color strains and it is the club's policy to adhere only to the following matings:

Color of Dane	Pedigree of Sire and Dam	Approved Breedings
1. FAWN	Pedigrees of FAWN or BRINDLE Danes *should not* carry BLACK, HARLEQUIN or BLUE upon them.	1. FAWN bred to FAWN or BRINDLE only.
1. BRINDLE		1. BRINDLE bred to BRINDLE or FAWN only.
2. HARLEQUIN	Pedigrees of HARLEQUIN or HARLEQUIN BRED BLACK Danes *should not* carry FAWN, BRINDLE or BLUE upon them.	2. HARLEQUIN bred to HARLEQUIN, BLACK from HARLEQUIN BREEDING or BLACK from BLACK BREEDING only.
2. BLACK (HARLEQUIN BRED)		2. BLACK from HARLEQUIN BREEDING bred to HARLEQUIN, BLACK from HARLEQUIN BREEDING or BLACK from BLACK BREEDING only.

3. BLUE

Pedigrees of BLUE or BLUE BRED BLACK Danes *should not* carry FAWN, BRINDLE or HARLEQUIN upon them.

**3. BLACK
(BLUE BRED)**

Pedigrees of BLACK BRED Danes *should not* carry FAWN, BRINDLE, HARLEQUIN or BLUE upon them.

**4. BLACK
(BLACK BRED)**

3. BLUE bred to BLUE, BLACK from BLUE BREEDING or BLACK from BLACK BREEDING only.

3. BLACK from BLUE BREEDING bred to BLUE, BLACK from BLUE BREEDING or BLACK from BLACK BREEDING only.

4. BLACK from BLACK BREEDING bred to BLACK, BLUE or HARLEQUIN only. (*See note below.*)

Note: Black Bred Great Danes may be bred to Blacks, Blues or Harlequins only; Puppies resulting from these breedings will become Blacks or Harlequins from Harlequin breeding (category 2 above), Blacks or Blues from Blue breeding (category 3 above) or Blacks from Black Breeding (category 4 above).

It is our belief that color mixing other than that set forth above is injurious to our breed.

ALL COLORS SHALL BE PURE COLOR BRED FOR FOUR (4) GENERATIONS

Breeders of Black, Blue or Harlequin Danes will be expected to clear their lines to provide pedigrees that are 4 generations pure color bred.

This pedigree is available only to those members who pledge and adhere to our Breeders Code of Ethics.

Gallery of Great Dane Stars

CH. REGGEN'S MADAS-L OF MARYDANE
The top winning Great Dane bitch of all time. Owned
by Mrs. Mary K. Johnston, Marydane Kennels.

253

CH. DEACON'S FURY v. GEORDON
Top winner of the mid-60's and sire of more than 25 champions.
Owned by Dr. and Mrs. M. J. Denio.

CH. BEAU JACK OF DOGGENBURG
Sire: Othello v.d. Doggenburg. Dam: Lynn v.d. Doggenburg
Breeder: Gustav Kley
Owned by Mr. and Mrs. Charles G. Staiger,
Sunningdane Kennels, Scarsdale, N. Y.

CH. DINRO'S NESHOBE CHIEF
Finished to championship in one month, with four majors.
Bred by Rosemarie Robert, and owned by Miss Rae Beardsley.

AM. & CAN. CH. SHEELA'S SCHEHERAZADE
Winner of 3 Bests in Show and 18 Groups.
Owned by Mr. and Mrs. James Blood.

CH. AMOR von MEISTERSINGER
Best in Show Harlequin of the early '60's.

CH. SILVER MOUNTAIN RHONDA
First blue Great Dane champion in the United States.
Bred by Mr. and Mrs. E. M. Cutler, and owned by Mrs. Frank Greco.

CH. VON NEFF'S CANNIBAL OF HEATHER
37½". Owned by Mr. and Mrs. Mel Neff.

Father and Son
CH. DINRO TABOO AGAIN and DINRO TALISMAN
Bred and owned by Rosemarie Robert.

The top winning Great Dane of all time—
CH. BIG KIM OF BELLA DANE
Whelped 1964. Bred by Kathleen Stebnitz.
Owned by Kathleen Stebnitz and Mabel Sheppard.
Handled to record by Lina Basquette.

261

CH. KENTS BRANDT OF NORTHCLIFF
Owners, Mr. and Mrs. Don Booxbaum.

CH. ASTRID'S BODO
Sire of 18 champions 1955-1961

CH. THENDARA HENRIETTE KEPPEN
Dam of many champions including Best in Show winner.
Ch. Honeygold von Overcup. Owned by Art and Marie White.

CH. GRETCHEN'S KHAN OF MOUNTDANIA
Best in Show winner of the mid-60's. Owned by Gretchen Wyler.

CH. ABNER LOWELL DAVIS
A top Western winner of the late '60's. Bred and owned
by Mr. and Mrs. Lowell K. Davis.

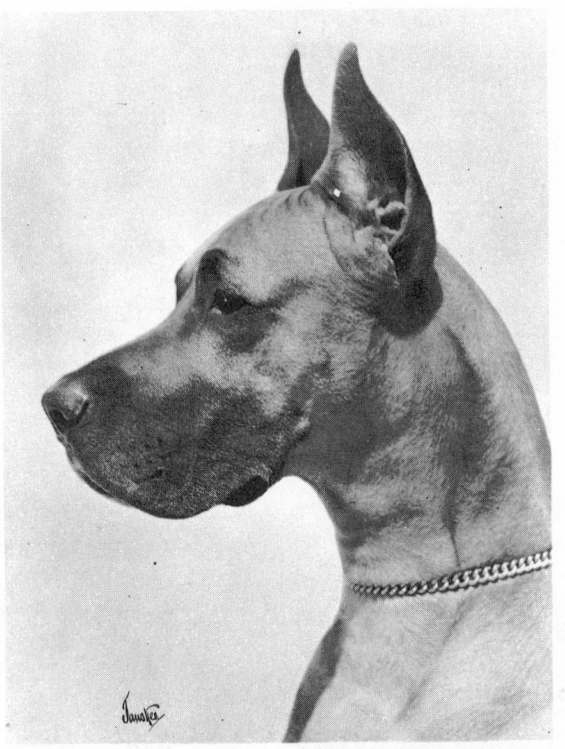

CH. STARLIGHT'S KING
Winner of 5 Bests in Show in the mid-60's.
Bred and owned by Mr. and Mrs. Charles C. Lipschultz.

CH. JANSEN-OF BRAE TARN
A Best in Show Winner of the 1940 era.
Owned by Ray Parker Stevens.

CH. CROCKERLY'S PRIMROSE
Best in Show bitch of the late '60's.

CH. SHALOTT'S LADY ALICIA
Best in Show winner of the '50's, and dam of 5 champions.
Owner, Mrs. Gilbert Freeman.

CH. HONEYGOLD von OVERCUP
Best in Show winner of the late '60's.
Owned by Mr. and Mrs. James Hatch, and handled by Doug Rodwell.

AM. CAN. & MEX. CH. JECAMO'S CAESAR OF AAA
Best in Show winner and sire of many champions.
Owned by Mr. and Mrs. Eugene Mitchell.

CH. HEATHER'S HROTHGAR
All-breed and Specialty Best in Show winner.
Owned by Philip and Carolyn Valenti.

CH. CROCKERLY'S HARMONY SIERS
A top winner of 1965 era
Bred and owned by Mr. and Mrs. James A. Blood

CH. CROCKERLY'S FOLLY
Top winning bitch of the 1962-64 era.
Owned by Mr. and Mrs. Norval Ayers.

CH. VAKECK'S GALLANT CAVALIER
Sire of 15 Champions
Sire: Ch. Vassall of Vakeck. Dam: Ch. Heide's Fantasy of Vakeck
Breeder-Owner: Vakeck Kennels

CH. FIDUS ACHATES
Sire: Vakeck's Gallant Cavalier.   Dam: Creighton's Sweet Sue
Breeder-Owner: Creighton B. Hayne

CH. DANERIDGE CALIBAN
Top winning Great Dane of 1963. Bred
and owned by Elizabeth R. Fawcett.

CH. DANE EDEN'S GOLDEN BARON, C.D., at right,
and his son, CH. DANE EDEN'S GOLDEN ZACHO, C.D.X.
Notable winners of the 1950's.

CH. DUCHESS of ZEL THOR II
(Ch. Dane Eden's Samson ex Ch. Cliza of Caldane)
Owned by G. Bordner

CH. LANE'S TURN GUNNAR
Best in Show winning brindle.
Bred and owned by Mrs. Leo Allen.

CH. HONEY HOLLOW BROADWAY JIM
An outstanding winner of the early '60's.
Owned by Mr. and Mrs. John E. Morris.

CH. DANELAGH'S FERGUS (wh. 1954)
(Ch. Dinro Aelric ex Ch. Astrid of Danelagh)
Owner, Miss Nancy Carroll-Draper.

CH. HONEY HOLLOW STORMI RUDIO
Top winner (7 Bests in Show and 41 Groups) of
the late 1950's. Bred by Lina Basquette and owned by Mrs. Cathryn Clarke.

CH. HONEY HOLLOW GREAT DONNER
Best in Show winner and sire of the early '60's.
Owners, Mr. and Mrs. James Childress.

CH. NERO'S ANTHONY, C.D.X. (wh. 1934)
First Great Dane in United States to win
C.D. and C.D.X. titles. Shown simultaneously in breed
and Obedience. Bred, trained, handled and owned by
Mrs. Henry M. Sabetti.

Three littermates who all finished to C.D. titles in 1965: (l. to r.):
CARMAC'S DANE THOR (Owner, J. Carmac),
STRANDJORD'S COUNTESS THYRA (Mr. and Mrs. R. M. Strandjord), and
LADY GRETA OF BLITZEN (Mr. and Mrs. Robert Hill).

CH. GILBERT'S DOLF'S CRUSADER
Sire of Ch. Senta's Astrid
Breeder: William J. Gilbert, Stirling, N. J.

OAKDANE'S BARBEE BELLE
Owned by Leroy S. and Barbara J. Marlin, Glendale, Calif.

283

CH. HEMING'S HEIDE-HO
(Ch. Bittel's Fawn Baron—Juno of Balmorholm)
Dam of 7 champions 1955-1961

AM. & CAN. CH. LAURADO'S PRINCE REBEL
An outstanding Best in Show winner of the late '60's.
Owner, Hazel E. Mage.

CH. LILLARD'S DEACON OF VIZIER
(Ch. Robertson's Valiant Vizier—Carliss Donna)
Sire of 11 champions 1955-1961

285

CH. BEAU'S ECSTASY
Sire: Ch. Vakeck's Gallant Cavalier. Dam: Creighton's Sweet Sue
Breeder: Creighton B. Hayne
Owner: Dorothea Smith, Middleburgh Hts., Ohio

CH. HEIDERE'S DEVIL-D of MARYDANE (wh. 1957)
Winner of 3 Bests in Show and 18 Groups and sire of more
than 30 champions including Ch. Reggen's Madas-L of Marydane.
Owner, Mrs. Mary K. Johnston.

CH. HONEY BUN
OF MARYDANE
(Danewehe's Deacon—
Ch. Clephadale
Audrowena)
Winner of 2 Bests in
Show, 7 Groups includ-
ing Westminster 1962

THE END

Part II

GENERAL CARE AND TRAINING
OF YOUR DOG

by

Elsworth S. Howell

Milo G. Denlinger

A. C. Merrick, D.V.M.

Training and
Simple Obedience

EVERY DOG that is mentally and physically sound can be taught good manners and simple obedience by any normal man, woman, or child over eight years old.

Certain requirements must be met by the dog, trainer and the environment if the training is to be enjoyable and effective. The dog must be rested and calm. The trainer must be rested, calm, gentle, firm, patient and persistent. The training site should be dry, comfortable and, except for certain exercises, devoid of distractions.

Proper techniques can achieve quick and sure results. Always use short, strong words for commands and always use the *same* word or words for the same command. Speak with authority; never scream or yell. Teach one command or exercise at a time and make sure the dog understands it and performs it perfectly before you proceed to the next step. Demand the dog's undivided attention; if he wavers or wanders, speak his name or pat him smartly or jerk his leash. Use pats and praise plentifully; avoid tidbit training if at all possible because tidbits may not always be available in an emergency and the dog will learn better without them. Keep lessons short; when the dog begins to show boredom, stop and do not resume in less than two hours. One or two ten-minute lessons a day should be ample, especially for a young puppy. Dogs have their good and bad days; if your well dog seems unduly lazy,

291

tired, bored or off-color, put off the lesson until tomorrow. Try to make lessons a joy, a happy time both for you and the dog, but do demand and get the desired action. Whenever correction or punishment is needed, use ways and devices that the dog does not connect with you; some of these means are given in the following instructions. Use painful punishment only as a last resort.

"NO!"

The most useful and easily understood command is "NO!" spoken in a sharp, disapproving tone and accompanied with a shaking finger. At first, speak the dog's name following with "NO!" until the meaning of the word—your displeasure—is clear.

"COME!"

Indoors or out, let the dog go ten or more feet away from you. Speak his name following at once with "COME!" Crouch, clap your hands, pick up a stick, throw a ball up and catch it, or create any other diversion which will lure the dog to you. When he comes, praise and pat effusively. As with all commands and exercises repeat the lesson, until the dog *always* comes to you.

THE FIRST NIGHTS

Puppies left alone will bark, moan and whine. If your dog is not to have the run of the house, put him in a room where he can do the least damage. Give him a Nylabone and a strip of beef hide (both available in supermarkets or pet shops and excellent as teething pacifiers). A very young puppy may appreciate a loud-ticking clock which, some dog trainers say, simulates the heart-beat of his former litter mates. Beyond providing these diversions, grit your teeth and steel your heart. If in pity you go to the howling puppy, he will howl every time you leave him. Suffer one night, two nights or possibly three, and you'll have it made.

The greatest boon to dog training and management is the wooden or wire crate. Any two-handed man can make a ⅜" plywood crate. It needs only four sides, a top, a bottom, a door on hinges and

292

with a strong hasp, and a fitting burlap bag stuffed with shredded newspaper, cedar shavings or 2″ foam rubber. Feed dealers or seed stores should give you burlap bags; be sure to wash them thoroughly to remove any chemical or allergy-causing material. The crate should be as long, as high and three times as wide as the dog will be full grown. The crate will become as much a sanctuary to your dog as a cave was to his prehistoric ancestor; it will also help immeasurably in housebreaking.

HOUSEBREAKING

The secret to housebreaking a healthy normal dog is simple: take him out every hour if he is from two to six months old when you get him; or the first thing in the morning, immediately after every meal, and the last thing at night if he is over six months.

For very young puppies, the paper break is indicated. Lay eight or ten layers of newspapers in a room corner most remote from the puppy's bed. By four months of age or after two weeks in a new home if older, a healthy puppy should not need the paper *IF* it is exercised outdoors often and *IF* no liquid (including milk) is given after 5 P.M. and *IF* it is taken out not earlier than 10 P.M. at night and not later than 7 A.M. the next morning.

When the dog does what it should when and where it should, praise, praise and praise some more. Be patient outdoors: keep the dog out until action occurs. Take the dog to the same general area always; its own traces and those of other dogs thus drawn to the spot will help to inspire the desired action.

In extreme cases where frequent exercising outdoors fails, try to catch the dog in the act and throw a chain or a closed tin can with pebbles in it near the dog but not on him; say "NO!" loudly as the chain or can lands. In the most extreme case, a full 30-second spanking with a light strap may be indicated but be sure you catch the miscreant *in the act*. Dog memories are short.

Remember the crate discussed under "THE FIRST NIGHTS." If you give the dog a fair chance, he will NOT soil his crate.

Do not rub his nose in "it." Dogs have dignity and pride. It is permissible to lead him to his error as soon as he commits it and to remonstrate forcefully with "NO!"

293

COLLAR AND LEASH TRAINING

Put on a collar tight enough not to slip over the head. Leave it on for lengthening periods from a few minutes to a few hours over several days. A flat collar for shorthaired breeds; a round or rolled collar for longhairs. For collar breaking, do NOT use a choke collar; it may catch on a branch or other jutting object and strangle the dog.

After a few days' lessons with the collar, attach a heavy cord or rope to it without a loop or knot at the end (to avoid snagging or catching on a stump or other object). Allow the dog to run free with collar and cord attached a few moments at a time for several days. Do not allow dog to chew cord!

When the dog appears to be accustomed to the free-riding cord, pick up end of the cord, loop it around your hand and take your dog for a walk (not the other way around!). DON'T STOP WALKING if the dog pulls, balks or screams bloody murder. Keep going and make encouraging noises. If dog leaps ahead of you, turn sharply left or right whichever is *away* from dog's direction—AND KEEP MOVING! The biggest mistake in leash training is stopping when the dog stops, or going the way the dog goes when the dog goes wrong. You're the leader; make the dog aware of it. This is one lesson you should continue until the dog realizes who is boss. If the dog gets the upper leg now, you will find it difficult to resume your rightful position as master. Brutality, no; firmness, yes!

If the dog pulls ahead, jerk the cord—or by now, the leash—backward. Do not pull. Jerk or snap the leash only!

JUMPING ON PEOPLE

Nip this annoying habit at once by bumping the dog with your knee on his chest or stepping with authority on his rear feet. A sharp "NO!" at the same time helps. Don't permit this action when you're in your work clothes and ban it only when dressed in glad rags. The dog is not Beau Brummel, and it is cruel to expect him to distinguish between denim and silk.

THE "PROBLEM" DOG

The following corrections are indicated when softer methods fail. Remember that it's better to rehabilitate than to destroy.

Biting. For the puppy habit of mouthing or teething on the owner's hand, a sharp rap with a folded newspaper on the nose, or snapping the middle finger off the thumb against the dog's nose, will usually discourage nibbling tactics. For the biter that means it, truly drastic corrections may be preferable to destroying the dog. If your dog is approaching one year of age and is biting in earnest, take him to a professional dog trainer and don't quibble with his methods unless you would rather see the dog dead.

Chewing. For teething puppies, provide a Nylabone (trade mark) and beef hide strips (see "THE FIRST NIGHTS" above). Every time the puppy attacks a chair, a rug, your hand, or any other chewable object, snap your finger or rap a newspaper on his nose, or throw the chain or a covered pebble-laden tin can near him, say "NO!" and hand him the bone or beef hide. If he persists, put him in his crate with the bone and hide. For incorrigible chewers, check diet for deficiencies first. William Koehler, trainer of many movie dogs including *The Thin Man's* Asta, recommends in his book, *The Koehler Method of Dog Training*, that the chewed object or part of it be taped crosswise in the dog's mouth until he develops a hearty distaste for it.

Digging. While he is in the act, throw the chain or noisy tin can and call out "NO!" For the real delinquent Koehler recommends filling the dug hole with water, forcing the dog's nose into it until the dog thinks he's drowning—and he'll never dig again. Drastic perhaps, but better than the bullet from an angry neighbor's gun, or a surreptitious poisoning.

The Runaway. If your dog wanders while walking with you, throw the chain or tin can and call "COME!" to him. If he persists, have a friend or neighbor cooperate in chasing him home. A very long line, perhaps 25 feet or more, can be effective if you permit the dog to run its length and then snap it sharply to remind him not to get too far from you.

Car Chasing. Your dog will certainly live longer if you make him car-wise; in fact, deathly afraid of anything on wheels. Ask a friend or neighbor to drive you in *his* car. Lie below the windows and as your dog chases the car throw the chain or tin can while your neighbor or friend says "GO HOME!" sharply. Another method is to shoot a water pistol filled with highly diluted ammonia at the dog. If your dog runs after children on bicycles, the latter device is especially effective but may turn the dog against children.

The Possessive Dog. If a dog displays overly protective habits, berate him in no uncertain terms. The chain, the noisy can, the rolled newspaper, or light strap sharply applied, may convince him that, while he loves you, there's no percentage in overdoing it.

The Cat Chaser. Again, the chain, the can, the newspaper, the strap—or the cat's claws if all else fails, but only as the last resort.

The Defiant, or Revengeful, Wetter. Some dogs seem to resent being left alone. Some are jealous when their owners play with another dog or animal. Get a friend or neighbor in this case to heave the chain or noisy tin can when the dog relieves himself in sheer spite.

For other canine delinquencies, you will find *The Koehler Method of Dog Training* effective. William Koehler's techniques have been certified as extremely successful by directors of motion pictures featuring dogs and by officers of dog obedience clubs.

OBEDIENCE EXERCISES

A well-mannered dog saves its owner money, embarrassment and possible heartbreak. The destruction of property by canine delinquents, avoidable accidents to dogs and children, and other unnecessary disadvantages to dog ownership can be eliminated by simple obedience training. The elementary exercises of heeling, sitting, staying and lying down can keep the dog out of trouble in most situations.

The only tools needed for basic obedience training are a slip collar made of chain link, leather or nylon and a strong six-foot leather leash with a good spring snap. Reviewing the requirements and basic techniques given earlier, let's proceed with the dog's schooling.

Heeling. Keep your dog on your left side, with the leash in your left hand. Start straight ahead in a brisk walk. If your dog pulls ahead, jerk (do not pull) the leash and say "Heel" firmly. If the dog persists in pulling ahead, stop, turn right or left and go on for several yards, saying "Heel" each time you change direction.

If your dog balks, fix leash *under* his throat and coax him forward by repeating his name and tapping your hip.

Whatever you do, don't stop walking! If the dog jumps up or "fights" the leash, just keep moving briskly. Sooner than later he will catch on and with the repetition of "Heel" on every correction, you will have him trotting by your side with style and respect.

Sit. Keeping your dog on leash, hold his neck up and push his rump down while repeating "Sit." If he resists, "spank" him lightly several times on his rump. Be firm, but not cruel. Repeat this lesson often until it is learned perfectly. When the dog knows the command, test him at a distance without the leash. Return to him every time he fails to sit and repeat the exercise.

Stay. If you have properly trained your dog to "Sit," the "Stay" is simple. Take his leash off and repeat "Stay" holding your hand up, palm toward dog, and move away. If dog moves toward you, you must repeat the "sit" lesson until properly learned. After your dog "stays" while you are in sight, move out of his sight and keep repeating "Stay." Once he has learned to "stay" even while you are out of his sight, you can test him under various conditions, such as when another dog is near, a child is playing close to him, or a car appears on the road. (Warning: do not tax your dog's patience on the "stay" until he has learned the performance perfectly.)

Down. For this lesson, keep your dog on leash. First tell him to "sit." When he has sat for a minute, place your shoe over his leash between the heel and sole. Slowly pull on the leash and repeat "Down" while you push his head down with your other hand. Do this exercise very quietly so that dog does not become excited and uncontrollable. In fact, this performance is best trained when the dog is rather quiet. Later, after the dog has learned the voice signal perfectly, you can command the "Down" with a hand signal, sweeping your hand from an upright position to a downward motion with your palm toward the dog. Be sure to say "Down" with the hand signal.

For more advanced obedience the following guides by Blanche Saunders are recommended:

The Complete Novice Obedience Course
The Complete Open Obedience Course
The Complete Utility Obedience Course (with Tracking)
Dog Training for Boys and Girls (includes simple tricks.)

All are published by Howell Book House at $3.00 each.

OBEDIENCE TRIALS

Booklets covering the rules and regulations of Obedience Trials may be obtained from The American Kennel Club, 51 Madison Avenue, New York, N.Y. 10010. In Canada, write The Canadian Kennel Club, 667 Yonge Street, Toronto, Ontario.

Both these national clubs can give you the names and locations of local and regional dog clubs that conduct training classes in obedience and run Obedience Trials in which trained dogs compete for degrees as follow: CD (Companion Dog), CDX (Companion Dog Excellent), UD (Utility Dog), TD (Tracking Dog) and UDT (Utility Dog, Tracking.)

The Exhibition
of Dogs

NOBODY should exhibit a dog in the shows unless he can win without gloating and can lose without rancor. The showing of dogs is first of all a sport, and it is to be approached in a sportsmanlike spirit. It is not always so approached. That there are so many wretched losers and so many supercilious winners among the exhibitors in dog shows is the reason for this warning.

The confidence that one's dog is of exhibition excellence is all that prompts one to enter him in the show, but, if he fails in comparison with his competitors, nobody is harmed. It is no personal disgrace to have a dog beaten. It may be due to the dog's fundamental faults, to its condition, or to inexpert handling. One way to avoid such hazards is to turn the dog over to a good professional handler. Such a man with a flourishing established business will not accept an inferior dog, one that is not worth exhibiting. He will put the dog in the best possible condition before he goes into the ring with him, and he knows all the tricks of getting out of a dog all he has to give. Good handlers come high, however. Fees for taking a dog into the ring will range from ten to twenty-five dollars, plus any cash prizes the dog may win, and plus a bonus for wins made in the group.

Handlers do not win all the prizes, despite the gossip that they do, but good handlers choose only good dogs and they usually finish at or near the top of their classes. It is a mistake to assume that this is due to any favoritism or any connivance with the judges; the handlers have simply chosen the best dogs, conditioned them well, and so maneuvered them in the ring as to bring out their best points.

The services of a professional handler are not essential, however. Many an amateur shows his dogs as well, but the exhibitor without previous experience is ordinarily at something of a disadvantage. If the dog is good enough, he may be expected to win.

The premium list of the show, setting forth the prizes to be offered, giving the names of the judges, containing the entry form, and describing the conditions under which the show is to be held, are usually mailed out to prospective exhibitors about a month before the show is scheduled to be held. Any show superintendent is glad to add names of interested persons to the mailing list.

Entries for a Licensed show close at a stated date, usually about two weeks before the show opens, and under the rules no entry may be accepted after the advertised date of closing. It behooves the exhibitor to make his entries promptly. The exhibitor is responsible for all errors he may make on the entry form of his dog; such errors cannot be rectified and may result in the disqualification of the exhibit. It therefore is wise for the owner to double check all data submitted with an entry. The cost of making an entry, which is stated in the premium list, is usually from six to eight dollars. An unregistered dog may be shown at three shows, after which he must be registered or a statement must be made to the American Kennel Club that he is ineligible for registry and why, with a request for permission to continue to exhibit the dog. Such permission is seldom denied. The listing fee for an unregistered dog is twenty-five cents, which must be added to the entry fee.

Match or Sanctioned shows are excellent training and experience for regular bench shows. Entry fees are low, usually ranging from fifty cents to a dollar, and are made at the show instead of in advance. Sanctioned shows are unbenched, informal affairs where the puppy may follow his owner about on the leash and become accustomed to strange dogs, to behaving himself in the ring, and to being handled by a judge. For the novice exhibitor, too, Sanctioned shows will provide valuable experience, for ring procedure is similar to that at regular bench shows.

The classes open at most shows and usually divided by sex are as follows: Puppy Class (often Junior Puppy for dogs 6 to 9 months old, and Senior Puppy for dogs 9 to 12 months); Novice Class, for dogs that have never won first in any except the Puppy Class; Bred-by-Exhibitor Class, for dogs of which the breeder and owner are the same person or persons; the American-bred Class, for dogs whose parents were mated in America; and the Open Class, which is open to all comers. The respective first prize winners of these various classes compete in what is known as the Winners Class for points toward championship. No entry can be made in the Winners Class, which is open without additional charge to the winners of the earlier classes, all of which are obligated to compete.

A dog eligible to more than one class can be entered in each of them, but it is usually wiser to enter him in only one. A puppy should, unless unusually precocious and mature, be placed in the Puppy Class, and it is unfair to so young a dog to expect him to defeat older dogs, although an exceptional puppy may receive an award in the Winners Class. The exhibitor who is satisfied merely that his dog may win the class in which he is entered is advised to place him in the lowest class to which he is eligible, but the exhibitor with confidence in his dog and shooting for high honors should enter the dog in the Open Class, where the competition is usually the toughest. The winner of the Open Class usually (but by no means always) is also the top of the Winners Class; the runner-up to this dog is named Reserve Winners.

The winner of each sex and any champions entered then compete for Best of Breed. Next, Winners Dog and Winners Bitch compete for Best of Winners and finally Best of Opposite Sex to Best of Breed is chosen. In the closing hours of the show, the Best of Breed or Best of Variety is eligible to compete in the respective Variety Group to which his breed belongs. And if, perchance, he should win his Variety Group, he is obligated to compete for Best Dog in Show. This is a major honor which few inexperienced exhibitors attain and to which they seldom aspire.

Duly entered, the dog should be brought into the best possible condition for his exhibition in the show and taught to move and to pose at his best. He should be equipped with a neat, strong collar without ornaments or spikes, a show lead of the proper length, width and material for his size and coat, and a nickel bench chain of strong links with which to fasten him to his bench. Food such as the dog is used to, a bottle of the water he is accustomed to drink, and all grooming equipment should be assembled in a bag the night before departure for the show. The exhibitor's pass, on which the dog is assigned a stall number, is sent by mail by the show superintendent and should not be left behind, since it is difficult to have the pass duplicated and it enables the dog's caretaker to leave and return to the show at will.

The time of the opening of the show is stated in the premium list, and it is wise to have one's dog at the show promptly. Late arrivals are subject to disqualification if they are protested.

Sometimes examination is made by the veterinarian at the entrance of the show, and healthy dogs are quickly passed along. Once admitted to the show, if it is a "benched" show, it is wise to find one's bench, the number of which is on the exhibitor's ticket, to affix one's dog to the bench, and not to remove him from it except for exercising or until he is to be taken into the ring to be judged. A familiar blanket or cushion for the bench makes a dog feel at home there. It is contrary to the rules to remove dogs from their benches and to keep them in crates during show hours, and these rules are strictly enforced. Many outdoor shows are not "benched," and you provide your own crate or place for your dog.

At bench shows some exhibitors choose to sit by their dog's bench, but if he is securely chained he is likely to be safe in his owner's absence. Dogs have been stolen from their benches and others allegedly poisoned in the shows, but such incidents are rare indeed. The greater danger is that the dog may grow nervous and insecure, and it is best that the owner return now and again to the bench to reassure the dog of his security.

The advertised program of the show permits exhibitors to know the approximate hour of the judging of their respective breeds. Although that time may be somewhat delayed, it may be depended upon that judging will not begin before the stated hour. The dog should have been groomed and made ready for his appearance in the show ring. When his class is called the dog should be taken unhurriedly to the entrance of the ring, where the handler will receive an arm band with the dog's number.

When the class is assembled and the judge asks that the dogs be paraded before him, the handler should fall into the counter-clock-wise line and walk his dog until the signal to stop is given. In moving in a circle, the dog should be kept on the inside so that he may be readily seen by the judge, who stands in the center of the ring. In stopping the line, there is no advantage to be gained in maneuvering one's dog to the premier position, since the judge will change the position of the dogs as he sees fit.

Keep the dog alert and facing toward the judge at all times. When summoned to the center of the ring for examination, go briskly but not brashly. It is unwise to enter into conversation with the judge, except briefly to reply to any questions he may ask. Do not call his attention to any excellences the dog may possess or excuse any shortcomings; the judge is presumed to evaluate the exhibit's merits as he sees them.

If asked to move the dog, he should be led directly away from the judge and again toward the judge. A brisk but not too rapid trot is the gait the judge wishes to see, unless he declares otherwise. He may ask that the movement be repeated, with which request the handler should respond with alacrity. It is best not to choke a dog in moving him, but rather to move him on a loose lead. The judge will assign or signal a dog to his position, which should be assumed without quibble.

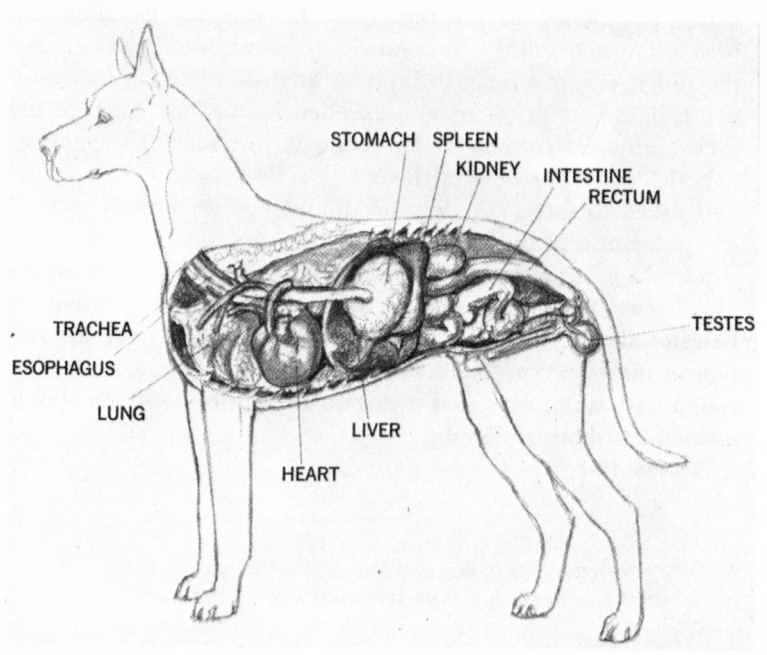

STOMACH SPLEEN
KIDNEY INTESTINE
RECTUM

TRACHEA

ESOPHAGUS

TESTES

LUNG

LIVER

HEART

The Feeding of Dogs, Constitutional Vigor

IN selecting a new dog, it is quite as essential that he shall be of sound constitution as that he shall be of the correct type of his own particular breed. The animal that is thoroughly typical of his breed is likely to be vigorous, with a will and a body to surmount diseases and ill treatment, but the converse of this statement is not always true. A dog may have constitutional vigor without breed type. We want both.

Half of the care and effort of rearing a dog is saved by choosing at the outset a puppy of sound constitution, one with a will and an ability to survive and flourish in spite of such adversity and neglect as he may encounter in life. This does not mean that the reader has any intention of obtaining a healthy dog and ill treating it, trusting its good constitution to bring it through whatever crises may beset it. It only means that he will save himself work, expense, and disappointment if only he will exercise care in the first place to obtain a healthy dog, one bred from sound and vigorous parents and one which has received adequate care and good food.

The first warning is not to economize too much in buying a dog. Never accept a cull of the litter at any price. The difference in first cost between a fragile, ill nourished, weedy, and unhealthy puppy and a sound, vigorous one, with adequate substance and the will to survive, may be ten dollars or it may be fifty dollars. But whatever it may be, it is worthwhile. A dog is an investment and it is not the cost but the upkeep that makes the difference. We may save fifty dollars on the first price of a dog, only to lay out twice or five times that sum for veterinary fees over and above what it would cost to rear a dog of sound fundamental constitution and structure.

The vital, desirable dog, the one that is easy to rear and worth the care bestowed upon him, is active, inquisitive, and happy. He is sleek, his eyes free from pus or tears, his coat shining and alive, his flesh adequate and firm. He is not necessarily fat, but a small amount of surplus flesh, especially in puppyhood, is not undesirable. He is free from rachitic knobs on his joints or from crooked bones resultant from rickets. His teeth are firm and white and even. His breath is sweet to the smell. Above all, he is playful and responsive. Puppies, like babies, are much given to sleep, but when they are awake the sturdy ones do not mope lethargically around.

An adult dog that is too thin may often be fattened; if he is too fat he may be reduced. But it is essential that he shall be sound and healthy with a good normal appetite and that he be active and full of the joy of being alive. He must have had the benefit of a good heredity and a good start in life.

A dog without a fundamental inheritance of good vitality, or one that has been neglected throughout his growing period is seldom worth his feed. We must face these facts at the very beginning. Buy only from an owner who is willing to guarantee the soundness of his stock, and before consummating the purchase, have the dog, whether puppy or adult, examined by a veterinarian in order to determine the state of the dog's health.

If the dog to be cared for has been already acquired, there is nothing to do but to make the best of whatever weaknesses or frailties he may possess. But, when it is decided to replace him with another, let us make sure that he has constitutional vigor.

SOME BRIEF PRECEPTS ABOUT FEEDING

Many dogs are overfed. Others do not receive adequate rations. Both extremes should be avoided, but particularly overfeeding of grown dogs. Coupled with lack of exercise, overfeeding usually produces excessive body weight and laziness, and it may result in illness and sterility. Prolonged undernourishment causes loss of weight, listlessness, dull coats, sickness, and death.

An adequate ration will keep most mature dogs at a uniform body weight and in a thrifty, moderately lean condition. Observation of condition is the best guide in determining the correct amount of food.

The axiom, "One man's meat is another man's poison," is applicable to dogs also. Foods that are not tolerated by the dog or those that cause digestive and other disturbances should be discontinued. The use of moldy, spoiled, or rotten food is never good practice. Food should be protected from fouling by rats or mice, especially because rats are vectors of leptospirosis. The excessive use of food of low energy content and low biological values will often result in poor condition and may cause loss of weight and paunchiness.

All feeding and drinking utensils must be kept scrupulously clean. They should be washed after each using.

It is usually desirable to reduce the food allotment somewhat during hot weather. Dogs should be fed at regular intervals, and the best results may be expected when regular feeding is accompanied by regular, but not exhausting, exercise.

Most dogs do not thrive on a ration containing large amounts of sloppy foods, and excessive bulk is to be avoided especially for hardworking dogs, puppies, and pregnant or lactating bitches. If the ration is known to be adequate and the dog is losing weight or is not in good condition, the presence of intestinal parasites is to be suspected. However, dogs sometimes go "off feed" for a day or two. This is cause for no immediate anxiety, but if it lasts more than two or three days, a veterinarian should be consulted.

THE FEEDING AND NUTRITION OF
THE ADULT DOG

The dog is a carnivore, an eater of meat. This is a truism that cannot be repeated too often. Dog keepers know it but are prone to disregard it, although they do so at their peril and the peril of their dogs. Despite all the old-wives' tales to the contrary, meat does not cause a dog to be vicious, it does not give him worms nor cause him to have fits. It is his food. This is by no means all that is needed to know about food for the dog, but it is the essential knowledge. Give a dog enough sound meat and he will not be ill fed.

The dog is believed to have been the first of the animals that was brought under domestication. In his feral state he was almost exclusively an eater of meat. In his long association with man, however, his metabolism has adjusted itself somewhat to the consumption of human diet until he now can eat, even if he cannot flourish upon, whatever his master chooses to share with him, be it caviar or corn pone. It is not to be denied that a mature dog can survive without ill effects upon an exclusive diet of rice for a considerable period, but it is not to be recommended that he should be forced to do so.

Even if we had no empirical evidence that dogs thrive best upon foods of animal origin, and we possess conclusive proof of that fact, the anatomy and physiology of the dog would convince us of it. An observation of the structure of the dog's alimentary canal, superimposed upon many trial and error methods of feeding, leads us to the conclusion that a diet with meat predominating is the best food we can give a dog.

To begin with, the dental formation of the dog is typical of the carnivores. His teeth are designed for tearing rather than for mastication. He bolts his food and swallows it with a minimum of chewing. It is harmless that he should do this. No digestion takes place in the dog's mouth.

The capacity of the dog's stomach is great in comparison with the size of his body and with the capacity of his intestines. The amounts of carbohydrates and of fats digested in the stomach are minimal. The chief function of the dog's stomach is the digestion of proteins. In the dog as in the other carnivores, carbohydrates and fats are digested for the most part in the small intestine, and absorption of food materials is largely from the small intestine. The enzymes necessary for the completion of the digestion of proteins which have not been fully digested in the stomach and for the digestion of sugars, starches, and fats are present in the pancreatic and intestinal juices. The capacity of the small intestine in the dog is not great and for that reason digestion that takes place there must be rapid.

The so-called large intestine (although in the dog it is really not "large" at all) is short and of small capacity in comparison with that of animals adapted by nature to subsist wholly or largely upon plant foods. In the dog, the large gut is designed to serve chiefly for storage of a limited and compact bulk of waste materials, which are later to be discharged as feces. Some absorption of water occurs there, but there is little if any absorption there of the products of digestion.

It will be readily seen that the short digestive tract of the dog is best adapted to a concentrated diet, which can be quickly digested and which leaves a small residue. Foods of animal origin (flesh, fish, milk, and eggs) are therefore suited to the digestive physiology of the dog because of the ease and completeness with which they are digested as compared with plant foods, which contain considerable amounts of indigestible structural material. The dog is best fed with a concentrated diet with a minimum of roughage.

This means meat. Flesh, milk, and eggs are, in effect, vegetation partly predigested. The steer or horse eats grain and herbage, from which its long digestive tract enables it to extract the food value and eliminate the indigestible material. The carnivore eats the flesh of the herbivore, thus obtaining his grain and grass in a concentrated form suitable for digestion in his short alimentary tract. Thus it is seen that meat is the ideal as a chief ingredient of the dog's ration.

Like that of all other animals, the dog's diet must be made up of proteins, carbohydrates, fats, minerals, vitamins, and water. None of these substances may be excluded if the dog is to survive. If he fails to obtain any of them from one source, it must come from another. It may be argued that before minerals were artificially supplied in the dog's diet and before we were aware of the existence of the various vitamins, we had dogs and they (some of them) appeared to thrive. However, they obtained such substances in their foods, although we were not aware of it. It is very likely that few dogs obtained much more than their very minimum of requirements of the minerals and vitamins. It is known that rickets were more prevalent before we learned to supply our dogs with ample calcium, and black tongue, now almost unknown, was a common canine disease before we supplied in the dog's diet that fraction of the vitamin B complex known as nicotinic acid. There is no way for us to know how large a portion of our dogs died for want of some particular food element before we learned to supply all the necessary ones. The dogs that survived received somewhere in their diet some of all of these compounds.

FOOD FOR THE STUD DOG

The stud dog that is used for breeding only at infrequent intervals requires only the food needed for his maintenance in good health, as set forth in the foregoing pages. He should be well fed with ample meat in his diet, moderately exercised to keep his flesh firm and hard, and not permitted to become too thin or too fat.

More care is required for the adequate nutrition of the dog offered at public stud and frequently employed for breeding. A vigorous stud dog may very handily serve two bitches a week over a long period without a serious tax upon his health and strength if he is fully nourished and adequately but not excessively exercised. Such a dog should have at least two meals a day, and they should consist of even more meat, milk (canned is as good as fresh), eggs, cottage cheese, and other foods of animal origin than is used in most maintenance rations. Liver and some fat should be included, and the vitamins especially are not to be forgotten. In volume this will be only a little more than the basic maintenance diet, the difference being in its richness and concentration.

An interval of an hour or two should intervene between a dog's meal and his employment for breeding. He may be fed, but only lightly, immediately after he has been used for breeding.

The immediate reason that a stud dog should be adequately fed and exercised is the maintenance of his strength and virility. The secondary reason is that a popular stud dog is on exhibition at all times, between the shows as well as at the shows. Clients with bitches to be bred appear without notice to examine a dog at public stud, and the dog should be presented to them in the best possible condition—clean, hard, in exactly the most becoming state of flesh, and with a gleaming, lively coat. These all depend largely upon the highly nutritious diet the dog receives.

FOOD FOR THE BROOD BITCH

Often a well fed bitch comes through the ordeal of rearing a large litter of puppies without any impairment of her vitality and flesh. In such case she may be returned to a good maintenance ration until she is ready to be bred again. About the time she weans her puppies her coat will be dead and ready to drop out, but if she is healthy and well fed a new and vigorous coat will grow in, and she will be no worse off for her maternal ordeal. Some bitches, either from a deficient nutrition or a constitutional disposition to contribute too much of their own strength and substance to the nutrition of the puppies, are thin and exhausted at the time of weaning. Such a bitch needs the continuance of at least two good and especially nutritious meals a day for a month or more until her flesh and strength are restored before she is returned to her routine maintenance ration, upon which she may be kept until time comes to breed her again.

At breeding time a bitch's flesh should be hard, and she should be on the lean side rather than too fat. No change in her regular maintenance diet need be made until about the fourth or fifth week of her pregnancy. The growth of the fetus is small up until the middle of the pregnancy, after which it becomes rapid.

The bitch usually begins to "show in whelp" in four to six weeks after breeding, and her food consumption should be then gradually stepped up. If she has been having only one meal a day, she should be given two; if she has had two, both should be larger. Henceforth until her puppies are weaned, she must eat not merely for two, as is said of the pregnant woman, but for four or five, possibly for ten or twelve. She is not to be encouraged to grow fat. Especial emphasis should be laid upon her ration's content of meat, including liver, milk, calcium phosphate, and vitamins A and D, both of which are found in cod-liver oil.

Some breeders destroy all but a limited number of puppies in a litter in the belief that a bitch will be unable adequately to nourish all the puppies she has whelped. In some extreme cases it may be necessary to do this or to obtain a foster mother or wet nurse to share the burden of rearing the puppies. However, the healthy bitch with normal metabolism can usually generate enough milk to feed adequately all the puppies she has produced, provided she is well enough fed and provided the puppies are fed additionally as soon as they are able to eat.

After whelping until the puppies are weaned, throughout the lactating period, the bitch should have all the nourishing food she can be induced to eat—up to four or five meals a day. These should consist largely of meat and liver, some fat, a small amount of cereals, milk, eggs, cottage cheese, calcium phosphate, and vitamins, with especial reference to vitamins A and D. At that time it is hardly possible to feed a bitch too much or to keep her too fat. The growth of the puppies is much more rapid after they are born than was their growth in the dam's uterus, and the large amount of food needed to maintain that rapid growth must pass through the bitch and be transformed to milk, while at the same time she must maintain her own body.

THE FEEDING OF PUPPIES

If the number of puppies in a litter is small, if the mother is vigorous, healthy, and a good milker, the youngsters up until their weaning time may require no additional food over and above the milk they suck from their dam's breasts. If the puppies are numerous or if the dam's milk is deficient in quality or quantity, it is wise to begin feeding the puppies artificially as soon as they are able and willing to accept food. This is earlier than used to be realized.

It is for the sake of the puppies' vigor rather than for the sake of their ultimate size that their growth is to be promoted as rapidly as possible. Vigorous and healthy puppies attain early maturity if they are given the right amounts of the right quality of food. The ultimate size of the dog at maturity is laid down in his germ plasm, and he can be stunted or dwarfed, if at all, only at the expense of his type. If one tries to prevent the full growth of a dog by withholding from him the food he needs, one will wind up with a rachitic, cowhocked dog, one with a delicate digestive apparatus, a sterile one, one with all of these shortcomings combined, or even a dead dog.

Growth may be slowed with improper food, sometimes without serious harm, but the dog is in all ways better off if he is forced along with the best food and encouraged to attain his full size at an early age. Dogs of the smaller breeds usually reach their full maturity several months earlier than those of the larger breeds. A well grown dog reaches his sexual maturity and can be safely used for limited breeding at one year of age.

As soon as teeth can be felt with the finger in a puppy's mouth, which is usually at about seventeen or eighteen days of age, it is safe to begin to feed him. His first food (except for his mother's milk) should be of scraped raw beef at body temperature. The first day he may have ¼ to 2 teaspoonfuls, according to size. He will not need to learn to eat this meat; he will seize upon it avidly and lick his chops for more. The second day he may have ⅓ to 3 teaspoonfuls, according to size, with two feedings 12 hours apart. Thereafter, the amount and frequency of this feeding may be rapidly increased. By the twenty-fifth day the meat need not be scraped, but only finely ground. This process of the early feeding of raw meat to puppies not only gives them a good start in life, but it also relieves their mother of a part of her burden of providing milk for them.

At about the fourth week, some cereal (thoroughly cooked oatmeal, shredded wheat, or dried bread) may be either moistened and mixed with the meat or be served to the puppies with milk, fresh or canned. It may be necessary to immerse their noses into such a mixture to teach them to eat it. Calcium phosphate and a small amount of cod-liver oil should be added to such a mixture, both of which substances the puppies should have every day until their maturity. At the fourth week, while they are still at the dam's breast, they may be fed three or four times a day upon this extra ration, or something similar, such as cottage cheese or soft boiled egg. By the sixth week their dam will be trying to wean them, and they may have four or five meals daily. One of these may be finely broken dog biscuit thoroughly soaked in milk. One or two of the meals should consist largely or entirely of meat with liver.

The old advice about feeding puppies "little and often" should be altered to "much and often." Each puppy at each meal should have all the food he will readily clean up. Food should not be left in front of the puppies. They should be fed and after two or three minutes the receptacle should be taken away. Young puppies should be roly-poly fat, and kept so up to at least five or six months of age. Thereafter they should be slightly on the fat side, but not pudgy, until maturity.

The varied diet of six-week-old puppies may be continued, but at eight or nine weeks the number of meals may be reduced to four, and at three months, to three large rations per day. After six months the meals may be safely reduced again to two a day, but they must be generous meals with meat, liver, milk, cod-liver oil, and calcium phosphate. At full maturity, one meal a day suffices, or two may be continued.

The secret of turning good puppies into fine, vigorous dogs is to keep them growing through the entire period of their maturation. The most important item in the rearing of puppies is adequate and frequent meals of highly nourishing foods. Growth requires two or three times as much food as maintenance. Time between meals should be allowed for digestion, but puppies should never be permitted to become really hungry. Water in a shallow dish should be available to puppies at all times after they are able to walk.

315

WHELPING CALENDAR

Find the month and date on which your bitch was bred in one of the left-hand columns. Directly opposite that date, in the right-hand column, is her expected date of whelping, bearing in mind that 61 days is as common as 63.

Date bred	Date due to whelp	Date bred	Date due to whelp	Date bred	Date due to whelp	Date bred	Date due to whelp	Date bred	Date due to whelp	Date bred	Date due to whelp	Date bred	Date due to whelp	Date bred	Date due to whelp	Date bred	Date due to whelp	Date bred	Date due to whelp	Date bred	Date due to whelp	Date bred	Date due to whelp
January	March	February	April	March	May	April	June	May	July	June	August	July	September	August	October	September	November	October	December	November	January	December	February
1	5	1	5	1	3	1	3	1	3	1	3	1	2	1	3	1	3	1	3	1	3	1	2
2	6	2	6	2	4	2	4	2	4	2	4	2	3	2	4	2	4	2	4	2	4	2	3
3	7	3	7	3	5	3	5	3	5	3	5	3	4	3	5	3	5	3	5	3	5	3	4
4	8	4	8	4	6	4	6	4	6	4	6	4	5	4	6	4	6	4	6	4	6	4	5
5	9	5	9	5	7	5	7	5	7	5	7	5	6	5	7	5	7	5	7	5	7	5	6
6	10	6	10	6	8	6	8	6	8	6	8	6	7	6	8	6	8	6	8	6	8	6	7
7	11	7	11	7	9	7	9	7	9	7	9	7	8	7	9	7	9	7	9	7	9	7	8
8	12	8	12	8	10	8	10	8	10	8	10	8	9	8	10	8	10	8	10	8	10	8	9
9	13	9	13	9	11	9	11	9	11	9	11	9	10	9	11	9	11	9	11	9	11	9	10
10	14	10	14	10	12	10	12	10	12	10	12	10	11	10	12	10	12	10	12	10	12	10	11
11	15	11	15	11	13	11	13	11	13	11	13	11	12	11	13	11	13	11	13	11	13	11	12
12	16	12	16	12	14	12	14	12	14	12	14	12	13	12	14	12	14	12	14	12	14	12	13
13	17	13	17	13	15	13	15	13	15	13	15	13	14	13	15	13	15	13	15	13	15	13	14
14	18	14	18	14	16	14	16	14	16	14	16	14	15	14	16	14	16	14	16	14	16	14	15
15	19	15	19	15	17	15	17	15	17	15	17	15	16	15	17	15	17	15	17	15	17	15	16
16	20	16	20	16	18	16	18	16	18	16	18	16	17	16	18	16	18	16	18	16	18	16	17
17	21	17	21	17	19	17	19	17	19	17	19	17	18	17	19	17	19	17	19	17	19	17	18
18	22	18	22	18	20	18	20	18	20	18	20	18	19	18	20	18	20	18	20	18	20	18	19
19	23	19	23	19	21	19	21	19	21	19	21	19	20	19	21	19	21	19	21	19	21	19	20
20	24	20	24	20	22	20	22	20	22	20	22	20	21	20	22	20	22	20	22	20	22	20	21
21	25	21	25	21	23	21	23	21	23	21	23	21	22	21	23	21	23	21	23	21	23	21	22
22	26	22	26	22	24	22	24	22	24	22	24	22	23	22	24	22	24	22	24	22	24	22	23
23	27	23	27	23	25	23	25	23	25	23	25	23	24	23	25	23	25	23	25	23	25	23	24
24	28	24	28	24	26	24	26	24	26	24	26	24	25	24	26	24	26	24	26	24	26	24	25
25	29	25	29	25	27	25	27	25	27	25	27	25	26	25	27	25	27	25	27	25	27	25	26
26	30	26	30	26	28	26	28	26	28	26	28	26	27	26	28	26	28	26	28	26	28	26	27
27	31	27	1 (May)	27	29	27	29	27	29	27	29	27	28	27	29	27	29	27	29	27	29	27	28
28	1 (Apr.)	28	2	28	30	28	30	28	30	28	30	28	29	28	30	28	30	28	30	28	30	28	1 (Mar.)
29	2			29	31	29	1 (July)	29	31	29	31	29	30	29	31	29	1 (Dec.)	29	31	29	31	29	2
30	3			30	1 (June)	30	2	30	1 (Aug.)	30	1 (Sep.)	30	1 (Oct.)	30	1 (Nov.)	30	1	30	1 (Jan.)	30	1 (Feb.)	30	3
31	4			31	2			31	2			31	2	31	2			31	2			31	4

Reproduction by courtesy of the Gaines Dog Research Center, N.Y.C.

THE PREGNANCY AND WHELPING
OF THE BITCH

The "period of gestation" of the bitch, by which is meant the duration of her pregnancy, is usually estimated at sixty-three days. Many bitches, especially young ones, have their puppies as early as sixty days after they are bred. Cases have occurred in which strong puppies were born after only fifty-seven days, and there have been cases that required as many as sixty-six days. However, if puppies do not arrive by the sixty-fourth day, it is time to consult a veterinarian.

For the first five to six weeks of her pregnancy, the bitch requires no more than normal good care and unrestricted exercise. For that period, she needs no additional quantity of food, although her diet must contain sufficient amounts of all the food factors, as is stated in the division of this book that pertains to food. After the fifth to sixth week, the ration must be increased and the violence of exercise restricted. Normal running and walking are likely to be better for the pregnant bitch than a sedentary existence but she should not be permitted to jump, hunt, or fight during the latter half of her gestation. Violent activity may cause her to abort her puppies.

About a week before she is due to whelp, a bed should be prepared for her and she be persuaded to use it for sleeping. This bed may be a box of generous size, big enough to accommodate her with room for activity. It should be high enough to permit her to stand upright, and is better for having a hinged cover. An opening in one side will afford her ingress and egress. This box should be placed in a secluded location, away from any possible molestation by other dogs, animals, or children. The bitch must be made confident of her security in her box.

A few hours, or perhaps a day or two, before her whelping, the bitch will probably begin arranging the bedding of the box to suit herself, tearing blankets or cushions and nosing the parts into the corners. Before the whelping actually starts, however, it is best to substitute burlap sacking, securely tacked to the floor of the box. This is to provide traction for the puppies to reach the dam's breast.

The whelping may take place at night without any assistance from the owner. The box may be opened in the morning to reveal the happy bitch nursing a litter of complacent puppies. But she may need some assistance in her parturition. If whelping is recognized to be in process, it is best to help the bitch.

As the puppies arrive, one by one, the enveloping membranes should be removed as quickly as possible, lest the puppies suffocate. Having removed the membrane, the umbilical cord should be severed with clean scissors some three or four inches from the puppy's belly. (The part of the cord attached to the belly will dry up and drop off in a few days.) There is no need for any medicament or dressing of the cord after it is cut.

The bitch should be permitted to eat the afterbirth if she so desires, and she normally does. If she has no assistance, she will probably remove the membrane and sever the cord with her teeth. The only dangers are that she may delay too long or may bite the cord too short. Some bitches, few of them, eat their newborn puppies (especially bitches not adequately fed during pregnancy). This unlikelihood should be guarded against.

As they arrive, it is wise to remove all the puppies except one, placing them in a box or basket lined and covered by a woolen cloth, somewhere aside or away from the whelping bed, until all have come and the bitch's activity has ceased. The purpose of this is to prevent her from walking or lying on the whelps, and to keep her from being disturbed by the puppies' whining. A single puppy should be left with the bitch to ease her anxiety.

It is best that the "midwife" be somebody with whom the bitch is on intimate terms and in whom she has confidence. Some bitches exhibit a jealous fear and even viciousness while they are whelping. Such animals are few, and most appear grateful for gentle assistance through their ordeal.

The puppies arrive at intervals of a few minutes to an hour until all are delivered. It is wise to call a veterinarian if the interval is greater than one hour. Though such service is seldom needed, an experienced veterinarian can usually be depended upon to withdraw with obstetrical forceps an abnormally presented puppy. It is possible, but unlikely, that the veterinarian will recommend a Caesarian section. This surgery in the dog is not very grave, but it should be performed only by an expert veterinarian. It is unnecessary to describe the process here, or the subsequent management of the patient, since, if a Caesarian section should be neces-

318

sary, the veterinarian will provide all the needed instructions.

Some bitches, at or immediately after their whelping period, go into a convulsive paralysis, which is called *eclampsia*. This is unlikely if the bitch throughout her pregnancy has had an adequate measure of calcium in her rations. The remedy for eclampsia is the intravenous or intramuscular administration of parenteral calcium. The bitch suspected of having eclampsia should be attended by a veterinarian.

Assuming that the whelping has been normal and without untoward incident, all of the puppies are returned to the bitch, and put, one by one, to the breast, which strong puppies will accept with alacrity. The less handling of puppies for the first four or five hours of their lives, the better. However, the litter should be looked over carefully for possible defectives and discards, which should be destroyed as soon as possible. There is no virtue in rearing hare-lipped, crippled, or mismarked puppies.

It is usually unwise to destroy sound, healthy puppies just to reduce the number in the litter, since it is impossible to sort young puppies for excellence and one may be destroying the best member of the litter, a future champion. Unless a litter is extraordinarily numerous, the dam, if well fed, can probably suckle them all. If it is found that her milk is insufficient, the litter may be artificially fed or may be divided, and the surplus placed on a foster mother if it is possible to obtain one. The foster mother need not be of the same breed as the puppies, a mongrel being as good as any. She should be approximately the same size as the actual mother of the puppies, clean, healthy, and her other puppies should be of as nearly the same age as the ones she is to take over as possible. She should be removed from her own puppies (which may well be destroyed) and her breasts be permitted to fill with milk until she is somewhat uncomfortable, at which time her foster puppies can be put to her breasts and will usually be accepted without difficulty. Unless the services of the foster mother are really required, it is better not to use her.

The whelping bitch may be grateful for a warm meal even between the arrivals of her puppies. As soon as her chore is over, she should be offered food in her box. This should be of cereal and milk or of meat and broth, something sloppy. She will probably not leave her puppies to eat and her meals must be brought to her.

319

It is wise to give a mild laxative for her bowels, also milk of magnesia. She will be reluctant to get out of her box even to relieve herself for about two days, but she should be urged, even forced, to do so regularly. A sensible bitch will soon settle down to care for her brood and will seldom give further trouble. She should be fed often and well, all that she can be induced to eat during her entire lactation.

As a preventive for infections sometimes occurring after whelping, some experienced breeders and veterinarians recommend injecting the bitch with penicillin or another antibiotic immediately following the birth of the last puppy. Oral doses of the same drug may be given daily thereafter for the first week. It is best to consult your veterinarian about this treatment.

ACID MILK

Occasionally a bitch produces early milk (colostrum) so acid that it disagrees with, sometimes kills, her puppies. The symptoms of the puppies are whining, disquiet, frequently refusal to nurse, frailty, and death. It is true that all milk is slightly acid, and it should be, turning blue litmus paper immersed in it a very light pink. However, milk harmfully on the acid side will readily turn litmus paper a vivid red. It seems that only the first two or three days milk is so affected. Milk problems come also from mastitis and other infections in the bitch.

This is not likely to occur with a bitch that throughout her pregnancy has received an adequate supply of calcium phosphate regularly in her daily ration. That is the best way to deal with the situation—to see to the bitch's correct nutrition in advance of her whelping. The owner has only himself to blame for the bitch's too acid milk, since adequate calcium in advance would have neutralized the acid.

If it is found too late that her milk is too acid, the puppies must be taken from her breast and either given to a foster mother or artificially fed from bottle or by medicine dropper. Artificial feeding of very young puppies seldom is successful. Sometimes the acidity of the dam's milk can be neutralized by giving her large doses of bicarbonate of soda (baking soda), but the puppies should not be restored to her breasts until her milk ceases to turn litmus paper red.

320

If it is necessary to feed the puppies artificially, "Esbilac," a commercial product, or the following orphan puppy formula, may be used.

7 oz. whole milk
1 oz. cream (top milk)
1 egg yolk
2 tbsp. corn syrup
2 tbsp. lime water

REARING THE PUPPIES

Puppies are born blind and open their eyes at approximately the ninth day thereafter. If they were whelped earlier than the full sixty-three days after the breeding from which they resulted, the difference should be added to the nine days of anticipated blindness. The early eye color of young puppies is no criterion of the color to which the eyes are likely to change, and the breeder's anxiety about his puppies' having light eyes is premature.

In breeds that require the docking of the tail, this should be done on the third day and is a surgical job for the veterinarian. Many a dog has had his tail cut off by an inexperienced person, ruining his good looks and his possibility for a win in the show ring. Dew claws should be removed at the same time. There is little else to do with normal puppies except to let them alone and permit them to grow. The most important thing about their management is their nutrition, which is discussed in another chapter. The first two or three weeks, they will thrive and grow rapidly on their mother's milk, after which they should have additional food as described.

Puppies sleep much of the time, as do other babies, and they should not be frequently awakened to be played with. They grow more and more playful as they mature.

After the second week their nails begin to grow long and sharp. The mother will be grateful if the puppies' nails are blunted with scissors from time to time so that in their pawing of the breast they do not lacerate it. Sharp nails tend to prompt the mother to wean the whelps early, and she should be encouraged to keep them with her as long as she will tolerate them. Even the small amount of milk they can drain from her after the weaning process is begun is the best food they can obtain. It supplements and makes digestible the remainder of their ration.

Many bitches, after their puppies are about four weeks of age, eat and regurgitate food, which is eaten by the puppies. This food is warmed and partly digested in the bitch's stomach. This practice, while it may appear digusting to the novice keeper of dogs, is perfectly normal and should not be discouraged. However, it renders it all the more necessary that the food of the bitch be sound, clean, and nutritious.

It is all but impossible to rear a litter of puppies without their becoming infested with roundworms. Of course, the bitch should be wormed, if she harbors such parasites, before she is bred, and her teats should be thoroughly washed with mild soap just before she whelps to free them from the eggs of roundworms. Every precaution must be taken to reduce the infestation of the puppies to a minimum. But, in spite of all it is possible to do, puppies will have roundworms. These pests hamper growth, reduce the puppies' normal resistance to disease, and may kill them outright unless the worms are eliminated.

Skin Troubles

THERE is a tendency on the part of the amateur dog keeper to consider any lesion of the dog's skin to be mange. Mange is an unusual condition in clean, well fed, and well cared for dogs. Eczema occurs much more frequently and is often more difficult to control.

MANGE OR SCABIES

There are at least two kinds of mange that effect dogs—sarcoptic mange and demodectic or red mange, the latter rare indeed and difficult to cure.

Sarcoptic mange is caused by a tiny spider-like mite (*Sarcoptes scabiei canis*) which is similar to the mite that causes human scabies or "itch." Indeed, the mange is almost identical with scabies and is transmissible from dog to man. The mite is approximately 1/100th of an inch in length and without magnification is just visible to acute human sight.

Only the female mites are the cause of the skin irritation. They burrow into the upper layers of the skin, where each lays twenty to forty eggs, which in three to seven days hatch into larvae. These larvae in turn develop into nymphs which later grow into adults. The entire life cycle requires from fourteen to twenty-one days for completion. The larvae, nymphs, and males do not burrow into the skin, but live under crusts and scabs on the surface.

The disease may make its first appearance on any part of the dog's body, although it is usually first seen on the head and muzzle, around the eyes, or at the base of the ears. Sometimes it is first noticed in the armpits, the inner parts of the thighs, the lower abdomen or on the front of the chest. If not promptly treated it may cover the whole body and an extremely bad infestation may cause the death of the dog after a few months.

Red points which soon develop into small blisters are the first signs of the disease. These are most easily seen on the unpigmented parts of the skin, such as the abdomen. As the female mites burrow into the skin, there is an exudation of serum which dries and scabs. The affected parts soon are covered with bran-like scales followed with grayish crusts. The itching is intense, especially in hot weather or after exercise. The rubbing and scratching favor secondary bacterial infections and the formation of sores. The hair may grow matted and fall out, leaving bare spots. The exuded serum decomposes and gives rise to a peculiar mousy odor which increases as the disease develops and which is especially characteristic.

Sarcoptic mange is often confused with demodectic (red) mange, ringworm, or with simple eczema. If there is any doubt about the diagnosis, a microscopic examination of the scrapings of the lesions will reveal the true facts.

It is easy to control sarcoptic mange if it is recognized in its earlier stages and treatment is begun immediately. Neglected, it may be very difficult to eradicate. If it is considered how rapidly the causative mites reproduce themselves, the necessity for early treatment becomes apparent. That treatment consists not only of medication of the dog but also of sterilization of his bedding, all tools and implements used on him, and the whole premises upon which he has been confined. Sarcoptic mange is easily and quickly transmissible from dog to dog, from area to area on the same dog, and even from dog to human.

In some manner which is not entirely understood, an inadequate or unbalanced diet appears to predispose a dog to sarcoptic mange, and few dogs adequately fed and cared for ever contract it. Once a dog has contracted mange, however, improvement in the amount of quality of his food seems not to hasten his recovery.

There are various medications recommended for sarcoptic mange, sulphur ointment being the old standby. However, it is messy, difficult to use, and not always effective. For the treatment of sarcoptic mange, there are available today such insecticides as lindane, chlordane, and DDT. The use of these chemicals greatly facilitates treatment and cure of the dogs affected with mange and those exposed to it.

A bath made by dissolving four ounces of derris powder (containing at least 5% rotenone) and one ounce of soap in one gallon of water has proved effective, especially if large areas of the surface of the dog's skin are involved. All crusts and scabs should be removed before its application. The solution must be well scrubbed into the skin with a moderately stiff brush and the whole animal thoroughly soaked. Only the surplus liquid should be taken off with a towel and the remainder must be permitted to dry on the dog. This bath should be repeated at intervals of five days until all signs of mange have disappeared. Three such baths will usually suffice.

The advantage of such all over treatment is that it protects uninfected areas from infection. It is also a precautionary measure to bathe in this solution uninfected dogs which have been in contact with the infected one.

Isolated mange spots may be treated with oil of lavender. Roll a woolen cloth into a swab with which the oil of lavender can be applied and rubbed in thoroughly for about five minutes. This destroys all mites with which the oil of lavender comes into contact.

Even after a cure is believed to be accomplished, vigilance must be maintained to prevent fresh infestations and to treat new spots immediately if they appear.

DEMODECTIC OR RED MANGE

Demodectic mange, caused by the wormlike mite *Demodex canis,* which lives in the hair follicles and the sebaceous glands of the skin, is difficult to cure. It is a baffling malady of which the prognosis is not favorable. The life cycle of the causative organism is not well understood, the time required from the egg to maturity being so far unknown. The female lays eggs which hatch into young of appearance similar to that of the adult, except that they are smaller and have but three pairs of legs instead of four.

One peculiar feature about demodectic mange is that some dogs appear to be genetically predisposed to it while others do not contract it whatever their contact with infected animals may be. Young animals seem to be especially prone to it, particularly those with short hair. The first evidence of its presence is the falling out of the hair on certain areas of the dog. The spots may be somewhat reddened, and they commonly occur near the eyes, on the hocks, elbows, or toes, although they may be on any part of the dog's body. No itching occurs at the malady's inception, and it never grows so intense as in sarcoptic mange.

In the course of time, the hairless areas enlarge, and the skin attains a copper hue; in severe cases it may appear blue or leadish gray. During this period the mites multiply and small pustules develop. Secondary invasions may occur to complicate the situation. Poisons are formed by the bacteria in the pustules, and the absorption of toxic materials deranges the body functions and eventually affects the whole general health of the dog, leading to emaciation, weakness, and the development of an acrid, unpleasant odor.

This disease is slow and subtle in its development, runs a casual course, and frequently extends over a period of two or even three years. Unless it is treated, it usually terminates in death, although spontaneous recovery occasionally occurs, especially if the dog has been kept on a nourishing diet. As in other skin diseases, correct nutrition plays a major part in recovery from demodectic mange, as it plays an even larger part in its prevention.

It is possible to confuse demodectic mange with sarcoptic mange, fungus infection, acne, or eczema. A definite diagnosis is possible only from microscopic examination of skin scrapings and of material from the pustules. The possibility of demodectic mange, particularly in its earlier stages, is not negated by the failure to find the mites under the microscope, and several examinations may be necessary to arrive at a definite diagnosis.

The prognosis is not entirely favorable. It may appear that the mange is cured and a new and healthy coat may be re-established only to have the disease manifest itself in a new area, and the whole process of treatment must be undertaken afresh.

In the treatment of demodectic mange, the best results have been obtained by the persistent use of benzine hexachloride, chlordane, rotenone, and 2-mercapto benzothiazole. Perseverance is necessary, but even then failure is possible.

EAR MITES OR EAR MANGE

The mites responsible for ear mange (*Ododectes cynotis*) are considerably larger than the ones which cause sarcoptic mange. They inhabit the external auditory canal and are visible to the unaided eye as minute, slowly moving, white objects. Their life history is not known, but is probably similar to that of the mite that causes sarcoptic mange.

These mites do not burrow into the skin, but are found deep in the ear canal, near the eardrum. Considerable irritation results from their presence, and the normal secretions of the ear are interfered with. The ear canal is filled with inflammatory products, modified ear wax, and mites, causing the dog to scratch and rub its ears and to shake its head. While ear mange is not caused by incomplete washing or inefficient drying of the ears, it is encouraged by such negligence.

The ear mange infestation is purely local and is no cause for anxiety. An ointment containing benzine hexachloride is very effective in correcting this condition. The ear should be treated every third or fourth day.

ECZEMA

Eczema is probably the most common of all ailments seen in the dog. Oftentimes it is mistaken for mange or ringworm, although there is no actual relationship between the conditions. Eczema is variously referred to by such names as "hot spots," "fungitch," and "kennel itch."

Some years ago there was near-unanimity of opinion among dog people that the food of the animal was the major contributing factor of eczema. Needless to say, the manufacturers of commercial dog foods were besieged with complaints. Some research on the cause of eczema placed most of the blame on outside environmental factors, and with some help from other sources it was found that a vegetative organism was the causative agent in a great majority of the cases.

Some dogs do show an allergic skin reaction to certain types of protein given to them as food, but this is generally referred to as the "foreign protein" type of dermatitis. It manifests itself by raising numerous welts on the skin, and occasionally the head, face, and ears will become alarmingly swollen. This condition can be controlled by the injection of antihistamine products and subsequent dosage with antihistaminic tablets or capsules such as chlortrimenton or benedryl. Whether "foreign protein" dermatitis is due to an allergy or whether it is due to some toxin manufactured and elaborated by the individual dog is a disputed point.

Most cases of eczema start with reddening of the skin in certain parts. The areas most affected seem to be the region along the spine and at the base of the tail. In house dogs this may have its inception from enlarged and plugged anal glands. The glands when full and not naturally expressed are a source of irritation. The dog will rub his hind parts on the grass in order to alleviate the itching sensation. Fleas, lice, and ticks may be inciting factors, causing the dog to rub and roll in the grass in an attempt to scratch the itchy parts.

In hunting dogs, it is believed that the vegetative cover through which the dogs hunt causes the dermatitis. In this class of dogs the skin becomes irritated and inflamed in the armpits, the inner surfaces of the thighs, and along the belly. Some hunting dogs are bedded down in straw or hay, and such dogs invariably show a general reddening of the skin and a tendency to scratch.

As a general rule, the difference between moist and dry eczema lies in the degree to which the dog scratches the skin with his feet or chews it with his teeth. The inflammation ranges from a simple reddening of the skin to the development of papules, vesicles, and pustules with a discharge. Crusts and scabs like dandruff may form, and if the condition is not treated, it will become chronic and then next to impossible to treat with any success. In such cases the skin becomes thickened and may be pigmented. The hair follicles become infected, and the lesions are constantly inflamed and exuding pus.

When inflammation occurs between the toes and on the pads of the feet, it closely resembles "athletes foot" in the human. Such inflammation generally causes the hair in the region to turn a reddish brown. The ears, when they are affected, emit a peculiar moldy odor and exude a brownish black substance. It is thought that most cases of canker of the ear are due to a primary invasion of the ear canal by a vegetative fungus. If there is a pustular discharge, it is due to the secondary pus-forming bacteria that gain a foothold after the resistance of the parts is lowered by the fungi.

Some breeds of dogs are more susceptible to skin ailments than are others. However, all breeds of dogs are likely to show some degree of dermatitis if they are exposed to causative factors.

Most cases of dermatitis are seen in the summer time, which probably accounts for their being referred to as "summer itch" or "hot spots." The warm moist days of summer seem to promote the growth and development of both fleas and fungi. When the fleas bite the dog, the resulting irritation causes the dog to scratch or bite to alleviate the itch. The area thus becomes moist and makes a perfect place for fungi spores to propagate. That the fungi are the cause of the trouble seems evident, because most cases respond when treated externally with a good fungicide. Moreover, the use of a powder containing both an insecticide and a fungicide tends to prevent skin irritation. Simply dusting the dog once or twice a week with a good powder of the type mentioned is sound procedure in the practice of preventive medicine.

(Editor's note: I have had some success with hydrogen peroxide in treating mild skin troubles. Saturate a cotton pad with a mixture of 2 parts 3% hydrogen peroxide to 1 part boiled water. Apply, but do NOT rub, to affected skin. Let dry naturally and when *completely* dry apply an antiseptic talcum powder like Johnson & Johnson's Medicated Powder. When this treatment was suggested to my veterinarian, he confirmed that he had had success with it. If the skin irritation is not noticeably better after two of these treatments, once daily, the case should be referred to a veterinarian.)

RINGWORM

Ringworm is a communicable disease of the skin of dogs, readily transmissible to man and to other dogs and animals. The disease is caused by specific fungi, which are somewhat similar to ordinary molds. The lesions caused by ringworm usually first appear on the face, head, or legs of the dog, but they may occur on any part of the surface of his body.

The disease in dogs is characterized by small, circular areas of dirty gray or brownish-yellow crusts or scabs partially devoid of hair, the size of a dime. As the disease progresses, the lesions increase both in size and in number and merge to form larger patches covered with crusts containing broken off hair. A raw, bleeding surface may appear when crusts are broken or removed by scratching or rubbing to relieve itching. In some cases, however, little or no itching is manifested. Microscopic examination and culture tests are necessary for accurate diagnosis.

If treatment of affected dogs is started early, the progress of the disease can be immediately arrested. Treatment consists of clipping the hair from around the infected spots, removing the scabs and painting the spots with tincture of iodine, five percent salicylic acid solution, or other fungicide two or three times weekly until recovery takes place. In applying these remedies it is well to cover the periphery of the circular lesion as well as its center, since the spots tend to expand outward from their centers. Scabs, hair, and debris removed from the dog during his treatments should be burned to destroy the causative organisms and to prevent reinfection. Precautions in the handling of animals affected with ringworm should be observed to preclude transmission to man and other animals. Isolation of affected dogs is not necessary if the treatment is thorough.

COAT CARE

Skin troubles can often be checked and materially alleviated by proper grooming. Every dog is entitled to the minimum of weekly attention to coat, skin and ears; ideally, a daily stint with brush and comb is highly recommended. Frequent examination may catch skin disease in its early stages and provide a better chance for a quick cure.

The outer or "guard" hairs of a dog's coat should glint in the sunlight. There should be no mats or dead hair in the coat. Wax in the outer ear should be kept at a minimum.

It is helpful to stand the dog on a flat, rigid surface off the floor at a height convenient to the groomer. Start at the head and ears brushing briskly *with* the lay of short hair, *against* the lay of long hair at first then with it. After brushing, use a fine comb with short teeth on fine, short hair and a coarse comb with long teeth on coarse or long hair. If mats cannot be readily removed with brush or comb, use barber's thinning shears and cut into the matted area several times until mat pulls free easily. Some mats can be removed with the fingers if one has the patience to separate the hair a bit at a time.

After brushing and combing, run your palms over the dog's coat from head to tail. Natural oils in your skin will impart sheen to your dog's coat.

The ears of some dogs secrete and exude great amounts of wax. Frequent examination will determine when your dog's ears need cleaning. A thin coating of clean, clear wax is not harmful. But a heavy accumulation of dirty, dark wax needs removal by cotton pads soaked in diluted hydrogen peroxide (3% cut in half with boiled water), or alcohol or plain boiled water if wax is not too thick.

There are sprays, "dry" bath preparations and other commercial products for maintaining your dog's coat health. Test them first, and if they are successful, you may find them beneficial time-savers in managing your dog's coat.

First Aid

JOHN STEINBECK, the Nobel Prize winning author, in *Travels with Charley in Search of America* bemoans the lack of a good, comprehensive book of home dog medicine. Charley is the aged Poodle that accompanies his illustrious author-owner on a motor tour of the U.S.A.

As in human medicine, most treatment and dosing of dogs are better left in the experienced, trained hands and mind of a professional—in this case, the veterinarian. However, there are times and situations when professional aid is not immediately available and an owner's prompt action may save a life or avoid permanent injury. To this purpose, the following suggestions are given.

The First Aid Kit

For instruments keep on hand a pair of tweezers, a pair of pliers, straight scissors, a rectal thermometer, a teaspoon, a tablespoon, and swabs for cotton.

For dressings, buy a container of cotton balls, a roll of cotton and a roll of 2" gauze. Strips of clean, old sheets may come in handy.

For medicines, stock ammonia, aspirin, brandy, 3% hydrogen peroxide, bicarbonate of soda, milk of bismuth, mineral oil, salt, tea, vaseline, kaopectate, baby oil and baby talcum powder.

Handling the Dog for Treatment

Approach any injured or sick dog calmly with reassuring voice and gentle, steady hands. If the dog is in pain, slip a gauze or sheet strip noose over its muzzle tying the ends first under the throat and then back of the neck. Make sure the dog's lips are not caught between his teeth, but make noose around muzzle *tight*.

If the dog needs to be moved, grasp the loose skin on the back of the neck with one hand and support chest with the other hand. If the dog is too large to move in this manner, slide him on a large towel, blanket or folded sheet which may serve as a stretcher for two to carry.

If a pill or liquid is to be administered, back the dog in a corner in a sitting position. For a pill, pry back of jaws apart with thumb and forefinger of one hand and with the same fingers of your other hand place pill as far back in dog's throat as possible; close and hold jaws, rubbing throat to cause swallowing. If dog does not gulp, hold one hand over nostrils briefly; he will gulp for air and swallow pill. For liquids, lift the back of the upper lip and tip spoon into the natural pocket formed in the rear of the lower lip; it may be necessary to pull this pocket out with forefinger. Do not give liquids by pouring directly down the dog's throat; this might choke him or make the fluid go down the wrong way.

After treatment keep dog quiet, preferably in his bed or a room where he cannot injure himself or objects.

Bites and Wounds

Clip hair from area. Wash gently with pure soap and water or hydrogen peroxide. If profuse bleeding continues, apply sheet strip or gauze tourniquet between wound and heart but nearest the wound. Release tourniquet briefly at ten-minute intervals. Cold water compresses may stop milder bleeding.

For insect bites and stings, try to remove stinger with tweezers or a dab of cotton, and apply a few drops of ammonia. If dog is in pain, give aspirin at one grain per 10 pounds. (An aspirin tablet is usually 5 grains.)

Burns

Clip hair from area. Apply strong, lukewarm tea (for its tannic acid content) on a sheet strip compress. Vaseline may be used for slight burns. Give aspirin as recommended if dog is in pain. Keep him warm if he seems to be in shock.

Constipation

Give mineral oil: one-quarter teaspoon up to 10 pounds; half teaspoon from 10 to 25 pounds; full teaspoon from 25 to 75 pounds; three-quarters tablespoon over 75 pounds.

Diarrhea

Give kaopectate in same doses by size as indicated for mineral oil above, but repeat within four and eight hours.

Fighting

Do not try forcibly to separate dogs. If available throw a pail of cold water on them. A sharp rap on the rump of each combatant with a strap or stick may help. A heavy towel or blanket dropped over the head of the aggressor, or a newspaper twisted into a torch, lighted and held near them, may discourage the fighters. If a lighted newspaper is used, be careful that sparks do not fall or blow on dogs.

Fits

Try to get the dog into a room where he cannot injure himself. If possible, cover him with a towel or blanket. When the fit ends, give aspirin one grain for every 10 pounds.

Nervousness

Remove cause or remove the dog from the site of the cause. Give the recommended dose of aspirin. Aspirin acts as a tranquilizer.

Poisoning

If container of the poison is handy, use recommended antidote printed thereon. Otherwise, make a strong solution of household salt in water and force as much as possible into the dog's throat using the lip pocket method. Minutes count with several poisons; if veterinarian cannot be reached immediately, try to get dog to an MD or registered nurse.

Shock

If dog has chewed electric cord, protect hand with rubber glove or thick dry towel and pull cord from socket. If dog has collapsed, hold ammonia under its nose or apply artificial respiration as follows: place dog on side with its head low, press on abdomen and rib cage, releasing pressure at one- or two-second intervals. Keep dog warm.

Stomach Upsets

For mild stomach disorders, milk of bismuth in same doses as recommended for mineral oil under *Constipation* will be effective. For more severe cases brandy in the same doses but diluted with an equal volume of water may be helpful.

Swallowing Foreign Objects

If object is still in mouth or throat, reach in and remove it. If swallowed, give strong salt solution as for *Poisoning*. Some objects that are small, smooth or soft may not give trouble.

Porcupines and Skunks

Using tweezers or pliers, twist quills one full turn and pull out. Apply hydrogen peroxide to bleeding wounds. For skunk spray, wash dog in tomato juice.

> WARNING! Get your dog to a veterinarian *soonest* for severe bites, wounds, burns, poisoning, fits and shock.

SIDING
TONGUE &
GROOVE

ASSEMBLED VIEW

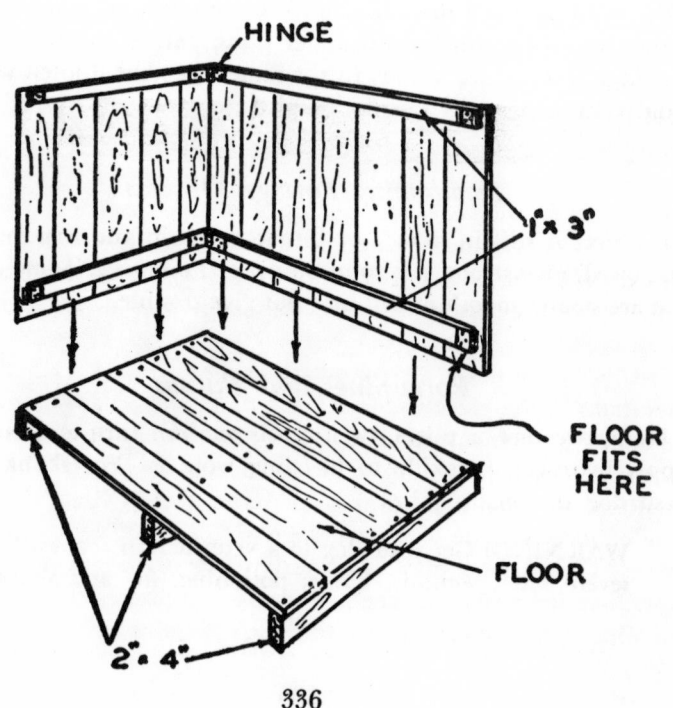

HINGE

1" x 3"

FLOOR
FITS
HERE

FLOOR

2" x 4"

336

Housing for Dogs

E VERY owner will have, and will have to solve, his own problems about providing his dog or dogs with quarters best suited to the dog's convenience. The special circumstances of each particular owner will determine what kind of home he will provide for his dogs. Here it is impossible to provide more than a few generalities upon the subject.

Little more need be said than that fit quarters for dogs must be secure, clean, dry, and warm. Consideration must be given to convenience in the care of kennel inmates by owners of a large number of dogs, but by the time one's activities enlarge to such proportions one will have formulated one's own concept of how best to house one's dogs. Here, advice will be predicated upon the maintenance of not more than three or four adult dogs with accommodations for an occasional litter of puppies.

First, let it be noted that dogs are not sensitive to aesthetic considerations in the place they are kept; they have no appreciation of the beauty of their surroundings. They do like soft beds of sufficient thickness to protect them from the coldness of the floors. These beds should be secluded and covered to conserve body heat. A box or crate of adequate size to permit the dog to lie full length in it will suffice. The cushion may be a burlap bag stuffed with shredded paper, *not straw, hay, or grass*. Paper is recommended, for its use will reduce the possibility of the dog's developing skin trouble.

337

Most dogs are allergic to fungi found on vegetative matter such as straw, hay, and grass. Wood shavings and excelsior may be used with impunity.

The kennel should be light, except for a retiring place; if sunshine is available at least part of the day, so much the better. Boxes in a shed or garage with secure wire runs to which the dogs have ready access suffice very well, are very inexpensive, and are easy to plan and to arrange. The runs should be made of wire fencing strong enough that the dogs are unable to tear it with their teeth and high enough that the dogs are unable to jump or climb over it. In-turning flanges of wire netting at the tops of the fences tend to obviate jumping. Boards, rocks, or cement buried around the fences forestall burrowing to freedom.

These pens need not be large, if the dogs are given frequent respites from their captivity and an opportunity to obtain needed exercise. However, they should be large enough to relieve them of the aspect of cages. Concrete floors for such pens are admittedly easy to keep clean and sanitary. However, they have no resilience, and the feet of dogs confined for long periods on concrete floors are prone to spread and their shoulders to loosen. A further objection to concrete is that it grows hot in the summer sunshine and is very cold in winter. If it is used for flooring at all, a low platform of wood, large enough to enable the dogs to sprawl out on it full length, should be provided in each pen.

A well drained soil is to be preferred to concrete, if it is available; but it must be dug out to the depth of three inches and renewed occasionally, if it is used. Otherwise, the accumulation of urine will make it sour and offensive. Agricultural limestone, applied monthly and liberally, will "sweeten" the soil.

Gates, hinges, latches, and other hardware must be trustworthy. The purpose of such quarters is to confine the dogs and to keep them from running at large; unless they serve such a purpose they are useless. One wants to know when one puts a dog in his kennel, the dog will be there when one returns. An improvised kennel of old chicken wire will not suffice for one never knows whether it will hold one's dogs or not.

Frequently two friendly bitches may be housed together, or a dog housed with a bitch. Unless one is sure of male friendships, it is seldom safe to house two adult male dogs together. It is better, if

338

possible, to provide a separate kennel for each mature dog. But, if the dogs can be housed side by side with only a wire fence between them, they can have companionship without rancor. Night barking can be controlled by confining the dogs indoors or by shutting them up in their boxes.

Adult dogs require artificial heat in only the coldest of climates, if they are provided with tight boxes placed under shelter. Puppies need heat in cold weather up until weaning time, and even thereafter if they are not permitted to sleep together. Snuggled together in a tight box with shredded paper, they can withstand much cold without discomfort. All dogs in winter without artificial heat should have an increase of their rations—especially as pertains to fat content.

Whatever artificial heat is provided for dogs should be safe, foolproof, and dog-proof. Caution should be exercised that electric wiring is not exposed, that stoves cannot be tipped over, and that it is impossible for sparks from them to ignite the premises. Many fires in kennels, the results of defective heating apparatus or careless handling of it, have brought about the deaths of the inmates. It is because of them that this seemingly unnecessary warning is given.

No better place for a dog to live can be found than the home of its owner, sharing even his bed if permitted. So is the dog happiest. There is a limit, however, to the number of dogs that can be tolerated in the house. The keeper of a small kennel can be expected to alternate his favorite dogs in his own house, thus giving them a respite to confinement in a kennel. Provision must be made for a place of exercise and relief at frequent intervals for dogs kept in the house. An enclosed dooryard will serve such a purpose, or the dog may be exercised on a lead with as much benefit to the owner as to the dog.

That the quarters of the dog shall be dry is even more important than that they shall be warm. A damp, drafty kennel is the cause of much kennel disease and indisposition. It is harmless to permit a dog to go out into inclement weather of his own choice, if he is provided with a sheltered bed to which he may retire to dry himself.

By cleanness, sanitation is meant—freedom from vermin and bacteria. A little coat of dust or a degree of disorder does not discommode the dog or impair his welfare, but the best dog keepers are orderly persons. They at least do not permit bedding and old bones to accumulate in a dog's bed, and they take the trouble to spray with antiseptic or wash with soap and water their dog's house at frequent intervals. The feces in the kennel runs should be picked up and destroyed at least once, and better twice, daily. Persistent filth in kennels can be counted on as a source of illness sooner or later. This warning appears superfluous, but it isn't; the number of ailing dogs kept in dirty, unsanitary kennels is amazing. It is one of the axioms of keeping dogs that their quarters must be sanitary or disease is sure to ensue.

GOOD DOG KEEPING PRACTICES

Pride of ownership is greatly enhanced when the owner takes care to maintain his dog in the best possible condition at all times. And meticulous grooming not only will make the dog look better but also will make him feel better. As part of the regular, daily routine, the grooming of the dog will prove neither arduous nor time consuming; it will also obviate the necessity for indulging in a rigorous program designed to correct the unkempt state in which too many owners permit their dogs to appear. Certainly, spending a few minutes each day will be well worth while, for the result will be a healthier, happier, and more desirable canine companion.

THAT DOGGY ODOR

Many persons are disgusted to the point of refusal to keep a dog by what they fancy is a "doggy odor." Of course, almost everything has a characteristic odor—everyone is familiar with the smell of the rose. No one would want the dog to smell like a rose, and, conversely, the world wouldn't like it very well if the rose smelled doggy. The dog must emit a certain amount of characteristic odor or he wouldn't be a dog. That seems to be his God-given grant. However, when the odor becomes too strong and obnoxious, then it is time to look for the reason. In most cases it is the result of clogged anal glands. If this be the case, all one must do to rid the pet of his odor is to express the contents of these glands and apply to the anal region a little soap and water.

If the odor is one of putrefaction, look to his mouth for the trouble. The teeth may need scaling, or a diseased root of some one or two teeth that need to be treated may be the source of the odor. In some dogs there is a fold or a crease in the lower lip near the lower canine tooth, and this may need attention. This spot is favored by fungi that cause considerable damage to the part. The smell here is somewhat akin to the odor of human feet that have been attacked by the fungus of athlete's foot.

The odor may be coming from the coat if the dog is heavily infested with fleas or lice. Too, dogs seem to enjoy the odor of dead fish and often roll on a foul smelling fish that has been cast up on the beach. The dog with a bad case of otitis can fairly "drive you out of the room" with this peculiar odor. Obviously, the way to rid the dog of odor is to find from whence it comes and then take steps to eliminate it. Some dogs have a tendency toward excessive flatulence (gas). These animals should have a complete change of diet and with the reducing of the carbohydrate content, a teaspoon of granular charcoal should be added to each feeding.

BATHING THE DOG

There is little to say about giving a bath to a dog, except that he shall be placed in a tub of warm (not hot) water and thoroughly scrubbed. He may, like a spoiled child, object to the ordeal, but if handled gently and firmly he will submit to what he knows to be inevitable.

The water must be only tepid, so as not to shock or chill the dog. A bland, unmedicated soap is best, for such soaps do not irritate the skin or dry out the hair. Even better than soap is one of the powdered detergents marketed especially for this purpose. They rinse away better and more easily than soap and do not leave the coat gummy or sticky.

It is best to begin with the face, which should be thoroughly and briskly washed with a cloth. Care should be taken that the cleaning solvent does not get into the dog's eyes, not because of the likelihood of causing permanent harm, but because such an experience is unpleasant to the dog and prone to prejudice him against future baths. The interior of the ear canals should be thoroughly cleansed until they not only look clean but also until no unpleasant odor comes from them. The head may then be rinsed and dried before proceeding to the body. Especial attention should be given to the drying of the ears, inside and outside. Many ear infections arise from failure to dry the canals completely.

With the head bathed and the surplus water removed from that part, the body must be soaked thoroughly with water, either with a hose or by dipping the water from the bath and pouring it over the dog's back until he is totally wetted. Thereafter, the soap or detergent should be applied and rubbed until it lathers freely. A stiff brush is useful in penetrating the coat and cleansing the skin. It is not sufficient to wash only the back and sides—the belly, neck, legs, feet, and tail must all be scrubbed thoroughly.

If the dog is very dirty, it may be well to rinse him lightly and repeat the soaping process and scrub again. Thereafter, the dog must be rinsed with warm (tepid) water until all suds and soil come away. If a bath spray is available, the rinsing is an easy matter. If the dog must be rinsed in standing water, it will be needful to renew it two or three times.

When he is thoroughly rinsed, it is well to remove such surplus water as may be squeezed with the hand, after which he is enveloped with a turkish towel, lifted from the tub, and rubbed until he is dry. This will probably require two or three dry towels. In the process of drying the dog, it is well to return again and again to the interior of the ears.

THE DOG'S TEETH

The dog, like the human being, has two successive sets of teeth, the so-called milk teeth or baby teeth, which are shed and replaced later by the permanent teeth. The temporary teeth, which begin to emerge when the puppy is two and a half to three weeks of age, offer no difficulty. The full set of milk teeth (consisting usually of six incisors and two canines in each jaw, with four molars in the upper jaw and six molars in the lower jaw) is completed usually just before weaning time. Except for some obvious malformation, the milk teeth may be ignored and forgotten about.

At about the fourth month the baby teeth are shed and gradually replaced by the permanent teeth. This shedding and replacement process may consume some three or four months. This is about the most critical period of the dog's life—his adolescence. Some constitutionally vigorous dogs go through their teething easily, with no

342

seeming awareness that the change is taking place. Others, less vigorous, may suffer from soreness of the gums, go off in flesh, and require pampering. While they are teething, puppies should be particularly protected from exposure to infectious diseases and should be fed on nutritious foods, especially meat and milk.

The permanent teeth normally consist of 42—six incisors and two canines (fangs) in each jaw, with twelve molars in the upper jaw and fourteen in the lower jaw. Occasionally the front molars fail to emerge; this deficiency is considered by most judges to be only a minor fault, if the absence is noticed at all.

Dentition is a heritable factor in the dog, and some dogs have soft, brittle and defective permanent teeth, no matter how excellent the diet and the care given them. The teeth of those dogs which are predisposed to have excellent sound ones, however, can be ruined by an inferior diet prior to and during the period of their eruption. At this time, for the teeth to develop properly, a dog must have an adequate supply of calcium phosphate and vitamin D, besides all the protein he can consume.

Often the permanent teeth emerge before the shedding of the milk teeth, in which case the dog may have parts of both sets at the same time. The milk teeth will eventually drop out, but as long as they remain they may deflect or displace the second teeth in the process of their growth. The incisors are the teeth in which a malformation may result from the late dropping of the baby teeth. When it is realized just how important a correct "bite" may be deemed in the show ring, the hazards of permitting the baby teeth to deflect the permanent set will be understood.

The baby teeth in such a case must be dislodged and removed. The roots of the baby teeth are resorbed in the gums, and the teeth can usually be extracted by firm pressure of thumb and finger, although it may be necessary to employ forceps or to take the puppy to the veterinarian.

The permanent teeth of the puppy are usually somewhat overshot, by which is meant that the upper incisors protrude over and do not play upon the lower incisors. Maturity may be trusted to remedy this apparent defect unless it is too pronounced.

An undershot mouth in a puppy, on the other hand, tends to grow worse as the dog matures. Whether or not it has been caused by the displacement of the permanent teeth by the persistence of

343

the milk teeth, it can sometimes be remedied (or at least bettered) by frequent hard pressure of the thumb on the lower jaw, forcing the lower teeth backward to meet the upper ones. Braces on dog teeth have seldom proved efficacious, but pressure and massage are worth trying on the bad mouth of an otherwise excellent puppy.

High and persistent fevers, especially from the fourth to the ninth month, sometimes result in discolored, pitted, and defective teeth, commonly called "distemper teeth." They often result from maladies other than distemper. There is little that can be done for them. They are unpleasant to see and are subject to penalty in the show ring, but are serviceable to the dog. Distemper teeth are not in themselves heritable, but the predisposition for their development appears to be. At least, at the teething age, the offspring from distemper toothed ancestors seem to be especially prone to fevers which impair their dentition.

Older dogs, especially those fed largely upon carbohydrates, tend to accumulate more or less tartar upon their teeth. The tartar generally starts at the gum line on the molars and extends gradually to the cusp. To rectify this condition, the dog's teeth should be scaled by a veterinarian.

The cleanliness of a dog's mouth may be brought about and the formation of tartar discouraged by the scouring of the teeth with a moist cloth dipped in a mixture of equal parts of table salt and baking soda.

A large bone given the dog to chew on or play with tends to prevent tartar from forming on the teeth. If tartar is present, the chewing and gnawing on the bone will help to remove the deposit mechanically. A bone given to puppies will act as a teething ring and aid in the cutting of the permanent teeth. So will beef hide strips you can buy in pet shops.

CARE OF THE NAILS

The nails of the dog should be kept shortened and blunted right down to the quick—never into the quick. If this is not done, the toes may spread and the foot may splay into a veritable pancake. Some dogs have naturally flat feet, which they have inherited. No pretense is made that the shortening of the nails of such a foot will obviate the fault entirely and make the foot beautiful or serviceable.

It will only improve the appearance and make the best of an obvious fault. Short nails do, however, emphasize the excellence of. a good foot.

Some dogs keep their nails short by digging and friction. Their nails require little attention, but it is a rare dog whose foot cannot be bettered by artificially shortening the nails.

Nail clippers are available, made especially for the purpose. After using them, the sides of the nail should be filed away as much as is possible without touching the quick. Carefully done, it causes the dog no discomfort. But, once the quick of a dog's nail has been injured, he may forever afterward resent and fight having his feet treated or even having them examined.

The obvious horn of the nail can be removed, after which the quick will recede to permit the removal of more horn the following week. This process may be kept up until the nail is as short and blunt as it can be made, after which nails will need attention only at intervals of six weeks or two months.

Some persons clip the nails right back to the toes in one fell swoop, disregarding injury to the quick and pain of the dog. The nails bleed and the dog limps for a day or two, but infection seldom develops. Such a procedure should not be undertaken without a general anesthetic. If an anesthetic is used, this forthright method does not prejudice the dog against having his feet handled.

NAIL TRIMMING ILLUSTRATED

The method here illustrated is to take a sharp file and stroke the nail downwards in the direction of the arrow, as in Figure 24, until it assumes the shape in Figure 25, the shaded portion being the part removed, a three-cornered file should then be used on the underside just missing the quick, as in Figure 26, and the operation is then complete, the dog running about quickly wears the nail to the proper shape.

345

Care for
the Old Dog

FIRST, how old is old, in a dog? Some breeds live longer than others, as a general rule. The only regularity about dog ages at death is their irregularity breed to breed and dog to dog.

The dog owner can best determine senility in his canine friend by the dog's appearance and behavior. Old dogs "slow down" much as humans do. The stairs are a little steeper, the breath a little shorter, the eye dimmer, the hearing usually a little harder.

As prevention is always better than cure, a dog's life may be happily and healthfully extended if certain precautionary steps are taken. As the aging process becomes quite evident, the owner should become more considerate of his dog's weaknesses, procrastinations and lapses. A softer, drier, warmer bed may be advisable; a foam rubber mattress will be appreciated. If a kennel dog has been able to endure record-breaking hot or cold, torrential or desert-dry days, he may in his old age appreciate spending his nights at least in a warm, comfy human house. And if the weather outside is frightful during the day, he should—for minimum comfort and safety—be brought inside before pneumonia sets in.

The old dog should NOT be required or expected to chase a ball, or a pheasant, or one of his species of different sex. The old bitch should not continue motherhood.

If many teeth are gone or going, foods should be softer. The diet should be blander—delete sweet or spicy or heavy tidbits—and there should be less of it, usually. The older dog needs less fat, less carbohydrate and less minerals unless disease and convalescence dictate otherwise. DON'T PERMIT AN OLD DOG TO GET FAT! It's cruel. The special diet known as PD or KD may be in order, if the dog has dietary troubles or a disease concomitant with old age. The veterinarian should be asked about PD or KD diets. Vitamin B-12 and other vitamin reinforcements may help.

The dog diseases of old age parallel many of the human illnesses. Senior male dogs suffer from prostate trouble, kidney disease and cancer. Senior bitches suffer from metritis and cancer. Both sexes suffer blindness, deafness and paralysis. Dogs suffer from heart disease; I know one old dog that is living an especially happy old age through the courtesy of digitalis. If the symptoms of any disease manifest themselves in an old dog the veterinarian MUST be consulted.

Many dog owners are selfish about old dogs. In their reluctance to lose faithful friends, they try to keep their canine companions alive in terminal illnesses, such as galloping cancer. If the veterinarian holds little or no promise for recovery of a pet from an illness associated with old age, or if the pet suffers, the kindest act the owner can perform is to request euthanasia. In this sad event, the kindest step the owner may take in *his* interest is to acquire a puppy or young dog of the same breed immediately. Puppies have a wonderful way of absorbing grief!

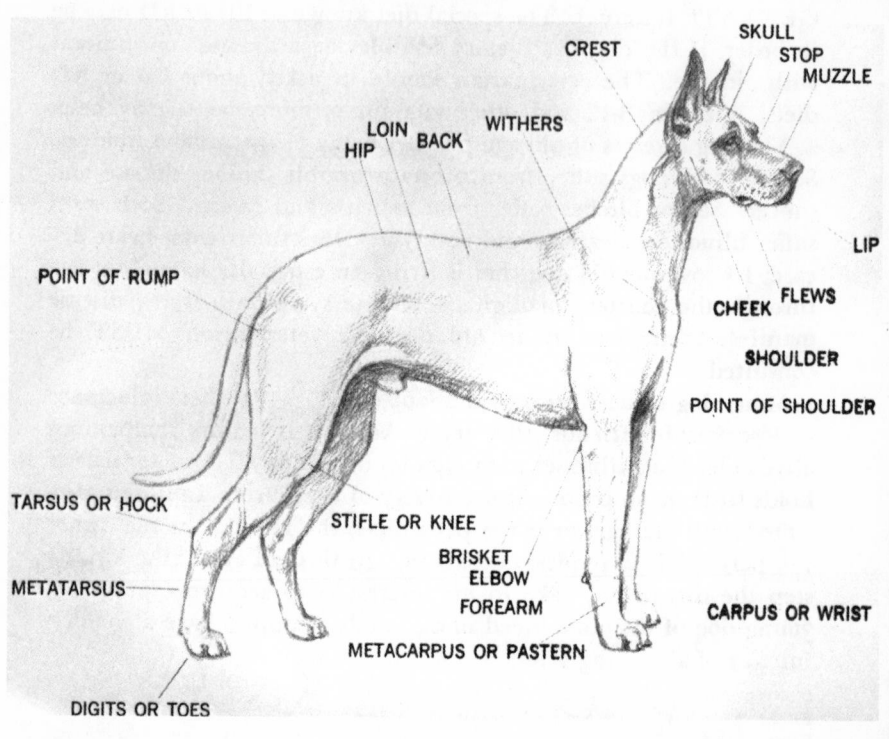

Glossary of Dog Terms

Achilles tendon: The large tendon attaching the muscle of the calf in the second thigh to the bone below the hock; the hamstring.

A.K.C.: The American Kennel Club.

Albino: An animal having a congenital deficiency of pigment in the skin, hair, and eyes.

American Kennel Club: A federation of member show-giving and specialty clubs which maintains a stud book, and formulates and enforces rules under which dog shows and other canine activities in the United States are conducted. Its address is 51 Madison Ave., New York, N. Y. 10010.

Angulation: The angles of the bony structure at the joints, particularly of the shoulder with the upper arm (front angulation), or the angles at the stifle and the hock (rear angulation).

Anus: The posterior opening of the alimentary canal through which the feces are discharged.

Apple head: A rounded or domed skull.

Balance: A nice adjustment of the parts one to another; no part too big or too small for the whole organism; symmetry.

Barrel: The ribs and body.

Bitch: The female of the dog species.

Blaze: A white line or marking extending from the top of the skull (often from the occiput), between the eyes, and over the muzzle.

Brisket: The breast or lower part of the chest in front of and between the forelegs, sometimes including the part extending back some distance behind the forelegs.

Burr: The visible, irregular inside formation of the ear.

Butterfly nose: A nose spotted or speckled with flesh color.

Canine: (Noun) Any animal of the family *Canidae,* including dogs, wolves, jackals, and foxes.
(Adjective) Of or pertaining to such animals; having the nature and qualities of a dog.

Canine tooth: The long tooth next behind the incisors in each side of each jaw; the fang.

Castrate: (Verb) Surgically to remove the gonads of either sex, usually said of the testes of the male.

Character: A combination of points of appearance, behavior, and disposition contributing to the whole dog and distinctive of the individual dog or of its particular breed.

Cheeky: Having rounded muscular padding on sides of the skull.

Chiseled: (Said of the muzzle) modeled or delicately cut away in front of the eyes to conform to breed type.

Chops: The mouth, jaws, lips, and cushion.

Close-coupled: Short in the loins.

Cobby: Stout, stocky, short-bodied; compactly made; like a cob (horse).

Coupling: The part of the body joining the hindquarters to the parts of the body in front; the loin; the flank.

Cowhocks: Hocks turned inward and converging like the presumed hocks of a cow.

Croup: The rear of the back above the hind limbs; the line from the pelvis to the set-on of the tail.

Cryptorchid: A male animal in which the testicles are not externally apparent, having failed to descend normally, not to be confused with a castrated dog.

Dentition: The number, kind, form, and arrangement of the teeth.

Dewclaws: Additional toes on the inside of the leg above the foot; the ones on the rear legs usually removed in puppyhood in most breeds.

Dewlap: The pendulous fold of skin under the neck.

Distemper teeth: The discolored and pitted teeth which result from some febrile disease.

Down in (or on) pastern: With forelegs more or less bent at the pastern joint.

Dry: Free from surplus skin or flesh about mouth, lips, or throat.

Dudley nose: A brown or flesh-colored nose, usually accompanied by eye-rims of the same shade and light eyes.

Ewe-neck: A thin sheep-like neck, having insufficient, faulty, or concave arch.

Expression: The combination of various features of the head and face, particularly the size, shape, placement and color of eyes, to produce a certain impression, the outlook.

Femur: The heavy bone of the true thigh.

Fetlock or Fetlock joint: The joint between the pastern and the lower arm; sometimes called the "knee," although it does not correspond to the human knee.

Fiddle front: A crooked front with bandy legs, out at elbow, converging at pastern joints, and turned out pasterns and feet, with or without bent bones of forearms.

Flews: The chops; pendulous lateral parts of the upper lips.

Forearm: The part of the front leg between the elbow and pastern.

Front: The entire aspect of a dog, except the head, when seen from the front; the forehand.

Guard hairs: The longer, smoother, stiffer hairs which grow through the undercoat and normally conceal it.

Hackney action: The high lifting of the front feet, like that of a Hackney horse, a waste of effort.

Hare-foot: A long, narrow, and close-toed foot, like that of the hare or rabbit.

Haw: The third eyelid, or nictitating membrane, especially when inflamed.

Height: The vertical distance from withers at top of shoulder blades to floor.

Hock: The lower joint in the hind leg, corresponding to the human ankle; sometimes, incorrectly, the part of the hind leg, from the hock joint to the foot.

Humerus: The bone of the upper arm.

Incisors: The teeth adapted for cutting; specifically, the six small front teeth in each jaw between the canines or fangs.

Knuckling over: Projecting or bulging forward of the front legs at the pastern joint; incorrectly called knuckle knees.

Leather: Pendant ears.

Lippy: With lips longer or fuller than desirable in the breed under consideration.

Loaded: Padded with superfluous muscle (said of such shoulders).

Loins: That part on either side of the spinal column between the hipbone and the false ribs.

Molar tooth: A rear, cheek tooth adapted for grinding food.

Monorchid: A male animal having but one testicle in the scrotum; monorchids may be potent and fertile.

Muzzle: The part of the face in front of the eyes.

Nictitating membrane: A thin membrane at the inner angle of the eye or beneath the lower lid, capable of being drawn across the eyeball. This membrane is frequently surgically excised in some breeds to improve the expression.

Occiput or occipital protuberance: The bony knob at the top of the skull between the ears.

Occlusion: The bringing together of the opposing surfaces of the two jaws; the relation between those surfaces when in contact.

Olfactory: Of or pertaining to the sense of smell.

Out at elbow: With elbows turned outward from body due to faulty joint and front formation, usually accompanied by pigeon-toes; loose-fronted.

Out at shoulder: With shoulder blades loosely attached to the body, leaving the shoulders jutting out in relief and increasing the breadth of the front.

Overshot: Having the lower jaw so short that the upper and lower incisors fail to meet; pig-jawed.

Pace: A gait in which the legs move in lateral pairs, the animal supported alternatively by the right and left legs.

Pad: The cushion-like, tough sole of the foot.

Pastern: That part of the foreleg between the fetlock or pastern joint and the foot; sometimes incorrectly used for pastern joint or fetlock.

Period of gestation: The duration of pregnancy, about 63 days in the dog.

Puppy: Technically, a dog under a year in age.

Quarters: The two hind legs taken together.

Roach-back: An arched or convex spine, the curvature rising gently behind the withers and carrying over the loins; wheel-back.

Roman nose: The convex curved top line of the muzzle.

Scapula: The shoulder blade.

Scissors bite: A bite in which the incisors of the upper jaw just overlap and play upon those of the lower jaw.

Slab sides: Flat sides with insufficient spring of ribs.

Snipey: Snipe-nosed, said of a muzzle too sharply pointed, narrow, or weak.

Spay: To render a bitch sterile by the surgical removal of her ovaries; to castrate a bitch.

Specialty club: An organization to sponsor and forward the interests of a single breed.

Specialty show: A dog show confined to a single breed.

Spring: The roundness of ribs.

Stifle or stifle joint: The joint next above the hock, and near the flank, in the hind leg; the joint corresponding to the knee in man.

Stop: The depression or step between the forehead and the muzzle between the eyes.

Straight hocks: Hocks lacking bend or angulation.

351

Straight shoulders: Shoulder formation with blades too upright, with angle greater than 90° with bone of upper arm.

Substance: Strength of skeleton, and weight of solid musculature.

Sway-back: A spine with sagging, concave curvature from withers to pelvis.

Thorax: The part of the body between the neck and the abdomen, and supported by the ribs and sternum.

Throaty: Possessing a superfluous amount of skin under the throat.

Undercoat: A growth of short, fine hair, or pile, partly or entirely concealed by the coarser top coat which grows through it.

Undershot: Having the lower incisor teeth projecting beyond the upper ones when the mouth is closed; the opposite to overshot; prognathous; underhung.

Upper arm: The part of the dog between the elbow and point of shoulder.

Weaving: Crossing the front legs one over the other in action.

Withers: The part between the shoulder bones at the base of the neck; the point from which the height of a dog is usually measured.